AN ILLUSTRATED TRAVELERS GUIDE

THE CIVIL WAR
IN GEORGIA

Historic Homes

Battlefields

Museums

Cemeteries

Memorials

Parks

Attractions

Maps

By Richard J. Lenz
Photography By Robb Helfrick

Published By Infinity Press

*Dedicated to all Georgians
who are proud of their rich heritage
in the epic struggle, 1861-65.*

About The Author and Designer: Richard J. Lenz is president of Lenz Design & Communications, Decatur, Georgia (404) 633-0501, an award-winning company specializing in marketing communications.

About The Photographer: Robb Helfrick is a photographer based in Woodstock, Georgia (770-928-2566) who specializes in creating historic, scenic and corporate images. He is represented by Aristock Photographic Stock Agency, Atlanta, Georgia (404-261-6150).

About The Publisher: A love of Georgia and an interest in its future brought together eight individuals who first met and shared their goals while participating in Leadership Georgia. Infinity Associates was created to promote a heightened awareness and appreciation of Georgia's natural and historic qualities by pooling the group's expertise and resources. The group includes Mr. Dennis M. Betz; Thomas E. Fitzgerald, M.D.; Mr. Allen Gudenrath; Mr. Calvin S. Hopkins, III; Mr. C. Eugene Kernaghan, III; Mr. W.H. (Dink) NeSmith, Jr.; E. Dale Threadgill, Ph.D.; and Mr. Philip A. Wilheit.

Acknowledgments: Special thanks to additional research, editorial, and graphic support from Sheila J. Lenz, Pamela J. Peel, and John R. Lenz. Special acknowledgment to Karen Helfrick. Special thanks to Bill Scaife, Gordon Jones, Billy Townsend and Douglas Young. Thank you to the Georgia Civil War Commission for their support of the project.

© Copyright 1995 by Infinity Associates

Published by Infinity Press, a division of Infinity Associates, 1100 Riverside Drive, Watkinsville, Georgia 30677

International Standard Book Number 0-9650305-0-4
Library of Congress Catalog Card Number 95-81860

Publisher's Cataloging-in-Publication

Lenz, Richard J.
      The Civil War In Georgia : an illustrated traveler's guide;
historic homes, battlefields, museums, cemeteries, memorials,
parks, attractions, maps / by Richard J. Lenz ; photography by Robb Helfrick.
        p.   cm.
      Includes bibliographical references and index
      ISBN 0-9650305-0-4
        1. Historic sites--Georgia--Guidebooks. 2. Georgia--Guidebooks.
    3. Georgia--History--Civil War, 1861-1865.   I. Title.

      F287.L36 1995   917.5804'43
                        QBI95-20740

Printed and bound in the United States of America.

How To Use This Book:

This book is intended to be a starting place for the Civil War enthusiast. For those seeking more information on a particular park or event, there are more detailed historical books and guides which focus on a single event or campaign in Civil War history. (See Appendix for supplemental reading.) This book is organized geographically by Georgia's official travel regions. Chattanooga is included (in the Northwest Georgia Mountain region) because of its proximity to Georgia and its role in Georgia's Civil War history. Frequently, historic events cross over several travel regions, requiring travelers to jump to different sections of this book if they are following a particular campaign or raid. Georgia's Civil War sites fall into the following categories: historic parks, battlefields, forts, homes, museums, buildings and ruins, and cemeteries and memorials. Some sites are a combination of categories. Some general advice on each:

Historic Parks

Georgia has four of the 22 national historic parks dedicated to the Civil War: **Chickamauga and Chattanooga National Battlefield Park; Kennesaw Mountain National Battlefield Park; Andersonville National Historic Site;** and **Fort Pulaski National Monument.** For the busy traveler with a casual interest in the Civil War, these parks offer the most to see and are well-prepared for the tourist. The state of Georgia and some towns have Civil War battlefield parks, many which are excellent and worth your time: **Pickett's Mill State Historic Site; Stone Mountain Park;** and **Fort McAllister State Historic Site.** Another state park with a Civil War aspect is **Sweetwater Creek State Conservation Park.** Good local parks include **Dug Gap Battle Park; Tanyard Creek Park; Fort Tyler; Gilgal Church Battle Site;** and **Fort Jackson.**

Historic Forts & Battlefields

Historic forts in Georgia vary widely from huge brick forts such as **Fort Pulaski** to small earthen fortifications barely perceptible to the eye (**Riverside Cemetery** in Macon). Battlefields in Georgia also run the gamut from a preserved national site cultivated to look like it did at the time of the battle, such as **Chickamauga**, to busy urban pavement noted by **historical markers**, such as the **Battle of Atlanta** (or Leggett's Hill or Bald Hill, depending on your nomenclature). Your interest in each will depend on how much of a buff you are or to what degree you are interested in that particular event.

Historic Homes

Most historic homes are in private hands but may be marked by a **Georgia historical marker**. Respect the owners' privacy and **do not** walk up and knock on the door for a private tour. A few homes are available for tours and are noted in this guide. Some Civil War historic homes are state parks and worth touring such as the **A.H. Stephens Historic Park and Confederate Museum; Robert Toombs' House Historic Site**, and, with much less Civil War history, the **Jarrell Plantation Historic Site**. Some non-state park historic homes worth touring are **Barnsley Gardens, Bellevue, Bulloch Hall, Hay House, Old Cannonball House, Old Governor's Mansion**, and the **Green-Meldrim House**. Some homes are available for tours during tour of homes held in many communities. Contact local Chambers of Commerce for details.

Museums

The museum with the best collection of Civil War artifacts is the **Atlanta History Center**, with approximately 1,200 objects on display in a new exhibit debuting in June 1996. The national and state parks have interesting collections, and some larger museums are definitely worth visiting: **Kennesaw Civil War Museum; Army Corps of Engineers Visitors Center; Cyclorama; State Capitol; Stone Mountain; National Infantry Museum;** and **Confederate Naval Museum.** Some of the smaller museums, despite smaller collections and irregular hours, may have more charm than the larger ones. Instead of employees you meet volunteers who have an intense interest in the subject matter and will tell you family stories you won't hear anywhere else. Good ones are the **Washington-Wilkes Historical Museum; Jefferson Davis Memorial Park; Blue & Gray Museum; Museum of Washington County; Midway Museum; Male Academy Museum;** and **DeKalb Historical Society Museum.**

Buildings & Ruins

There are many Civil War era buildings around the state which played a role in the War. Some are open to the public but most are not. There are ruins, generally of old mills, located around the state. The most impressive are at **Sweetwater Creek State Conservation Park,** and **Sope Creek Mills** in the Chattahoochee National Recreation Area. **Barnsley Gardens,** a ruined mansion, has much to offer: gardens, plant shop, and restaurant.

Cemeteries, Memorials, and Monuments

There are so many fascinating Civil War cemeteries in the state that they are listed separately in the appendix of this book. Almost all are open to the public. While Civil War veterans can be found in graveyards all across Georgia, the mass plots or "Confederate Sections" of unknown soldiers are less plentiful. Georgia has the world's largest Civil War memorial (or memorial from any war) with **Stone Mountain.** Many other kinds of memorials are found including more than 100 county memorials erected after the War. One can find memorials to various brigades, women, and others.

Do's and Don'ts:

Do respect private property. Much of Georgia's Civil War history — battlefields, historic homes, forts, and memorials — is on private property. **Don't trespass.**

Do call ahead. Many of Georgia's smaller history museums and historic homes available for tour operate with irregular hours. Many times, published hours are incorrect or changed. **Don't drive several hours only to be disappointed.**

Do get a good supply of maps and travel with a companion. It is easy to get lost even in Georgia's smaller towns, and a general road atlas is sometimes insufficient for finding a special site. Most towns have welcome centers or Chambers of Commerce that have maps or advice on how to find a particular site and are eager to help. One can secure county maps from the Georgia Department Of Transportation at Att: Map Sales, 2 Capital Square, Atlanta, Georgia 30334, (404) 656-5336 for $1.50 each. Traveling with a friend helps you navigate safely on many of Georgia's busy streets and highways. **Don't get lost.**

Do be careful. Some history occurred on land which later became urbanized and may be more unsafe today than during the original Civil War event. Travel with a companion and during the day. Be alert and park and lock your car in a safe place. Some historic land is located on busy streets, so be careful if you plan to swerve over to the shoulder to read a historical marker. **Don't get hurt.**

Do respect historic ground and artifacts. In museums across Georgia there are many fragile items. At battlefield parks, stay on the marked trails, and don't climb on statues, fences, or battlements. **Don't destroy history — leave it for others to enjoy hundreds of years from today.**

Do support historic preservation. There are many organizations, museums, and associations committed to preserving history, and they can use your support. Some are listed in the appendix of this book. **Don't let this important chapter of history be lost.**

TABLE OF CONTENTS

Cannon on Snodgrass Hill, Chickamauga & Chattanooga National Military Park.

GEORGIA'S CIVIL WAR HISTORY is remarkable for its richness and variety. Not only is Georgia the site of the second-bloodiest battle of the Civil War — **Chickamauga** — but it is also the site of many significant and varied historic events and developments in the Civil War. In Georgia, the Civil War buff can visit the bloody grounds of the **Atlanta Campaign**, where huge armies of the North and South fought in what many call the final turning point of the War. One can reexperience the horror of the most notorious prison camp in the War at **Andersonville**, or retrace the **"Great Locomotive Chase,"** the most famous and daring raid of the War. One can follow the path Sherman took on his famous **"March to the Sea"** or study improvements in the art of war at **Fort Pulaski** near Savannah, where the rifled cannon made the brick fort obsolete. One can examine Confederate ironclads at the Columbus **Confederate Naval Museum** or improvements in military communication at the **Signal Corps Museum** near Augusta. Georgia is where the defiant Confederate president Jefferson Davis fled and was captured by Union pursuers. A museum is located at the spot in Irwinville. The largest memorial to the Confederacy (and world's largest carving) is in Georgia at Stone Mountain. Find a memorial to **Nathan Bedford Forrest** in Rome, in tribute to that Confederate genius' rout and capture of an invading Union force of cavalry riding mules. Black troops invaded Georgia, and the famous **Massachusetts 54th**, featured in the movie *Glory*, helped burn the coastal town of Darien. **Wilson's Raiders**, a massive, 14,000-man cavalry force which swept across Alabama and Georgia near the end of the War, may have been the forerunner to the blitzkrieg tactics used by the Germans in World War II, and was called the most successful use of Union cavalry in the War. Wilson's Raiders fought what some call the last battle of the War in **Columbus**. At LaGrange, a brigade of Wilson's Raiders was met by an armed contingent of Georgia women called the **Nancy Harts,** named for the Revolutionary War heroine. **LaGrange** was spared a burning and is today one of Georgia's prettiest towns to tour.

Many beautiful Civil War cemeteries are found throughout Georgia, giving silent testimony to the brave soldiers, both Confederate and Union, who made the ultimate sacrifice in support of their cause. Georgia provided the second-highest per capita number of soldiers, 112,000, considered to be among the Confederacy's most able, along with many leading statesmen of the day, and you can tour some of these leaders' antebellum homes. At least 3,466 black Georgians ably served the Union side.

Frequently, history comes alive in the details.

You can visit a **Macon** home which received a calling card from Union cavalry in the form of a cannon ball. Lying on the floor of the front hallway is a cannon ball. There's a couch Sherman slept on in **Sandersville** during his "March to the Sea," there are bloodstains on the floor of a church used as a hospital in **Ringgold**, there are bulletholes in the siding of an antebellum home at **Barnsley Gardens**, there's a tunnel at **Kennesaw National Park** where trapped Union forces tried to dig under Confederate fortifications to blow them up. You may notice the medicine bottles of sickly vice president of the Confederacy, Alexander H. Stephens at his home in Crawfordville or while gazing at a photo at the **Savannah History Museum**, wonder what was said when retired Confederate generals Robert E. Lee and Joseph E. Johnston met for the final time after the War in Savannah, where Johnston made his home after the War. Enjoy your journey into Georgia's Civil War history!

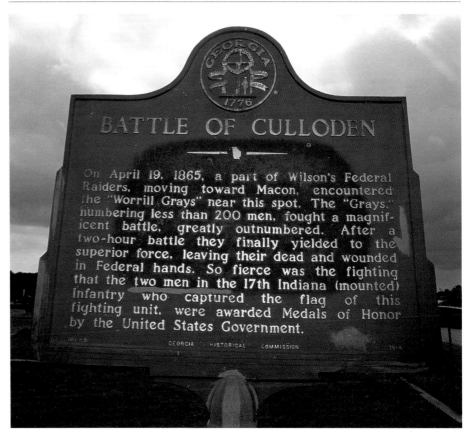

Georgia historical marker at Culloden, Georgia.

Georgia's Historical Markers

If you spend any time touring the state's historic sites, you will inevitably come in contact with Georgia's historical markers. Many historians consider these markers to be remarkably accurate, leading those of us who read them to wonder who wrote them, when, and how.

There are approximately 2,000 of the aluminum markers statewide, with text covering historic events that range from the American Revolution to the Civil Rights movement. The historical marker program began in the 1950s as part of preparations for the Civil War centennial. The State Historical Commission, which oversees the marker program, was established in 1952, and the first Georgia marker was erected in June, 1952, a Civil War marker in Cobb County titled "Davis' Cross Roads."

The State Historical Commission hired two Civil War historians to research, write, and place the Civil War markers. Wilbur G. Kurtz, Sr. was responsible for the markers from Chattanooga to Atlanta. Col. Allen P. Julian handled the series of markers that stretches from Atlanta to Savannah. The two historians' main sources were the *Official Record of the War of the Rebellion* and interviews with Civil War veterans. By walking the battlefields with these veterans, Kurtz and Julian accurately marked sites that otherwise may never have been recorded.

Today, there are approximately 700 Civil War related historical markers statewide, with new ones still being researched and erected.

CHRONOLOGY

1860

Nov. 6 .... Abraham Lincoln is elected president of the United States.

1861

Jan. 3 .... Georgia troops seize Fort Pulaski in Savannah.

Jan. 19 .... Delegates at Georgia's Secession Convention in Milledgeville vote 208 to 89 to secede from the Union.

Jan. 24 .... Augusta Arsenal is surrendered to Georgia troops.

Feb. 8 .... At the convention of seceded states in Montgomery, Alabama, the Confederate Constitution is adopted.

Feb. 9 .... In Montgomery, Jefferson Davis is elected president of the Confederacy and Alexander Stephens, of Georgia, is elected vice president. Davis appoints Robert Toombs, of Georgia, secretary of state.

Mar. 4 .... President Lincoln is inaugurated.

Apr. 12 .... Confederates fire on Fort Sumter, committing the first act of war.

Apr. 13 .... Fort Sumter surrenders to the Confederates.

July 21 .... Confederates defeat the Federals in the first great battle of the war, the Battle of First Bull Run or Manassas, Virginia.

Oct. 19 .... Augustus McLaughlin negotiates a contract with David S. Johnston's Southern Confederate States Navy Yard at Saffold, for the building of the gunboat C.S.S. *Chattahoochee*.

1862

Feb. 6 – 16 .... In Tennessee, Confederates surrender Forts Henry and Donelson.

Mar. 9 .... Off the coast of Virginia, the first battle between ironclad vessels, the U.S.S. *Monitor* and the C.S.S. *Virginia*, is a draw. Strategically, the advantage goes to the Federals.

Mar. 23 – June 9 .. Gen. Stonewall Jackson's Confederate forces are successful in the Shenandoah Valley Campaign in Virginia.

Apr. 6 – 7 .... The Federals are victorious in the Battle of Shiloh, Tennessee, but they do not succeed in gaining new positions.

Apr. 10 – 11 ..... Fort Pulaski, a brick fort guarding the mouth of the Savannah River, falls to Federal forces using rifled cannon.

Apr. 12 .... In the "Great Locomotive Chase," James R. Andrews and his Union volunteers attempt to head north from Big Shanty in the Confederate locomotive, the *General*. Fuller and the Confederate crew of the *Texas* chase the *General* in reverse and capture it north of Ringgold.

June 7 .... Andrews, leader of the Union raiders in the "Great Locomotive Chase," is hanged in Atlanta.

Sept. 17 .... Confederates hold their position in the Battle of Antietam or Sharpsburg, one of the bloodiest battles of the Civil War.

Dec. 11 – 13 ..... Federals fail to take Fredericksburg, Virginia in the Battle of Fredericksburg.

1863

Jan. 1 .... President Lincoln signs the Emancipation Proclamation, freeing slaves in the Confederate states.

Mar. 29 – July 4 .. On Independence Day, Confederates surrender Vicksburg, Mississippi to Federals under Gen. U.S. Grant.

Apr. 11 – May 3 .. With his men riding mules, U.S. Col. Abel Streight conducts a cavalry raid aimed to reach deep into Georgia. Confederate forces under Nathan B. Forrest stop Streight in eastern Alabama, saving Rome, Georgia and Southern railroads from being destroyed.

May 10 .... After being wounded at Chancellorsville and having his arm amputated, Gen. Stonewall Jackson dies of pneumonia south of Fredericksburg, Virginia.

May 27 .... The C.S.S. *Chattahoochee* suffers an accidental boiler explosion on the Chattahoochee River, and 18 men are killed. The gunboat is taken to Columbus for repairs where, at the end of the war, it is destroyed to prevent Federal capture.

June 11 .... Darien is burned by Union troops, including the 2nd South Carolina and one company of the Massachusetts 54th.

June 16 .... The *Atlanta*, an ironclad built in Savannah, launches a diversionary attack in an attempt to save Charleston, South Carolina. After taking several severe hits, the Confederate ship surrenders.

July 1 – 3 .... Confederates under Gen. Robert E. Lee are defeated in the Battle of Gettysburg, the bloodiest battle ever fought on American soil. Total casualties number 43,000.

Sept. 19 – 20 .... Confederate forces under Gen. Braxton Bragg are victorious in the Battle of Chickamauga, the second bloodiest battle of the Civil War with 34,000 total casualties. Gen. William S. Rosecrans' Federals retreat into Chattanooga, and Confederates lay siege by positioning troops on Lookout Mountain and Missionary Ridge.

Oct. 16 .... Grant takes command of the Western armies, including the army at Chattanooga.

Nov. 24 .... In a fight known as the "Battle Above the Clouds," Federal troops under Grant climb and take Lookout Mountain.

Nov. 25 .... Union forces take Chattanooga by pushing the Confederates back into Georgia in the Battle of Missionary Ridge. Confederates retreat into Ringgold, Georgia.

Nov. 27 .... Confederate forces conclude the campaign for Chattanooga with rear guard fighting at Ringgold Gap and retreat into Dalton for the winter.

Dec. 2 .... In Dalton, Bragg turns over command of the Army of Tennessee. Lt. Gen. William Hardee assumes temporary command.

Dec. 27 .... In Dalton, Gen. Joseph E. Johnston assumes command of the Army of Tennessee.

1864

Mar. 10 .... Grant is commissioned General-in-Chief of the U.S. Armies.

Mar. 11 .... Gen. William T. Sherman is appointed commander of the Western Theater.

Feb. 27 .... Federal prisoners begin arriving at the Confederacy's largest prison, Camp Sumter, at Andersonville, near Americus.

May 7 .... Sherman's Federals advance through Ringgold Gap to begin the Atlanta Campaign.

May 7 – 12 .... Rocky Face Ridge Phase of the Atlanta Campaign.

May 8 .... In the Battle of Dug Gap, Union forces unsuccessfully attempt to flank Confederates in Dalton.

May 9 .... Gen. James B. McPherson leads the Federal Army of the Tennessee through Snake Creek Gap, pushing toward Resaca to get at Johnston's rear. When faced with Confederate resistance at Resaca, he pulls back, wasting an opportunity to destroy Johnston.

May 12 – 13 ..... Johnston's Confederate forces evacuate Dalton.

May 13 – 15 ..... In the Battle of Resaca, Johnston's Confederates repulse Sherman's direct attack, but because of the danger of being flanked with the river at his back, Johnston withdraws during the night. Confederates move toward Calhoun and Adairsville.

May 15 – 18 ..... Despite heavy fortifications, Rome falls into Union hands in the Battle of Rome. Federals cross the Oostanaula River and occupy the city until May 24.

May 18 .... Sherman assumes all Johnston's Confederate forces marched from Adairsville to Kingston. When Sherman's men arrive in Kingston, they realize Johnston's men are 5.5 miles east at Cassville.

May 18 – 19 ..... At Cassville, Johnston commands Gen. John Bell Hood to attack separated units of Sherman's army, but Hood fails to attack. Johnston's generals counsel retreat, and the Confederates retire through Cartersville and across the Etowah River to Allatoona.

May 25 .... Confederates repulse Gen. Joseph Hooker's Federals in the Battle of New Hope Church.

May 27 ....Union forces are pushed back at Pickett's Mill.

May 28 ....Johnston attacks near Dallas, but the Confederates are thrown back.

June 1 – 4 ....Sherman captures Allatoona Pass and moves his three armies northeastward, closer to this important supply line. Johnston shifts his army to three high points (Lost, Pine, and Brush Mountains) north of Marietta.

June 14 ....Confederate Gen. Leonidas Polk is killed while observing Union troop movements from atop Pine Mountain.

June 15 – 17 .....Battle of Gilgal Church.

June 15 – 18 .....Federals fail to take Petersburg, Virginia by assault, so they put the city under siege.

June 22 ....Hood leads a strong attack against Federals at Kolb's Farm. The Confederates lose greatly.

June 24 ....In the Battle of LaFayette, Watkins' Federal forces occupying the town are attacked by Gen. Gideon Pillow's Confederate cavalry. When Union reinforcements arrive, Confederate forces withdraw.

June 27 ....Sherman attacks Kennesaw Mountain and is defeated, suffering heavy losses.

July 4 ....Union forces succeed in the Battle of Ruff's Mill. This attack, combined with one on Johnston's right at Smyrna, pushes the Confederate line back to the Chattahoochee River.

July 8 ....At the mouth of Soap Creek, Federal forces cross the Chattahoochee River for the first time, leaving Johnston no choice but to fall back across the river closer to Atlanta.

July 18 ....Hood replaces Johnston as commander of the Army of Tennessee. Kenner Garrard's Federal cavalry division and one of McPherson's infantry brigades reach Stone Mountain Depot, drive off Confederate guards, seize the depot, and destroy railroad track.

July 20 ....Confederate assaults under Hood fail in the Battle of Peachtree Creek. Sherman's armies control almost half the perimeter of Atlanta.

July 21 – 24 ......Garrard's Federal cavalrymen leave a path of destruction through Covington, Conyers, and Social Circle that cuts off the Confederate Army of Tennessee from supplies and reinforcements from the Eastern Confederacy.

July 22 ....Gen. Joseph Wheeler's Confederate cavalrymen strike the Army of the Tennessee's wagon train at Decatur. Federals save their wagons, and Confederates withdraw to reinforce the fight in Atlanta.

July 22 ....Confederate forces are beaten in the Battle of Atlanta, the bloodiest battle of the campaign with over 10,000 casualties. Union Gen. McPherson is killed by skirmishers when he refuses to surrender and tries to escape. While directing his troops toward the battlefield, Confederate Gen. William H.T. Walker is shot from his horse and killed.

July 28 ....Confederate forces are defeated in the Battle of Ezra Church.

July 30 ....While attempting to cut railways south of Atlanta, Union Gen. Edward McCook meets Wheeler's Confederate cavalry three miles south of Newnan. Wheeler saves Newnan in the Battle of Brown's Mill.

July 30 ....On a mission to cut railways south of Atlanta and free prisoners at Andersonville, Gen. George Stoneman's Federal cavalry wreck railway facilities at Griswoldville, Gordon, McIntyre, and Toomsboro and burn trains, trestles, and the railway bridge over the Oconee River. They shell Macon briefly and attempt to retreat while being pursued by Confederate cavalry.

July 31 ....At Sunshine Church, Stoneman surrenders to Confederate cavalrymen under Georgia Gen. Alfred Iverson, Jr. Before surrendering, Stoneman covers the escape of Lt. Col. Silas Adams' and Col. Horace Capron's brigades, which march toward Eatonton. At Murder Creek, the two brigades separate.

Aug. 1 ....After looting food and grain in Eatonton, Adams' brigade burns supplies and valuable industrial property in Madison. That night, Adams' and Capron's brigades camp near Athens. The Federals intend to head to Athens next, but they are turned back at the bridge over the Middle Oconee River by Home Guard units with artillery. Adams turns west and by avoiding towns, reaches Union lines near Marietta on Aug. 4.

Aug. 1 ....After the failure of the Union cavalry raids, the siege of Atlanta begins. Although Union forces had fired shells into the city previously, Sherman officially begins siege operations when he instructs generals John Schofield, George Thomas, and Oliver O. Howard's men to fire into Atlanta simultaneously.

Aug. 2 ....Capron stops briefly at Jug Tavern (now Winder) and again at King's Tanyard, where he is attacked before dawn on Aug. 3. In the Battle of King's Tanyard, 430 of Capron's men are captured. Only Capron and six of his men finally reach the Union lines four days later.

Aug. 6 ....Sherman fails to cut Confederate railroads south of Atlanta in the Battle of Utoy Creek.

Aug. 7 – Oct. 19 ...Gen. Philip Sheridan's Union forces sweep through the Shenandoah Valley in a wave of destruction comparable to Sherman's forthcoming "March to the Sea." Federals take control of the Valley, demolishing railroad lines, burning crops and barns, and killing livestock.

Aug. 18-22 ....Gen. Judson Kilpatrick's Federal cavalry raid Lovejoy's Station, but their efforts to destroy the Macon and Western Railroad are blocked.

Aug. 25 ....The guns of Sherman's forces shelling Atlanta fall silent. Sherman orders Hooker's old 20th Corps to hold its position on the Chattahoochee River, and on the 26th, he sends all of his remaining forces in a bold flanking move to the west and south to cut the railway lines near Jonesboro.

Aug. 31 ....Confederate attacks are repulsed by the Army of the Tennessee in the first day of the Battle of Jonesboro, south of Atlanta. Federals cut the Macon and Western Railroad below Rough and Ready, between Jonesboro and Atlanta.

Sept. 1 ....Confederates evacuate Atlanta. The Battle of Jonesboro reopens when Confederate corps meet Union forces at Rough and Ready. Confederate forces are almost destroyed.

Sept. 2 ....Atlanta surrenders to Sherman, and the Confederate army gathers around Lovejoy's Station. Lincoln receives a telegraph from Sherman which reads, "Atlanta is ours and fairly won." Lincoln declares a national day of thanksgiving.

Sept. 7 ....Sherman orders the evacuation of civilians from Atlanta.

Oct. 5 ....Hood assaults Sherman's supply lines north of Atlanta but does not take the important railroad pass at Allatoona.

Oct. 9 ....Gen. John Winder leaves Andersonville to run Camp Lawton in Millen.

Oct. 12 – 17 .....Hood continues his offensive to the north with skirmishes at Resaca, Coosaville Road near Rome, and Dalton. The Army of Tennessee gives up trying to cut Sherman's supply line and moves toward Alabama.

Nov. 5 ....Cassville is burned by Federal troops, never to be rebuilt.

Nov. 8 ....Lincoln reelected President of the United States.

Nov. 9 – 10 ....Sherman organizes his army into a right and left wing, planning to march deeper into Georgia toward the sea. He departs from Kingston, leaving behind a path of destruction.

Nov. 11 ....As Federals leave Rome to join Sherman in Atlanta, they destroy the railroad and burn property including bridges, foundries, mills, shops, and warehouses.

Nov. 12 – 15 .....Federals burn the city of Atlanta and cut their own lines of communication with the North. Sherman's "March to the Sea" begins.

Nov. 18 ....At Rutledge, Union forces destroy the depot, water tank, warehouses and other railroad facilities. The Georgia state capitol is moved to Macon, its home until March 11, 1865.

CHRONOLOGY

Nov. 19 .... Federal forces burn Madison for a second time, destroying the depot, water tank, warehouses, railroad facilities, and quantities of corn and supplies.

Nov. 20 .... Confederates withdraw from Gordon to defend Ball's Ferry, a crossing on the Oconee River.

Nov. 22 .... Federal infantry defeat Georgia troops in the Battle of Griswoldville.

Nov. 22 .... Sherman's forces press toward Millen, so in the course of three days, Camp Lawton is emptied. Thousands of sick prisoners are dropped in Savannah, and the rest head to a prison camp near Blackshear.

Nov. 22 – 25 ..... Sherman's Federals occupy Milledgeville, the capital of Georgia, after the legislature flees in panic. Union forces plunder private and public buildings, including the State House where soldiers conduct a mock session of the legislature.

Nov. 24 – 25 ..... Skirmishes at Ball's Ferry delay Union forces trying to cross the Oconee River. Confederate forces withdraw, and three days later, on Nov. 26, the Federals finally cross.

Nov. 25 – 26 ..... Sherman's troops skirmish with Wheeler's Confederate cavalry at Sandersville. Sherman burns Sandersville.

Nov. 28 .... Wheeler's Confederate cavalrymen skirmish with Kilpatrick's Federals around Buckhead Church. When Kilpatrick crosses Buckhead Creek east of the church, Wheeler crosses upstream and attacks. Kilpatrick retreats.

Dec. 3 .... Sherman's Seventeenth Corps arrive at Millen.

Dec. 4 .... After nine days of action in the Waynesboro area, Kilpatrick's Federals drive Wheeler's Confederate cavalrymen from their position.

Dec. 5 .... As a result of Sherman's progress toward the sea, 5,000 prisoners in Blackshear are transported southwest to a temporary prison camp at Thomasville.

Dec. 8 .... Federals file across Ebenezer Creek and destroy their pontoon bridge behind them, leaving over 600 slaves in the hands of Confederate forces.

Dec. 10 – 21 ..... Sherman arrives in front of Savannah. He decides to besiege the city rather than assault it.

Dec. 13 .... Sherman captures Fort McAllister on the Ogeechee River below Savannah.

Dec. 13 .... Col. Eli Murray's brigade of Kilpatrick's Federal cavalry advance to Midway Church. On the 14th, Kilpatrick establishes his headquarters there, and on the 17th, Gen. Joseph Mower's division, en route to destroy railroad from McIntosh to the Altamaha River, halts at Midway Church for the night.

Dec. 17 .... Lee can spare no troops from Virginia to help relieve Savannah. Sherman demands surrender from Gen. William J. Hardee, and Hardee rejects.

Dec. 19 .... Atkins' division of Kilpatrick's Federal cavalry destroys trestle work past Morgan's Lake but cannot capture the Savannah and Gulf Railroad bridge over the Altamaha River at Doctortown nor cross the bridge and attack the Doctortown battery. Atkins finally withdraws, marches through Hinesville, and rejoins Kilpatrick at the Ogeechee River.

Dec. 20 .... Surviving prisoners at Thomasville are ordered to begin traveling by foot back to Andersonville. The majority of them complete the journey by Dec. 24.

Dec. 20 .... Hardee sneaks out of Savannah under the cover of night. Confederate forces sink the ironclad ships *Savannah* and *Georgia*, burn steamers and gunboats, spike heavy guns, and destroy powder and ammunition. After crossing the Savannah River, the evacuating troops burn Fort Jackson's barracks.

Dec. 21 .... Federal troops occupy Savannah.

1865

Mar. 22 – July 2 .. Union Gen. James H. Wilson leads the Civil War's largest cavalry force, Wilson's Raiders, in a raid against the heart of Georgia and Alabama.

Apr. 2 .... The siege of Petersburg ends. As Federals drive into Petersburg, the Confederate government, including President Davis, evacuates Richmond, Virginia.

Apr. 3 .... Union troops occupy Petersburg and Richmond, Virginia.

Apr. 6 .... Confederates are defeated at Sayler's Creek, Virginia, the last major engagement between the Army of Northern Virginia and the Army of the Potomac.

Apr. 9 .... Lee surrenders to Grant at Appomattox Court House, Virginia.

Apr. 14 .... President Lincoln is assassinated by John Wilkes Booth at Ford's Theatre in Washington, D.C.

Apr. 16 .... A brigade of Wilson's Raiders capture Fort Tyler, the last Confederate fort to fall during the Civil War. The Federals secure passage over the bridge there to the extensive railroad yard at West Point.

Apr. 16 .... In the last significant land battle of the Civil War east of the Mississippi River, Wilson's main cavalry force is victorious in the fight for Columbus.

Apr. 17 .... Federals burn Columbus' cotton warehouses and industries and destroy the ironclad gunboat, C.S.S. *Muscogee* or *Jackson*.

Apr. 17 .... Outside LaGrange, the Nancy Harts, a company of women soldiers, stand up to Union cavalry forces. No fighting takes place, but the Nancy Harts protect the town from destruction.

Apr. 18 – 19 ..... Wilson marches from Columbus to Macon and crosses the Flint River at Double Bridges. The Raiders fan out in a wave of destruction through Thomaston and Griffin, burning railroad facilities and warehouses.

Apr. 19 .... Confederate forces, calling themselves the "Worrill Grays," yield to Wilson's Raiders near Culloden.

Apr. 20 .... Wilson's subordinates move into Macon, refusing to accept word of Generals Sherman and Johnston's settlement. Realizing the futility of resistance, Confederate forces surrender.

Apr. 26 .... Federal troopers burn the barn where John Wilkes Booth, charged with the assassination of President Lincoln, is hiding. Booth is killed.

Apr. 26 .... Near Durham Station, North Carolina, Sherman's Carolinas Campaign ends with Johnston's Confederate surrender.

May 4 .... President Davis crosses the Savannah River and arrives in Washington. Capturing Davis remains the principal duty of Wilson's Raiders.

May 5 .... In Washington, President Davis meets with his Confederate Cabinet for the last time.

May 10 .... Wilson's Raiders follow Jefferson Davis to Irwinville, and a skirmish breaks out between confused Federals, killing two. President Davis attempts to escape but is forced to surrender to Federal cavalrymen.

May 12 .... In Kingston, the last Confederate forces in Georgia surrender.

July 7 .... At the Washington Arsenal, the Booth conspirators are executed for their role in the assassination of President Lincoln.

Nov. 10 .... On the same platform where the Lincoln conspirators were hanged, Captain Henry Wirz, Commandant of the Andersonville Prison is executed for cruelty to Federal prisoners of war.

Oct. 30 .... Georgia repeals the Act of Secession and adopts a new constitution which ratifies the Thirteenth Amendment abolishing slavery. In 1868, the State is readmitted into the Union after agreeing to ratify the Fourteenth Amendment, protecting the rights of citizenship and the Fifteenth Amendment, protecting voting rights for all races.

With the most widespread military action in Georgia during the Civil War, Northwest Georgia is an area with much history, including the Battle of Chickamauga, Sept. 19-20, 1863; the Battle of Chattanooga, Nov. 23-25, 1863; much of the Atlanta Campaign, May 8-Sept. 2, 1864; and much of the "Great Locomotive Chase," April 12, 1862. The site with the most to see would be the **Chicamauga and Chattanooga National Military Park**, which was the first and largest Civil War park in the country. Many of the towns involved in the Atlanta Campaign have markers, monuments, cemeteries and historic homes dealing with this military event. **Pickett's Mill State Historic Site** has what some call the best preserved battlefield of the Civil War, and in the Visitors Center you can test your military skill in a computer simulation game. **Sweetwater Creek State Conservation Park** has extraordinary mill ruins and a fascinating story to tell. Northwest Georgia features beautiful mountain ranges, deep valleys, and wild rivers, and is the historic land of the Cherokee Indian nation.

Headstone at Cassville Confederate Cemetery, Cassville, Georgia.

Florida state monument at Chickamauga.

CHICKAMAUGA AND CHATTA-nooga National Military Park is the oldest and largest military park in the nation, preserving large portions of the battlefields from the two major battles fought here in the fall of 1863. Of all the sites in this book, this one may have the most to see and experience. There are approximately 700 monuments, 250 cannon, and 650 markers, scattered over 8,000 acres in two states, ranging from the lofty heights of Lookout Mountain to the dense woods, thick underbrush and open meadows near Chickamauga creek. The park is composed of several separate areas: **Chickamauga** battlefield, seven miles south of Chattanooga on U.S. 27; **Point Park** and **Lookout Mountain** battlefield near Chattanooga; a series of parks called reservations along **Missionary Ridge**; **Orchard Knob Reservation** in Chattanooga; and **Signal Point** reservation north of Chattanooga. *(For attractions in the Chattanooga area of Chattanooga and Chickamauga Military Park, see Chattanooga section, pp. 14-17.)*

Chickamauga & Chattanooga National Military Park (Chickamauga, Georgia)

AC CK CT GI GLC

U.S. 27, Ft. Oglethorpe 706-866-9241

I-75 to exit 141. GA 2 (Battlefield Parkway) five miles to U.S. 27. Go left to Visitors Center.

At **Chickamauga Battlefield**, start your tour at the **Visitors Center** where exhibits and an excellent **multimedia presentation** explain the battle and its significance in the Civil War. Also at the center is the **Fuller Gun Collection**, which displays 355 shoulder weapons. Outside is an **artillery display**, illustrating the various cannon used by the light field artillery during the War. The major highlights of the battlefield can be seen in a 7-mile, self-guided **automobile tour**. Monuments and metal tablets, in red for Confederate and blue for Union, show where various units were positioned during the battle. Twenty-nine states provided a total of 124,000 fighting men (the largest battle in the Western Theater), resulting in 34,000 casualties, the second bloodiest battle fought on American soil. Large triangular stacks of cannonballs mark the locations where eight brigade commanders died on the battlefield, including Lincoln's brother-in-law, Benjamin H. Helm. You will find monuments to various units all across the park, with the Northern forces having more monuments than the impoverished Southern forces. Points on the battlefield not to miss: the historic **Brotherton Cabin**, where Georgia native Confederate Gen. James Longstreet charged with his troops through the gap in the Union line, starting the rout; the **Wilder Tower** (commemorating Col. John Wilder and his mounted infantry whose 2,000 men armed with 7-shot Spencer repeating carbines poured deadly fire on Longstreet's veterans but could not stop them) where you get an excellent view of the battlefield; and **Snodgrass Hill**, the knob where U.S. Gen. George H. Thomas earned his nickname "Rock of Chickamauga" when he rallied a small portion of disorganized U.S. troops into a defense force, giving time for Gen. William S. Rosecrans' army to retreat into Chattanooga; and the 87-foot **Georgia Monument**, the largest on the battlefield, with its figures representing the infantry, artillery and cavalry. Reenactments: The Battle of Chickamauga Anniversary Commemoration and the Battles for Chattanooga Anniversary Commemoration occur on weekends closest to the anniversary to the battles (but not on Thanksgiving weekend).

The Brotherton Cabin is located in the path of Gen. James Longstreet's Confederate charge which routed the Union army at Chickamauga.

The Georgia state monument, the tallest on the Chickamauga battle-field, looks out on a field which witnessed terrible carnage in 1863. More than 120,000 men fought in these blood-soaked meadows over two days, resulting in more than 34,000 casualties. Witnesses said Chickamauga was a confusing "soldier's battle," with poorly co-ordinated and managed tactics and action by both sides. The land be-came the first Civil War park in the nation, and has been used ex-tensively by the U.S. Military War Colleges.

Lee and Gordon's Mill
[HM] 🏠 ⚔ ⚙ **AC CK CT GI**
Lee and Gordon's Mill Rd., Chickamauga

U.S. 27 south from Chickamauga Visitors Center 4 miles to stoplight. Turn left onto Lee & Gordon's Mill Rd.

The owner of the **Gordon-Lee Mansion**, James Gordon, built the first mill at this site in 1836, making it one of the oldest mills in Georgia. The mill, a Chickamauga battlefield landmark, was alternately seized by Confederate and Union forces during the campaign, and was the scene of constant skirmishing as it was between the lines for most of the battle. Confederate Gen. Braxton Bragg used it as a headquarters from September 7-10, 1863, later moving his headquarters to LaFayette. The mill was then seized by Union Gen. Thomas Crittenden for his headquarters from Sept. 10-20, 1863, forcing Gordon's son-in-law James Morgan Lee, who operated the mill, to grind corn for the Federals. Later, Confederate Gen. Leonidas Polk established his headquarters here. The mill burned in 1867 but was rebuilt.

Gordon-Lee Mansion
[HM] 🏠 🏛 **AC CK**
217 Cove Rd., Chickamauga 706-375-4728

U.S. 27 south from Chickamauga Visitors Center, at stoplight, turn right onto Lee and Gordon's Mill Rd. Travel apx. 0.5 mile, and turn left on Crittenden Ave. Turn left on Cove Rd., and the mansion will be the fourth building on the right.

Now a bed and breakfast inn, the **mansion** was completed in 1847 by James Gordon and is one of the few remaining structures from the Battle of Chickamauga. It served as the headquarters of Gen. William S. Rosecrans, leader of the 58,000-man Union Army before the Battle of Chickamauga. James Garfield, who would later become president of the U.S., served as Rosecrans' chief-of-staff here. During the battle, the house and grounds became the main hospital for the second bloodiest battle of the Civil War, with 30 Union doctors remaining behind to work on the wounded after the Confederate victory. A **museum** is on the second floor.

Top, beautiful Chickamauga Creek, an Indian word meaning "River of Death," flows peacefully today; but in 1863 it was the scene of much suffering and death. Above, the Gordon-Lee Mansion, used as a hospital and headquarters during the Civil War, today serves as a bed and breakfast.

The Battles of Chickamauga and Chattanooga

Chickamauga was the biggest battle fought in the Western Theater, and the bloodiest, with more than 34,000 casualties. The name for the muddy creek comes from the Cherokee, and has been translated to mean the "river of death." U.S. Maj. Gen. William S. Rosecrans' troops had maneuvered Gen. Braxton Bragg's Confederate troops out of Chattanooga without a fight by threatening his supply lines. Bragg had moved his headquarters to LaFayette, where he planned his next move. Rosecrans, thinking Bragg was in full retreat, dangerously divided his three corps along a 40-mile front, pursuing Bragg's men through the rugged Northwest Georgia mountains. Bragg hoped to destroy the isolated fragments of the Union army as they emerged from the mountains, but his goal was not realized when his subordinate officers failed to execute their orders. Rosecrans recognized the vulnerability of his troops, and quickly concentrated his men west of Chickamauga Creek near **Lee & Gordon's Mill** on the Chattanooga-LaFayette road. With news of reinforcements, Bragg regained confidence and began the Battle of Chickamauga on the morning of Sept. 19, 1863, with Confederates attacking the Union left flank under Gen. George H. Thomas, in a sequence of attacks from north to south. Bragg was trying to push the Federals into a mountain hollow known as McLemore's Cove, but at the end of the day, the battered Union troops had held fast. That evening, Bragg was reinforced by troops from Virginia, under Lt. Gen. James Longstreet, tipping the numerical scales in the Confederates' favor, with approximately 66,000 Rebels versus 58,000 Yankees. The next day, the Confederate attacks resumed, with the turning point coming from a mistake on the Union side. A Union officer reported erroneously that a gap existed in his line. Without verifying whether this was true, Rosecrans ordered a division to pull out of position to plug the alleged gap, thereby creating a real gap. As luck would have it, at this precise spot and time, Longstreet had sent thousands of charging Confederate troops, which had the effect of routing four Union divisions and sending them fleeing back to Chattanooga. Some Union troops did not run, and Gen. George Thomas gathered them at a small elevation called Snodgrass Hill, and fought a bloody rearguard action that successfully allowed the Federal army to retreat before being totally destroyed. When sundown came, Thomas, later to be nicknamed the "Rock of Chickamauga," guided the remain-

Above left, Union Gen. U.S. Grant, who personally commanded Federal forces trapped in Chattanooga. His first move was to open supply lines by a sneak night attack on the Tennessee River. Above right, U.S. Army transport on the Tennessee River in 1863.

der of the army through a mountain gap back to Chattanooga. Senior officers under Bragg urged him to immediately pursue the disorganized Federals, but he ignored their advice and possibly missed an opportunity to completely destroy a major part of the Union army.

The battles for Chattanooga, coming two months later from Nov. 23-25, 1863, was a Union victory that set the stage for the Atlanta Campaign. Rosecrans had retreated into the river town and waited for help. The Confederates had taken the heights at Missionary Ridge and Lookout Mountain, and entrenched in the Chattanooga Valley between, and managed to cut the city's rail and river supply lines, placing the Union troops under siege. Rosecrans' troops were subsisting on starvation rations which came to town over a thin, 60-mile supply line. Into this situation came Gen. U.S. Grant, who had been promoted to command of the Union armies in the Western Theater in mid-October. After the disaster at Chickamauga, he had replaced Rosecrans with Thomas, ordered reinforcements to Chattanooga, including two corps from Virginia under Maj. Gen. Joseph Hooker and four divisions from Vicksburg led by Maj. Gen. William T. Sherman, and worked to resupply the trapped men. On Oct. 27, Union troops quietly floated down the Tennessee River at night to capture Brown's Ferry, allowing Union steamboats to transport supplies within eight miles of Chattanooga. Meanwhile on the Confederate side, Bragg was losing control of his army. His senior officers thought him incompetent, and unanimously voiced their lack of confidence in his command to Confederate President Davis, but Davis refused to act. At Davis' suggestion, Bragg sent Longstreet and his 15,000 men to Knoxville, to be rid of one of his big-

gest critics. The effect was to reduce Bragg's fighting strength. By the time Sherman's troops arrived in mid-November, the Union supplies were flowing to Federal troops, and the Union forces numbered nearly 70,000 versus 46,000 Confederates. On Nov. 23, Thomas' troops captured Orchard Knob, a small hill that was the forward position of the Confederates. The next day, Sherman's men launched an attack on Maj. Gen. Patrick R. Cleburne's men at the right flank of the Confederates and Missionary Ridge, but got bogged down when they discovered a deep valley between them and their goal. Meanwhile that day, Gen. Joe Hooker's men had achieved success in taking Lookout Mountain in the "Battle Above the Clouds." The next day, Sherman continued to assault Cleburne's troops but with little success, as Hooker worked his way across the Chattanooga Valley to Bragg's left. Grant, impatient at his command post on Orchard Knob, ordered Thomas' men toward the first row of trenches at the bottom of Missionary Ridge to relieve the pressure on Sherman. Thomas' men, consisting of four divisions, accomplished the task quickly, but realized that they were exposed to fire from trenches located above them. In a spontaneous move, the Federals charged up the 500-foot hill, shocking both Grant on Orchard Knob and the Confederates on Missionary Ridge, and winning the battle as they sent the Rebels retreating into Georgia. A rearguard action by Cleburne at Ringgold, Georgia, saved the Confederate troops from ruin. The Confederates lost approximately 6,700 men to the Union's 5,000 casualties, but more importantly, the Confederates lost a strategic transportation hub.

Point Park

🏠 ⚔ 🏛 🏞 AC CK CT GI

Lookout Mt., Chattanooga, TN 423-821-7786

From downtown Chattanooga, take Broad St. to Lookout Mt. Park is at intersection of W. Brow and E. Brow Roads on Lookout Mt.

Point Park, at 2,100 feet above sea level, features beautiful views of the Tennessee River Valley. Three **gun batteries** mark a small segment of the siege lines that encircled Chattanooga. The 95-foot **Peace Monument**, constructed from pink Massachusetts granite and Tennessee marble, features on top of its shaft a Union and Confederate soldier shaking hands under one flag. The **visitors center** has the historic James Walker painting of "The Battle Above The Clouds," measuring 13 feet by 33 feet, along with an audio program discussing the work, and a book store. A set of stairs leads 500 feet down to **The Ochs Museum and Overlook**, with great views of the valley. A ledge nearby is **Umbrella Rock**, where many Union soldiers had their photo taken, including Gen. U.S. Grant. To the left of the museum is the **Bluff Trail**, the main hiking trail of the park which will take you to the **Cravens House.**

The Cravens House

🏠 ⚔ 🏞 CT GI

Lookout Mountain, TN 423-821-6161

Follow Scenic Hwy. past Ruby Falls. Before crossing the Incline, turn on Cravens Terrace Rd.

Built around 1854 by Robert Cravens, this **house** was the site of the fiercest fighting on the mountain and is the only remaining structure of the Civil War period on the battlefield. Confederate officers used the house as a headquarters for their fortifications on Lookout Mountain, only to be pushed out by Union Gen. "Fighting" Joe Hooker on Nov. 24, 1863 during the "Battle Above the Clouds." Only open for tours on Sat. & Sun. Grounds are always open.

Above left, view from Point Park on Lookout Mountain. Top right, Point Park entrance.

Chickamauga & Chattanooga National Military Park (Chattanooga, TN)

🏠 ⚔ 🚂 R.I.P. 🏛 🏞

AC CK CT GI GLC

Chattanooga Park headquarters are at Point Park. See directions to Point Park.

A variety of **parks, monuments, scenic views, museums** and **historic structures** are featured in the Tennessee portion of the Chickamauga and Chattanooga Battlefield Park. These sites focus on the Battles For Chattanooga, which occurred two months after Chickamauga. Besieged Union forces under Gen. U.S. Grant in Chattanooga defeated Confederate forces under Gen. Braxton Bragg on Lookout Mountain and then Missionary Ridge.

The Tennessee River and Chattanooga (at top right in photo) from Point Park on Lookout Mountain.

Signal Point Reservation

HM CT GI

Signal Mountain, TN

Hwy. 27 to Signal Mt. Blvd. exit. Follow to top of mountain and take first street to the left. Follow signs.

Signal Point Reservation, to the north and directly opposite Lookout Mountain marks the spot where Native Americans, Confederates, and Union forces communicated through the use of signals. When the Federal army was trapped in Chattanooga in the fall of 1863, the U.S. Signal Corps was able to communicate up to 25 miles through the use of flags. Exhibits are displayed along the terrace, which affords a beautiful view of the Tennessee River Valley.

Orchard Knob Reservation

HM CT

Orchard Knob Ave., Chattanooga, TN

At Orchard Knob Ave. and East Third St.

Orchard Knob Reservation marks the site of Gen. U.S. Grant's headquarters during the Union assaults of Confederate forces holding Missionary Ridge on Nov. 25, 1863. It was here that Grant and Gen. George "Rock of Chickamauga" Thomas watched in amazement as Union troops — without orders — charged up Missionary Ridge, knocking Gen. Braxton Bragg's Confederates back into Georgia. Or-

chard Knob was the forward position of the Confederate siege line, until Grant attacked on Nov. 23, when he suspected the Rebel forces might be lifting their siege. A half-hour battle secured the hill for the Union. Located in the park are **monuments, memorials, descriptive metal plaques,** and **cannon.**

Missionary Ridge Reservations

HM CT GI

Crest Road, Chattanooga, TN

Follow Crest Rd. from Glass St.

Missionary Ridge is a 400-foot high, 20-mile long mountain barrier running east of the city of Chattanooga. Along this ridge were the seemingly impregnable, entrenched Confederate forces and gun batteries, laying siege to U.S. forces in Chattanooga. A series of military reservations, with **monuments, cannon** and **explanatory tablets,** mark significant spots on the ridge. The **Sherman Reservation** marks the area where Gen. William T. Sherman tried in vain to break through the Confederate eastern flank commanded by Gen. Patrick Cleburne. The **De Long Reservation** contains a large monument to the 2nd Minnesota Regiment, which fought gallantly at Chickamauga and was among the first to reach the crest of Missionary Ridge. The **Ohio Reservation** honors troops who fought in the Chattanooga Campaign. The **Ohio Monument** was dedicated by then Ohio Gov. William McKinley, who later became

president of the U.S. The **Bragg Reservation** marks the site of Confederate Gen. Braxton Bragg's headquarters, who resigned his commission after his defeat at Chattanooga. The monument here honors Illinois troops.

Georgia Monument, Chickamauga National Military Park.

Left, Andrews' Raiders monument at Chattanooga National Cemetery. Top right, Andrews' grave. Lower right, Ohio Monument on Missionary Ridge.

National Cemetery

HM R.I.P. AC CK CT GI GLC

1200 Bailey Ave., Chattanooga, TN 615-855-6590

I-24 West to Fourth Ave. exit, make a right at the light. Go left at the next light. When you get to Holtzclaw, go right. Main cemetery entrance will be on the left.

This national **cemetery**, located on 124 acres of gently rolling hills, contains the reinterred Union dead from Chickamauga, Chattanooga and other actions in the area. Estab-lished in 1865 by Gen. George H. Thomas, a total of 12,956 Union soldiers are known to be buried here, approximately 5,000 with iden-tities unknown. Confederate dead from the Battle of Chattanooga were buried in the Con-federate Cemetery in Chattanooga, and the Confederate dead from Chickamauga were buried in Marietta. Today more than 31,000 veterans from many American wars are bur-ied in the National Cemetery, which was offi-cially established by the 1867 Act to Estab-lish and Protect National Cemeteries. This is also the last resting place of eight of the 24 Andrews Raiders of the famous "Great Loco-motive Chase," (see page 37) including James Andrews, who were executed in Atlanta, bur-ied in Oakland Cemetery, but later reinterred here. (Except for Andrews, who was buried in an unmarked grave in Atlanta and later rein-terred here.) Just inside the main gate is a large monument with a bronze likeness of the *Gen-eral*, the locomotive stolen near Marietta, Georgia and recaptured just north of Ringgold, Georgia. Tried as spies, Andrews and seven of his men were hanged. Four of those buried here were among the first recipients of the Con-gressional Medal of Honor. The monument was dedicated on Memorial Day, 1891.

Confederate Cemetery

R.I.P. AC CK CT GI

East Third St., Chattanooga, TN

Located from East Third to East Fifth near downtown Chattanooga.

After the war, in 1865, returning Confederate veterans decided to establish a **Confederate cemetery** for those who were killed in various actions around Chattanooga or died in hospitals and then were buried in plots and graveyards around the city. Organizers decided on the east side of the Citizens Cemetery and gathered the dead and had them reinterred. Commemorative **tablets** line the walks identifying the units but not individuals, unless they were veterans. Notice the **Confederate flag on the main gate and the metal plaque** erected in 1901. A large stone **obelisk** stands on the hill.

This diorama at the Battles for Chattanooga Museum explains the history of the battles.

Chattanooga Confederate obelisk honors Chattanooga's Confederate dead.

The Battles For Chattanooga Museum

CT GI

3742 Tennessee Ave., Chattanooga, TN 615-821-2812

I-24 to exit 178, left on South Broad to Tennessee Ave.

Their motto, "Visit Here First," is good advice. At this tourist attraction, one can get a feel for what happened in Chattanooga before going to Point Park. A large, three-dimensional **battle map**, with 5,000 miniature soldiers, 650 lights, sound effects, and smoking cannons, is an excellent primer for adults and children. The museum also has Civil War artifacts and a bookstore.

National Medal Of Honor Museum of Military History

GI

400 Georgia Ave., Chattanooga, TN 615-267-1737

I-24 to Hwy. 27. exit 1C (Fourth St. exit) to fifth light.

The **National Medal of Honor Museum** highlights the heroic deeds of American Servicemen and one woman who won the nation's greatest honor. The Medal of Honor, established during the Civil War, was awarded first to the Andrews Raiders, some of whom are buried in the **Chattanooga National Cemetery** not far from this museum.

Here you find history and some unusual artifacts of the Civil War (first cannon ball fired into Chattanooga), Spanish American War, WWI, WWII (a brick from Hitler's house), Korean War, Vietnam War and Persian Gulf War; plus the individual stories of Medal of Honor recipients. The museum is raising funds to build a permanent site for its artifacts and exhibits.

RINGGOLD WAS A VERY IMPORTANT railroad town on the Western & Atlantic and the scene of much activity during the Civil War. The "Great Locomotive Chase" ended just a few miles north of the town when James Andrews and his raiders, pursued by William Fuller in the *Texas*, abandoned the stolen *General* and fled to the woods only to be quickly captured. A **marker** is erected at the spot, two miles north of Ringgold on the Ooltewah Road.

In 1862-63, Ringgold was the site of many hospitals, treating more than 20,000 injured and sick troops. In early October, 1863, the hospitals were moved south to avoid capture by advancing U.S. forces. Gen. William S. Rosecrans' Union army and Gen. Braxton Bragg's Confederates fought nine miles west of Ringgold at Chickamauga. A **historical marker** notes that after Chickamauga, "food became so scarce that mule meat was fed to these sick and wounded men."

When Bragg's army was forced off Missionary Ridge and retreated toward Dalton, Confederate Brig. Gen. Patrick Cleburne was ordered to take a position in Ringgold Gap and delay Union forces, which saved the Confederate army, supply trains, and artillery from capture. The Battle of Ringgold Gap, on Nov. 27, 1863, earned Cleburne the nickname of "Stonewall of the West." The area around Ringgold became a no-man's land between the Union and Confederates in the winter of 1863, after the battle for Chattanooga and before the Atlanta Campaign. The town of Ringgold was the forward position of Union forces after the Battle of Ringgold Gap, and the **Whitman-Anderson House** at 309 Tennessee Street, served as temporary headquarters for Gen. U.S. Grant.

Atlanta Campaign Pavilion #1

HM 🏞 AC

U.S. 41, Ringgold

I-75 to exit 139. North on U.S. 41. Marker is one mile south of Ringgold.

During the Great Depression in the 1930s, the Works Project Administration (WPA) erected five interpretive Atlanta Campaign pavilions for the National Park Service to mark and explain this significant event in the Civil War. These attractive **fieldstone constructions**, now owned by the state, feature a giant bronze relief map of the area, plaques describing the actions that took place nearby, and picnic tables for travelers looking to pause and reflect on Civil War history. Unfortunately, some of these **pavilions** have been at-

tacked by vandals and are in need of repair. The first pavilion explains the entire Atlanta Campaign. Other pavilions are found at Rocky Face Ridge, Resaca, Cassville, and New Hope Church. A short walk behind the pavilion and across the railroad tracks takes you to a large **monument** marking the battle position of Col. David Ireland's New York brigades, which were defeated during the Battle of Ringgold Gap.

Stone Presbyterian Hospital

HM 🏠 AC CK CT GI

U.S. 41, Ringgold

South of Ringgold on U.S. 41 at intersection of 41/76 and GA Hwy. 2.

This sandstone building, erected in 1850 from rock quarried from White Oak Mountain to the north, was used as a Confederate hospital after the Battle of Ringgold on Nov. 27, 1863. Bloodstains are reportedly still vis-

Top, Stone Presbyterian Church served as a hospital during the Civil War. Below left, Atlanta Campaign marker; on right, Ringgold's historic depot.

ible on the floor. The **church**, on the National Register of Historic Places, has been used by many religious denominations and was purchased by the Catoosa County Historical Society.

Western & Atlantic Depot

HM 🏠 AC CK CT GI GLC

U.S. 41, Ringgold

On U.S. 41 south of downtown Ringgold.

Built in 1849 of locally quarried sandstone block with 14-inch thick walls, this large **depot** served a bigger market than Chattanooga in the early 1850s. Large quantities of wheat were shipped from this depot. Now listed on the National Register of Historic Places, the depot was badly damaged by U.S. Gen. Joe Hooker's guns during the Battle of Ringgold, Nov. 27, 1863, and was repaired with lighter-colored limestone block, a testament to the damage it received.

THE TOWN OF TUNNEL HILL WAS AN important railroad town on the Western and Atlantic Railroad during the Civil War, used for supplying the Confederates during the Chickamauga and Chattanooga battles and for supplying the Union during the Atlanta Campaign. Hospitals were located here, and several antebellum homes and buildings remain, as do breastworks constructed by both armies.

Railroad Tunnel

Ⓗⓜ ✕ ◎ **AC CK CT GI GLC**

Clisby Austin Rd., Tunnel Hill

Exit 137 off I-75, north on U.S. 41 apx. 3.5 miles; turn right on Cherry St., go to railroad at Clisby Austin Rd.

Tunnel Hill was the scene of much activity during the Civil War. Goods and supplies going from the Western Frontier via Chattanooga to the Atlantic Coast had to pass through this 1,447-foot long tunnel. An engineering marvel when it was finished in 1850, the tunnel was built by two separate parties who started on either side of Chetoogeta Mountain and dug to the center. It remained in use until 1920 when a larger tunnel was dug next to it. The oldest tunnel in the southeastern U.S. — the first south of the Mason-Dixon line — it was contested at least four times between Confederate and U.S. forces in 1864, and U.S. Gen. William T. Sherman began the Atlanta Campaign on May 7, 1864 by seizing Tunnel Hill, where Confederates had maintained a camp after the Battles of Chattanooga. "The Great Locomotive Chase" raced through the tunnel. A fertilizer company has part of the old **Tunnel Hill Depot**, where Confederate President Jefferson Davis stopped and gave a rousing speech early in the War. The Battle of Tunnel Hill Reenactment is held the first weekend after Labor Day. During this weekend, tours of **Clisby Austin** are offered, with profits going to preservation of Tunnel Hill War sites.

Clisby Austin House

Ⓗⓜ 🏠 ✕ **AC CK GI MTS**

Clisby Austin Rd., Tunnel Hill

See directions to Tunnel Hill. House across from Covered Bridge on Clisby Austin Rd.

The **Clisby Austin House** was used as a Confederate hospital following the Battle of Chickamauga and Gen. John Bell Hood recovered here after having his leg amputated

Abandoned today, this railroad tunnel was an engineering feat in the 1800s.

due to injuries suffered on the Chickamauga battlefield. U.S. Gen. William T. Sherman headquartered here from May 7-12, 1864, during the fighting around Dalton at the beginning of the Atlanta Campaign. The house is privately owned.

Prater's Mill

Ⓗⓜ 🏠 ✕ ◎ **AC A**

Hwy. 2, Varnell 705-275-6455

I-75 to exit 138, north on Hwy. 201 to Hwy. 2; turn right and travel 2.6 miles to mill on left.

This three-story **grist mill**, established in 1855, is on the National Register of Historic Places, and is one of Georgia's best examples of the mills which played an important economic role in the riverine South. It was the camp site for 600 U.S. soldiers in February 1864 after skirmishing near Dalton. Confederate Gen. Joseph Wheeler set up camp here with 2,500 men en route to Tunnel Hill in April 1864. Grounds are open during daylight

hours and the buildings are open during the Prater's Mill Country Fair held annually on Mother's Day weekend and the second weekend in October.

The Varnell House

Ⓗⓜ 🏠 ✕ **AC**

Hwy. 201, Varnell

Apx. 1 mile south of Varnell on Hwy. 201. Look for historical marker.

The **Varnell House**, built in 1847 by "Dry Dan Dold," was used as a Confederate and Federal hospital and was headquarters for several Federal generals. A number of skirmishes were fought around the house, including a Confederate victory when Confederate cavalry great, "Fighting" Joe Wheeler swung around the Union left flank on May 12, 1864, taking the town, inflicting casualties, and capturing 100 prisoners, including nine officers.

The rough, steep terrain of Dug Gap helped Confederates beat back Union attacks during the Atlanta Campaign.

army had to retreat south when threatened on their flank near Resaca.

Dalton was an important railroad town on the Western and Atlantic Railroad which connected Chattanooga with Atlanta. A northern line, the East Tennessee and Georgia, connected east Tennessee with Dalton. Also an important hospital town, Dalton had four buildings dedicated to caring for the wounded and sick; and the "Great Locomotive Chase" came through here. With 32, more Civil War **historical markers** are found in Whitfield County than in any other county in the state.

Dug Gap Battlefield Park

HM ✗ 🚋 AC

Dug Gap Battlefield Rd., Dalton

Exit 136 off I-75, west 1.6 miles on Walnut Ave./Dug Gap Battlefield Rd. Park on right.

Dug Gap Battlefield Park, located on a rocky ridge, is a great place to see the difficulty of fighting on this steep terrain. A path leads to a 1,237-foot long segment of the stone breastworks which protected outnumbered Confederates who successfully held off Union attacks Feb. 25 and May 8, 1864. The Confederates used not only bullets but huge boulders, which they rolled down on screaming Federals.

The Blunt House & Cook House

HM 🏠 AC

Blunt House: 506 S. Thornton Ave., Dalton
Cook House: 314 N. Selvidge St., Dalton

Exit 136 off I-75 North, east 1.6 miles on Walnut Ave., turn left on Thorton, Blunt house on third block on left.

Built in 1848 by Ainsworth Blunt, Dalton's first mayor, the **Blunt House** was used as a Union hospital in 1864. The house is on the National Register of Historic Places and owned by the Whitfield-Murray Historical Society. Call 706-278-0217 for information. The **Cook (Huff) House** was Confederate Gen. Johnston's headquarters during the winter of 1863-64 and was the scene of C.S. Brig. Gen. Patrick Cleburne's controversial proposal to emancipate and arm slaves to assist the southern cause.

D ALTON WAS THE WINTER CAMP of Gen. Joseph E. Johnston's Army of Tennessee in 1863, the place where the second main army of the Confederacy had its morale restored to health after the disaster at Chattanooga under Gen. Braxton Bragg.

Dalton was also the Confederate headquarters when U.S. Gen. W.T. Sherman opened the Atlanta Campaign in May 1864 with the battles near Rocky Face Ridge, including the battle of Rocky Face Ridge, Buzzard's Roost (or Mill Creek Gap) and Dug Gap. Johnston's

A rare statue of C.S. Gen. Joseph Johnston is found in Dalton, where he camped before the Atlanta Campaign. Above, the Dalton Depot.

C.S. Gen. Joe Johnston Statue

 AC

Hamilton and Crawford streets, Dalton

Dalton Central Business District.

This is reportedly the only **statue** in the country dedicated to Confederate Gen. Joseph E. Johnston. On the Register of National Historic Places, it was erected in 1912 by the United Daughters of the Confederacy.

Confederate Cemetery

AC CK CT GI

Emory St., Dalton

Exit 136 off I-75, east 1.6 miles on Walnut Ave., turn left onto Greenwood and drive 0.3 mile to the stop sign at Emory. Cemetery entrance is straight ahead.

From 1862 to Sept. 1863, when hospitals were relocated farther south, four main Confederate hospitals treated the injured and sick. West Hill contains the remains of 421 unknown and four known Confederates and four unknown Union soldiers. Some died in the battles of Stones River, Perryville, Chickamauga, Lookout Mountain, Chattanooga, Missionary Ridge and other battles north of Dalton. Others died of disease and sickness in Dalton's Confederate hospitals. A **monument** was erected in 1892 to commemorate the Confederate soldiers who died in the battles of Dalton, Rocky Face, Chickamauga and Resaca.

Crown Gardens/Archives

GI

715 Chattanooga Ave., Dalton 706-278-0217

Exit 137 off I-75, east 16 miles on U.S. 41, south 1 mile on Chattanooga Ave. Gardens on right.

This is the home of the **Whitfield-Murray Historical Society**, which houses Civil War artifacts (some from the Orphan Brigade excavated by the Dalton Civil War Roundtable), and research material on the Civil War.

Atlanta Campaign Pavilion #2

 AC

U.S. 41, Dalton

U.S. 41 north of Dalton to Georgia Highway Patrol Post.

The second **Atlanta Campaign pavilion and relief map** is located in Mill Creek Gap. Here the Confederates dammed Mill Creek to create a lake and block the gap, stopping Gen. George Thomas's Federal forces. The map features the events that occurred around Dalton.

The Blunt House.

The Hamilton House

AC

Intersection of Matilda St. & Chattanooga Ave., Dalton

From Joe Johnston statue go north on Hamilton. At 0.2 mile, turn left onto Hawthorne and immediately right onto Chattanooga Ave. House will be on the left.

This beautiful home, built by John Hamilton about 1840, served as headquarters for the celebrated Brig. Gen. John H. Lewis' Kentucky Orphan Brigade. Lewis had his tent near the **spring house**.

The Resaca battlefield as photographed by George N. Barnard in 1864. Below center, Resaca reenactors.

THE FIRST SERIOUS FIGHTING OF the Atlanta Campaign occurred in the Dalton area on May 8, 1864, with fighting at Rocky Face Ridge, Buzzard's Roost, and Dug Gap. Union Gen. W.T. Sherman's plan was to attack and hold Confederate Gen. Joseph Johnston's men at these positions, while sending Gen. James B. McPherson's troops on a wide, flanking move to Snake Creek Gap, where he could cut Johnston's supply line at Resaca, ten miles south of Dalton, and isolate and destroy the Army of Tennessee. McPherson easily seized Snake Creek Gap, discovering that Johnston had failed to guard it, but on the next day he encountered 4,000 entrenched troops outside of Resaca. Imagining what could go wrong, McPherson cautiously retired his superior forces back into Snake Creek Gap, missing an opportunity, as Sherman said, that doesn't come twice in a lifetime. An upset Sherman ordered his armies to Snake Creek Gap, and

Johnston abandoned Dalton, retreating to Resaca. The first major battle of the Atlanta Campaign happened in Resaca, a small town located where the Western and Atlantic Railroad meets the Oostanaula River. Although casualty estimates vary, the Battle of Resaca on May 14-15, 1864 may have been one of

the bloodier battles of the Atlanta Campaign, with approximately 6,100 casualties: 3,500 Union and 2,600 Confederate. Looking down from entrenched high ground east of Camp Creek, C.S. Gen. Joseph Johnston put his Confederate left flank on the Oostanaula River and right flank on the Conasauga River, with the railroad and town to his back and a marshy creek in his front. From this position Johnston withstood attacks from Union Gen. W.T. Sherman's Union men, who had to come down from their high ground and cross Camp Creek Valley. From the **Lafayette Road Route 136 looking north**, you can view the natural amphitheater the Resaca battlefield creates. Federal forces were able to threaten the Confederate rear by crossing at Lay's Ferry, and Johnston had to retreat south to Calhoun. **Entrenchments** remain, but they are on private property. A popular **living history reenactment** occurs in Resaca in May.

Atlanta Campaign Pavilion #3

🪦 🎖 AC

U.S. 41, Resaca

North on U.S. 41 from Resaca apx. 2 miles.

The third in a series of **Atlanta Campaign** pavilions and relief maps is located where the rear of the Confederate line was during the Battle of Resaca. The map explains the events at the Battle of Resaca and the Federal flanking movement at Lay's Ferry, which resulted in Johnston's withdrawal south over the Oostanaula River along the Western and Atlantic Railroad to Calhoun and then Cassville.

Confederate Cemetery

🪦 ⚔ R.I.P. 🎖 AC GLC

County Rd. 297, Resaca

North on U.S. 41 from Resaca apx. 2 miles, right on County Road 297.

This haunting **cemetery** is located close to the site of the fiercest fighting at Resaca, where Confederate Lt. General John Bell Hood almost broke Sherman's left flank when he attacked Major Gen. Joseph Hooker's men. Shortly after the battles, a local resident, Miss Mary J. Green, organized Resaca's women to give the dead a decent burial. More than 400 Confederates are buried in the cemetery. On the wall of the stone gate is a **marker** placed by the Atlanta Chapter of the United Daughters of the Confederacy to the memory of Mary Green "who established this Resaca cemetery — the first in this state — for our Confederate soldiers."

The Resaca Living History Reenactment, held every May in Resaca, is one of the most popular in the South.

BECAUSE OF ROME'S LOCATION AT the head of the Coosa River (where the Etowah and Oostanaula rivers meet) and rail connection to the main line between Atlanta and Chattanooga, the town was a rising center for manufacturing and transportation in northwest Georgia. The city became a major location for troop movements from 1862 through 1864. Rome's farms in the surrounding countryside supplied food for the Confederacy, the Noble Brothers Foundry manufactured cannons and other military goods, and the city's hospitals treated thousands of wounded and sick. Because of its value to the Confederacy, Rome became a target of several Union military campaigns. In May 1863, Union Col. Abel Streight led a raid toward Rome, which was thwarted by Gen. Nathan Bedford Forrest. This raid led to the building of earthen fortifications around the city. In mid-May, while the Battle of Resaca of the Atlanta Campaign was underway, Union Gen. Jefferson C. Davis, with his 2nd Infantry Division,

First Presbyterian Church in Rome.

was looking for a bridge that didn't exist to cross the Oostenaula south of the Confederates in Resaca. Without orders, Davis decided to push on to Rome, where he took the city on May 18, 1864. Davis told Sherman that Rome was "the strongest fortified place I have seen in Dixie." Union forces garrisoned the city during the Atlanta Campaign and strengthened fortifications after Gen. John Bell Hood moved north to strike at Sherman's supply lines after the fall of Atlanta. Sherman made Rome his headquarters in October and November 1864. From Rome, Sherman telegraphed U.S. Grant with his plan to "March to the Sea," and when it was approved, he burned Rome Nov. 10-11, 1864, then did the same to Atlanta four days later. Leaving Rome, he wired Gen. George Thomas in Nashville, "Last night we burned Rome, and in two or more days will burn Atlanta." Rome was the first to feel Sherman's wrath. An encampment and reenactment are held annually to commemorate the Siege of Rome.

First Presbyterian Church stained glass.

First Presbyterian Church
Saint Paul A.M.E. Church

HM 🏠 AC

First Presbyterian: 101 East Third Ave., Rome
Saint Paul A.M.E.: E. 6th Ave. and W. 2nd St.
Rome

From the Rome Visitors Center, take Turner McCall Blvd. to Broad St. Turn right on Broad to historic downtown.

First Presbyterian Church, dedicated in 1856, was used by Union troops for food storage and reportedly as a hospital during the Civil War. The pews were removed and used for the construction of a pontoon bridge across one of Rome's rivers and for the construction of horse stalls. **Saint Paul A.M.E. Church** was built in 1852 and used by occupying Union forces as a stable for their horses.

Noble Brothers cannon lathe.

Noble Brothers Foundry

HM ◉ AC GI

Broad St. and Myrtle St., Rome

Travel south on Broad St. Marker is on the left before you cross the Coosa river.

The Noble Brothers Foundry, an important Confederate arms manufacturing center, was destroyed by Sherman when he burned the city to go on his "March to the Sea," Nov. 10-11, 1864. A **marker** can be seen at the former site of the foundry, which was situated between the railroad tracks and the Etowah River. A giant lathe belonging to the Noble Brothers and used to turn out approximately 70 cannon is found at the **Rome Visitors Center**. The face plate still bears marks from sledgehammers used unsuccessfully by Sherman's men, who were unable to destroy it due to its huge size.

Fort Norton

HM ✕ 🚂 AC GI HTC

Jackson Hill, Rome

Fort Norton is located near the Rome Visitors Center on a dirt road behind the building.

Fort Norton, with intact earthworks and interlocking trenches, is located near the visitors center in Rome on Jackson Hill. After U.S. Col. Abel Streight's defeated raid on Rome in May of 1863 — stopped just west of the city in Alabama near the Lawrence Plan-

tation — local residents were spurred to fortify the city. Later, their efforts came under the command of C.S. Gen. Braxton Bragg and his successor Joseph Johnston. Fort Norton, named for a local Confederate soldier who died in the War, saw action when troops in the fort fired cannon and shoulder arms on Union Gen. Jefferson C. Davis as he attacked the city. Union troops, who controlled the city and feared an attack from Confederate troops moving north under Gen. John Bell Hood after the fall of Atlanta, worked to improve the fortifications in 1864. A local effort is underway to study and conserve the fort.

Left, statue of Nathan Bedford Forrest, who saved Rome from Union raiders, located at Myrtle Hill Cemetery. Above, Confederate mass graves at Myrtle Hill Cemetery. Below, John B. Gordon Hall.

Myrtle Hill Cemetery
Confederate Monument
Nathan B. Forrest Statue
C.S. Women's Monument

HM ⚒ R.I.P. 🏃 **AC GI**

South Broad St. and Myrtle St., Rome

South on Broad St. Cemetery is on the right after crossing the Coosa River.

During the Civil War, Myrtle Hill was the site of **Fort Stovall**. Today, there stands an impressive **Confederate monument** marking the spot and commemorating the Floyd countians who gave their lives for the Confederacy. Near the base of the Myrtle Hill Cemetery, established as the second city cemetery in 1857, is a **Confederate cemetery** containing 363 Confederate and two Union soldiers. Close to the Confederate cemetery are two distinctive monuments: one to **Confederate Gen. Nathan Bedford Forrest** for saving Rome and the other to the **Women of the Confederacy**. In one of the greatest deceptions of the War, Forrest, with only 425 men, stopped U.S. Col. A.D. Streight and his 1,500 men in nearby Alabama on May 3, 1863. Forrest tricked Streight into believing he was outnumbered after a running battle of three days. (In an unusual innovation of the War, Streight's men were infantry mounted on mules.) Forrest was subsequently the toast of the town and presented with a fine horse and $1,000 to care for his sick and wounded. The monument was erected on the anniversary of the event in 1908. The **women's monument** is believed to be the first monument dedicated to women in the Western hemisphere. Erected in 1910, it honors the women who cared for the wounded and sick of both sides in the Civil War and is one of three major women's monuments in Georgia. Woodrow Wilson wrote one of the inscriptions. Notice the **historical marker** telling the story of John Wisdom, **"Georgia's Paul Revere,"** a native of Rome who rode more than 60 miles from Gadsen, Alabama, to warn that the "Yankees are coming, the Yankees are coming!"

LAFAYETTE

John B. Gordon Hall

HM 🏠 ⚔ 🏃 **AC CK**

304 N. Main St., LaFayette 706-638-1272 (City Manager's Office)

Follow U.S. 27 Business into LaFayette.

Built in 1836, this two-story red-brick academy on the National Register of Historic Places was Gen. Braxton Bragg's headquarters of the Army of Tennessee, from September 10 to 17, 1863, while he planned the Battle of Chickamauga. A stack of cannonballs honors him. Later, the building was in the line of fire during the **Battle of LaFayette**. On June 18, 1864, Union forces of approximately 450 men occupied the town to "endeavor to rid the country of several guerilla bands." On June 24 at 3 a.m., Union forces were attacked by Confederate Brig. Gen Gideon J. Pillow and his 1,600 cavalry. The next morning, Union reinforcements arrived after being alerted by an escaped Federal picket and drove off the Confederate attackers, leaving a total of 219 casualties from the battle. Tours are allowed by appointment only. The **LaFayette Presbyterian Church** was used as a field hospital by both armies during the Civil War.

Barnsley Mansion and Gardens was visited by Union troops in 1864.

Adairsville Depot

⬛ 🏠 AC GI GLC

Public Square, Adairsville 770-773-3451 (City Hall)

Exit 128 off I-75, west on GA 140. Turn left onto Main St., and right onto Public Square Rd.

Adairsville was the scene of the last leg of the "Great Locomotive Chase" on April 12, 1862. It was here that Captain William Fuller boarded the southbound *Texas*, dropped the freight cars and roared out in reverse in pursuit of James Andrews and the *General*. Both trains were exceeding 60 miles an hour on their way north to Calhoun. The original depot, next to the railroad tracks, is on the National Register of Historic Places. On May 17, 1864 during the Atlanta Campaign, Confederate forces under Johnston, looking for a place to fight, temporarily set up a defensive line north of the town, which resulted in skirmishing with Sherman's men. Finding the position untenable, Johnston sent Hood and Polk to Cassville and Hardee to Kingston to split Sherman's forces and set a trap. Divisions of the Union Army of the Cumberland and Army of the Tennessee marched through Adairsville on May 18 in pursuit of the Confederates. The Great Locomotive Chase Festival is held every year on the first weekend in October.

Barnsley Gardens

⬛ ✕ 🏠 R.I.P. 🏛 AC GI

Barnsley Gardens Rd., Adairsville 770-773-7480

Exit 128 off I-75, west on GA 140. Travel 1.5 miles and go left on Hall Station Rd. Travel 5.5 miles and go right on Barnsley Gardens Rd. Travel 2.5 miles to entrance on left.

Barnsley Gardens, with its fascinating history and beautiful gardens, is a unique Civil War site. Its full story would make a great Gothic romance or television mini-series with fortunes won and lost, romances, ghosts, death and destruction, and renewal. In 1824, Godfrey Barnsley, at 18, came penniless to America from England. In ten years he became one of the wealthiest cotton merchants in the South and married Julia Scarborough, the daughter of a wealthy Savannah shipping merchant. Wanting to leave Savannah's unhealthy climate, Barnsley purchased 3,680 acres in northwest Georgia and developed Woodlands Manor, creating an English estate, complete with surrounding gardens, in the wilds of America. His 14-room Italianate Gothic mansion was made of the finest materials, with black marble from Italy and pink marble from France; doors and panelling from England; silver latches on the windows; and many fine art objects and furniture to decorate the house, such as a 40-person mahogany table from Emperor Don Pedro of Brazil. The mansion also featured many innovations of the day, such as hot and cold running water, flush toilets, and a hot-air powered rotisserie stove which could cook meals for 150 people. His garden was an eclectic mix of hundreds of plants collected from around the world, including many rare trees. It featured a sunken bog garden with aquatic plants, and many unusual roses.

During the Civil War, Barnsley did not condone the "secession fever" sweeping the south, but believed England would inevitably join the Southern side because of its dependence on cotton. He invested a large portion of his cash assets in Confederate bonds and donated his sailing ships to the Confederate Navy after the Union naval blockade stopped his shipping business. His two sons, George and Lucien, joined the Confederate Army. He sold metals in his buildings to the Noble foundry in Rome.

When Sherman's men, under Gen. James B. McPherson, moved south from Resaca to Kingston in mid-May 1864, Barnsley had his lead water pipes removed and melted into bullets. As McPherson's army advanced toward the Gardens on May 18, C.S. Col. Richard Earle rode into Woodlands to warn the Barnsleys that the "Yankees are coming." As he turned to go out the door, he was killed by a sharpshooter. (The family buried him close to where he fell and today you can visit his grave.) Earle's death enraged his men, who charged the forward forces of the Union, capturing more than a hundred prisoners. As more Union troops arrived, a battle raged near the manor until the Confederates gave way. McPherson, calling Barnsley Gardens "a little piece of heaven," forbid his troops to hurt the manor and grounds. It was only after the main army moved on that the stragglers and looters ransacked the Barnsley home. The Civil War ruined Barnsley's fortune, and he died in 1873 as penniless as he began.

Today, the manor is in ruins not from Union forces but from a tornado which blew the roof off the structure in 1906, leading to rapid deterioration. Today, the gardens and structures have been undergoing extensive and expensive restoration work by the Prince Fugger family. A restaurant is established in a recently relocated historic home, which is scarred by bullets from a cavalry battle. A Civil War encampment is sponsored on the first or second week in July each year.

KINGSTON WAS ANOTHER ONE of Georgia's important railroad towns on the Western and Atlantic during the Civil War. A spur west went to Rome. A chapter of the "Great Locomotive Chase" occurred here April 12, 1862, as did a chapter of the Atlanta Campaign in May 1864. Confederate Lt. Gen. and Georgia native William Hardee brought his army through here on May 18, 1864, then turned east to Cassville to meet up with the rest of the Confederate army five miles away. Union Gen. W.T. Sherman believed the Confederate army to be gathering just south of Kingston and ordered his forces to concentrate here. His troops started arriving in Kingston on the 19th of May and discovered Sherman's error.

Sherman retired to Kingston after the action in Cassville and planned the Dallas portion of the Atlanta Campaign. He returned in October after the fall of Atlanta, chasing Confederate Gen. John Bell Hood north. When Sherman left Kingston, he burned the town. It was the site of eight Confederate hospitals and the location where the last Confederate troops were surrendered in the state. Kingston claims to be the first town in the U.S. to hold a Confederate Memorial Day (or Decoration Day) in April 1864, a tradition which continues to this day.

The remains of the old Kingston depot's stone foundation.

Kingston Depot & City Park

HM 🏠 🖼 AC GI GLC MTS

Downtown Kingston

Ruins visible in park next to tracks.

The stone foundation of the ruined **Kingston Depot** can be seen near the park. The business district was located on this side of the tracks, but Sherman burned it when he left Kingston for his "March to the Sea." Across from the park is the once-renowned but now abandoned **DeSoto Hotel**, on the National Register of Historic Places. Built in 1890, it burned in 1911. The depot was the scene of an important chapter of the "Great Locomotive Chase," when James Andrews' Union Raiders and the *General* were delayed here for an hour by southbound train traffic. Pursuing William Fuller abandoned the *Yonah* here because of the time it would take to move the southbound trains, and pursued on foot until he requisitioned the *William R. Smith*, under steam and ready to roll just north of the town. A **monument** across the street facing the park honors the site of the Wayside Home, the first Confederate hospital in Kingston — established in August 1861 to treat some of the 10,000 injured and sick troops attended here.

Confederate Cemetery

HM R.I.P. 🖼 AC

Johnson Street, Kingston

From Shaw St. drive across railroad tracks and continue to end of park. Turn right at four-way stop and turn left on Johnston. Continue to cemetery.

On a hill looking down on Kingston is a **Confederate cemetery** with 249 unknown dead, one known, and two unknown Union soldiers. These men were wounded in the battles of Perryville, Chickamauga, Missionary Ridge, and the Dalton-Kingston Campaign and died in hospitals in Kingston, run by Surgeon B.W. Avent. These hospitals were moved in May 1864 when Union troops approached. They were later reopened by the Federals. The solemn **obelisk** in the middle of the cemetery was erected in 1874. Across from the Confederate section is a more recent **memorial** to Confederate vets from Kingston.

McCravey-Johnson House Methodist Church

HM 🏠 AC GI

Church Street, Kingston

Located opposite the park.

The **McCravey-Johnson House** was the headquarters of Confederate Brig. Gen. William T. Wofford. On May 12, 1865, he arranged the last surrender of Georgia's remaining troops, numbering approximately 4,000, to U.S. Brig Gen. Henry M. Judah. The troops surrendered in the park and were issued rations. Wofford is buried in the Cassville Confederate cemetery.

The **Methodist Church**, built in 1854, was the only church remaining after Gen. W.T. Sherman marched through here. It was open to all denominations and was used as a school. Pastor here was Confederate Gen. Clement A. Evans, famous Georgian general under Gen. Robert E. Lee, methodist preacher, and editor of the *Confederate Military History*. The large, superbly crafted bell that hangs in the church tower was a gift from John Pendleton King, a U.S. Senator, president of the Western & Atlantic Railroad, and for whom the town is named.

Kingston Presbyterian Church was used as a hospital. C.S. Gen. Clement A. Evans pastored here.

ALTHOUGH THE NAME CASS-ville can be found on maps, the original town no longer exists. At the time of the Civil War, Cassville, founded in 1833, was a growing town of 1,300 in the beautiful Etowah Valley, with a courthouse, two four-year colleges, four hotels, stores, a newspaper, and many fine homes. Even when the Western & Atlantic Railroad was relocated two miles west of the town, Cassville continued to flourish, regarding itself as the educational and cultural center for all of northern Georgia. In 1861, at Gov. Joe Brown's suggestion, the Georgia legislature changed the county's name to Bartow County to honor Georgia General Francis B. Bartow, who died at Manassas. Cassville was the scene of a battle and eight hospitals.

At Cassville, Confederate Gen. Joseph E. Johnston set a trap for Sherman's Union forces — called by some the "Cassville Controversy." Retreating from Resaca during the Atlanta Campaign, Confederate Gen. Johnston divided his force along two diverging roads at Adairsville and quickly concentrated them at Cassville, hoping Sherman would do the same. He hoped to attack one part of Sherman's army before reinforcements could arrive. Sherman, believing the Confederates were in Kingston, did split his army, ordering most of his army to Kingston and just his 20th and 23rd corps under Schofield and Hooker to Cassville, making this column vulnerable to attack from the

Cassville Confederate Cemetery.

flank and front. Hood was to lead the attack on the flank, and Hardee and Polk's corps were to attack from the front. But the trap never sprung. Hood did not attack. On May 19, 1864, when Union cavalry appeared at Hood's rear, he redeployed his forces, and the great opportunity was lost. In a meeting between the generals, Hood and Polk advised Johnston to retreat over the Etowah to better ground.

Johnston called the position "the best that I saw occupied during the war." (In their memoirs written after the war, Hood and Johnston are in sharp disagreement over what happened at Cassville.) When Sherman realized the imminent peril of his separated column, he rushed his forces to Cassville. Killed in fighting at Cassville was Legare Hill, son of Joshua Hill, the mayor of Madison.

Cassville Cemetery Monuments
Atlanta Campaign Pavilion #4

HM 🏠 ✕ R.I.P. 👥 AC GI

Cemetery: Pine Log Rd., Cassville
Monuments: Cassville/White Rd., Cassville
Atlanta Campaign Pavilion: Intersection of U.S. 41 and Cassville/White Rd., Cassville

Cassville Confederate Cemetery, on the eastern slope of a hill shaded by old cedar trees and a huge **obelisk**, holds approximately 300 unknown Confederate soldiers who died in hospitals in Cassville. Headstones were added in 1899. The cemetery rests on part of the Cassville battleground. Also interred here is Cassville native **Gen. William T. Wofford**, a Confederate hero in the Eastern Theater who surrendered the last Georgia troops. He died in Cassville on May 22, 1884. Half a mile from the cemetery is the historic **Methodist Church**, which remains from Civil War times. A fourth **Atlanta Campaign Pavilion**, the largest of the five, is found near Cassville. It is in terrible condition, with weeds growing up through a hole where the campaign relief map is supposed to be. As you proceed down the Cassville/White road, you will see a small **WPA marker** to the disappeared town of Cassville, located on the old courthouse grounds. Sherman burned this town of 1,300 on Nov. 5, 1864, after the fall of Atlanta, reportedly because he suspected it of supporting Confederate guerilla activities. The town was never rebuilt and the county seat was moved to Cartersville.

The Confederate Monument at Cassville Confederate Cemetery.

CARTERSVILLE GREW TO PROMInence after the Civil War. The county seat was moved here when Cassville, renamed Manassas, was burned by Sherman's troops. Cartersville was also burned by Sherman. It was from here that he last communicated with the north on Nov. 13, 1864, cutting himself adrift from his base of operations on his "March to the Sea," with his final message to Gen. Thomas in Nashville, "All is well ...," interrupted as the wire was severed. There are several interesting Civil War sites in the Cartersville/Allatoona area.

Cartersville Depot

HM 🏠 ⚔ **AC GI GLC**

Main St., Railroad tracks, Cartersville

I-75 to Cartersville exit 124, which is Main St.

The **Cartersville depot**, still used today, was the scene of a skirmish on May 20, 1864 during the Atlanta Campaign. A rear guard of Confederate Gen. Johnston's retreat barricaded themselves inside the depot, knocking out bricks for gun ports. A **25-by-40 foot section** of the original structure remains and is identified by the older brick.

The Bartow History Center

🏛 **AC GI**

13 Wall St., Cartersville 770-382-3818

The **Bartow History Center** has exhibits featuring the county's role in the Civil War, with displays of weapons, artifacts, photos, and maps from war times.

Roselawn

🏠 🏛 **AC GI**

224 West Cherokee Ave., Cartersville 770-387-5162

Roselawn was the home of Sam P. Jones, the most famous evangelist of the late 1800s. The Victorian mansion, on the National Register of Historic Places, houses a small Civil War collection upstairs. Across the street is the antebellum **First Baptist Church**, which received $4,000 in 1904 in restitution from the U.S. Government for damage done 40 years earlier by Sherman's men.

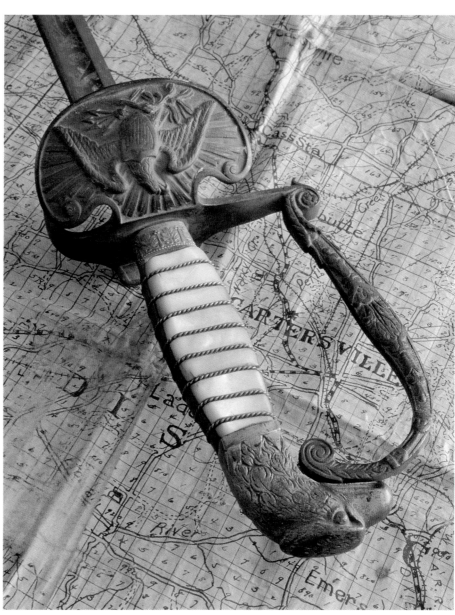

Top, the Cartersville Depot, the scene of a skirmish during the Atlanta Campaign. Bottom, a Militia Sword on display at the Bartow History Center.

IN THE ALLATOONA AREA, YOU will find the **ruins** of an important iron furnace on the Etowah River, a **visitor's center** with Civil War relics and exhibits, and the site of the famous Battle of Allatoona Pass. During the Atlanta Campaign of 1864, Confederate Gen. Joseph Johnston retreated from Cassville to the steep, 1,000-foot high Allatoona mountains, a virtually impregnable natural fortress south of the Etowah River. The Western & Atlantic Railroad passed through a 65-foot deep cut in the mountains here. Sherman, who was familiar with the terrain having surveyed it as a young man in 1844, spent several days in Kingston contemplating his next move. He decided to sweep his army around Johnston, travelling southeast on a network of primitive roads to Dallas. If they moved quickly enough, he could move from here on to Atlanta, perhaps unopposed by the Confederate Army.

After the fall of Atlanta, Hood moved his battered army north to threaten Sherman's supply line and draw him out of Atlanta. On Oct. 5, 1864, Hood's men attacked two forts on either side of the mountain cut at Allatoona Pass in a bloody and unsuccessful attempt to destroy the railroad here. The battle, with 30 percent casualties (Confederate Gen. Samuel G. French had 70 officers killed or wounded), was given extensive play in the Northern press. During the battle, Union Gen. James M. Corse signalled Sherman for help, whose reported famous reply — "Hold the Fort, I am Coming" — became a beloved hymn.

U.S. Army Corps of Engineers Visitor Center

🄷🄼 🏛 🖼 AC GI

Hwy. 294/Spur 20, Cartersville 770-382-4700

Exit 125 off I-75. Turn right off the exit ramp, and turn right on Spur 20. Travel apx. 4 miles.

This museum features Civil War exhibits, relics, artifacts, and the story and memorabilia of Mark Cooper and his iron works. Outside the museum, walk to the dam overlook and notice the white **obelisk** on the right, called the **Friendship Monument**, erected by Cooper to 38 friends who loaned him $100,000 during the financial panic of 1857 to keep him solvent. In 1860, he repaid his friends and erected a monument in their honor. Markers nearby tell the story of Allatoona Pass.

Right, Cooper's Iron Furnace stone structure on the Etowah River.

Grave of Unknown Confederate Hero at Allatoona Pass.

Cooper's Furnace Historic Site Day Use Area

🄷🄼 ◉ AC GI

River Rd., Cartersville

U.S. 41 to River Road at the Etowah River. Follow signs.

A beautiful park on the Etowah River south of Allatoona dam was the location of Mark Cooper's **Etowah Iron Works**, a rolling mill, flour mill, and factories for the production of guns, railroad iron, and tools, stretching more than a mile down the river. More than 600 people worked in these factories and lived in a town nearby called Etowah, which is now under Allatoona Lake. Cooper sold his factories to the Confederacy in 1862, which needed iron to fight the war. Found here are the remnants of an enormous stone furnace used to create more than 20 tons of pig iron a week. Union Gen. John M. Schofield's men destroyed the iron works shortly after C.S. Gen. Joseph Johnston abandoned Cassville on May 22, 1864. After the war, there was an attempt to rebuild, but the mill couldn't compete with the more modern northern mills. Notice the five **stone bridge supports** in the Etowah River. A retreating Johnston burned the bridge here, and it was never rebuilt. The "Great Locomotive Chase" raced across these supports on April 12, 1862, and Union raider Andrews in the *General* unwisely didn't destroy the bridge. Pursuing him was Fuller on a handcar, which he abandoned here to borrow the Cooper's Furnace yard engine, *Yonah*, which motorized his pursuit to Kingston.

Allatoona Pass Battlefield and Forts

HM 🏠 ✕ 🚂 R.I.P. 🏞 AC GI

GA 397, Allatoona

Park near the dam and walk northwest on a closed dirt road, the old railroad bed. As you enter the cut, marked by steep rock sides, notice the highest point, approximately 65 feet from the roadbed. On top of the cut on the left is the **Star Fort** or western redoubt, located on private property; on the right, approximately 250 yards up, is the eastern redoubt, located on U.S. Army Corps of Engineers property. The **forts** are in a remarkable state of preservation. The eastern redoubt can be reached on foot by a steep, unpaved road back near where you entered the cut. Across the Emerson/Allatoona Road is the **Clayton/Mooney House**, a private residence which was used as a headquarters prior to the battle and as a hospital after the battle to treat some of the 1,500 casualties. The house has bullet holes in the gables. Notice the marble **gravestone** commemorating 21 unknown Confederates killed at Allatoona Pass and buried on the grounds. Approximately 600 yards south of the house and across the railroad tracks is the **grave** of "An Unknown Hero" protected by a wrought iron fence.

Allatoona, then and now, clockwise from middle left shows the deep cut and Clayton House; the Clayton/Mooney House today; the deep cut; the Etowah River Bridge supports today; and the Etowah River Bridge and Confederate defenses during the Atlanta Campaign.

The "Hell Hole" at New Hope Church by George N. Barnard, 1864.

T HE AREA AROUND DALLAS, heading northeast to Pickett's Mill State Park, was the scene of three desperate and bloody battles along the same line — New Hope Church, Pickett's Mill, and Dallas — of the Atlanta Campaign from May 25, 27, and 28, 1864 respectively. Two were Confederate victories. Union Gen. W.T. Sherman tried to get around C.S. Gen. Joseph Johnston and Allatoona Pass by leaving the railroad and moving southeast to Dallas, but Johnston responded by sidestepping his armies and placing them between the Union armies and Atlanta. The rough, wild countryside and narrow roads made maneuvering slow and difficult. For ten days along a ten-mile front, there was constant skirmishing and three major battles. At New Hope Church, Sherman believed he was beyond the left flank of the enemy and ordered an attack by Gen. Joe Hooker's men, who formed a column. Confederate Maj. Gen. A.P. Stewart's division of Gen. John Bell Hood's corps poured

deadly fire into the narrow front, inflicting heavy casualties until a violent thunderstorm erupted with heavy rain, stopping the battle. The next day, the opposing armies regrouped and entrenched. Sherman, with his love of flanking movements, ordered Maj. Gen. Oliver O. Howard's men to turn the Confederate right flank at Pickett's Mill. The Union forces, lost and disorganized in the brushy thickets of the area, were slaughtered by Confederates under Patrick Cleburne. Two defeats convinced Sherman to move back north toward his supply line. Sensing a weakness on Sherman's right at Dallas, Johnston's Confederates probed the area to see if Sherman's forces were vulnerable to attack. A mix-up in signals led to a Confederate attack, which was destroyed by withering Union fire from entrenched Federal forces. Sherman eventually moved back north to Acworth, located south of Allatoona Pass but northwest of Kennesaw Mountain. Johnston took position across Lost, Pine, and Brush mountains.

Pickett's Mill State Historic Park

HM ✕ 🚂 ◎ 🏛 AC GI

2640 Mt. Tabor Rd., Dallas 770-443-7850

Located 5 miles northeast of Dallas. From GA Hwy. 381 north, turn right onto Due West Rd. and then turn left onto Mt. Tabor Rd.

A tour of this phase of the Atlanta Campaign should start at **Pickett's Mill**, one of the best preserved Civil War battlefields in the nation and one of the few Confederate victories in the Atlanta Campaign. Guided and self-guided tours are available along three different routes through 765 acres of the **battlefield**, taking up to an hour and a half. You can see **earthworks** constructed by soldiers and the ravines where many men died. At the excellent **museum and visitors center**, a 17-minute video explains what happened at Pickett's Mill. Don't miss your chance to see how you rate as a general in an interactive computer game which tests your skill in the heat of a battle. The **Battle of Pickett's Mill Living History Encampment** takes place each year on the first weekend in June.

Above, reenactors at Pickett's Mill State Historic Park.

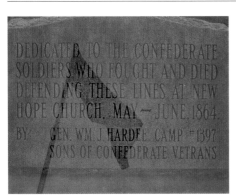

New Hope Church Monument.

Atlanta Campaign Pavilion #5
New Hope Church Monument

HM 🚶 AC

Dallas

GA Hwy. 381 three miles northeast of Dallas.

At the intersection of several roads is the "new" **New Hope Baptist Church**. Next to the church is the final **Atlanta Campaign Pavilion**, with a plaque and relief map explain-

ing this phase of the Atlanta Campaign. Notice the **WPA marker** inserted in the large boulder dedicated to "the Northern and the Southern men who gave their all for cherished principles, undivided union, and state's rights, in the battle fought here in May 1864." Across the highway to the right is an old graveyard, where some Confederates took positions behind gravestones to hold off the attacking Union forces. The stone building to the left of the graveyard occupies the original site of New Hope Church. Across the highway to the left is a Confederate **memorial** next to some original **trenches** from the battle.

The brushy thickets of Pickett's Mill Creek contributed to a Union loss on May 27, 1864. In the Battle of Pickett's Mill, Sherman ordered three brigades to attempt a flank attack of the Confederate line. Johnston anticipated the Union move and placed Confederates under Patrick Cleburne at the end of his line. The attacks were poorly coordinated and the Yankee brigades got lost in the dense forest and deep ravines. When they emerged to attack the Confederates, "the Rebel fire swept the ground like a hailstorm," punishing the Federals. After the encounter, a Confederate captain reported that he saw "50 dead men within 30 feet of me. A great number of them have their skulls bursted open and their brains running out ..." It was the second humiliating defeat for Sherman in two days.

Sweetwater Creek State Conservation Park

HM ◉ AC GI

Mt. Vernon Rd., Lithia Springs 770-732-5871

Exit 12 off I-20 West. Turn left off the exit ramp. Travel apx. 0.4 mile to Blairsbridge Rd. and turn right. Go 2 miles and turn left onto Mt. Vernon Rd.

The 1,986-acre park features a wide mix of activities, including fishing, boating, picnicking, and hiking. The park was established to protect the ruins of New Manchester Manufacturing Company, a Civil War-era **textile mill** which Sherman's forces burned, and sent its women workers north on trains to Indiana. A hiking trail leads to the old raceway and impressive mill ruins next to the rocky Sweetwater Creek. A living history event, including an encampment, called New Manchester Days is held each September.

Georgia was one of the south's largest textile producing states, and the New Manchester Mill on Sweetwater Creek was one of the South's largest mills. The five-story factory building, with a 50,000-pound water wheel, was reputed to be the tallest building in the Atlanta area. The mill, built in 1849, converted raw cotton into thread and the thread into cloth. Approximately 17 structures made up New Manchester and an estimated 500 people resided in the town, with approximately 100 working at the mill. On July 2, 1864, portions of Union Maj. Gen. George Stoneman's cavalry rode into New Manchester without opposition. They ordered the mill shut down and the cloth distributed to the millworkers. Meanwhile, in Roswell on July 5, other textile mills were seized and shut down, and Sherman ordered the mills burned and the workers deported to the North. (At one time, Sherman sought permission to send "treasoners" to Honduras, San Domingo, or British or French Guiana) His orders also applied to New Manchester.

On July 9, Major Thompkins and eight men burned the New Manchester factory. According to unconfirmed reports, they destroyed the 300-foot long dam, and let the swift waters of Sweetwater Creek do the rest, destroying several hundred thousand dollars worth of property in the flood. The operatives and their managers were charged with treason and ordered to Marietta. A shortage of transport wagons resulted in cavalrymen taking a second rider — mostly women — on their horses and carrying them 16 miles on July 10 to the Georgia Military Institute. One Illinois soldier wrote home saying it "was a very fine sight" and "one we do not often see in the army." "The employees were all women and they were really good looking." Accounts of sexual activity between the men and women were reported but it's unclear whether it was consensual or rape.

In Marietta they joined the Roswell workers and totalling approximately 500, the women were loaded on trains with their families and shipped first to Nashville, Tennessee on July 15, then Louisville, Kentucky on July 20, and later across the Ohio River to nearby Indiana. They came to be collectively known as the "Roswell Women," and their ultimate fate remains unknown. Reportedly not one of the women ever returned.

Extensive ruins of New Manchester textile mill burned by Union troops are found in Sweetwater Creek State Conservation Park.

THE NORTHEAST GEORGIA Mountain travel region, a popular tourist destination due to the beauty of its mountains, does not have much in the way of Civil War historic sites. The area was more sparsely settled than other regions of the state, with poorer transportation routes. Some of the hardscrabble mountain folk in the area were even more independent than the fire-eating secessionists. Some in the mountains were pro-union.

Gainesville, a mill town on the Chattahoochee River, was the boyhood home of Confederate Lt. Gen. James T. Longstreet. When Gen. Robert E. Lee reorganized the Army of Northern Virginia, he placed Longstreet in charge of the First Corps and General Thomas J. "Stonewall" Jackson in command of the Second Corps. This trio won fame as a fighting force early in the War with many victories against larger and better equipped Union armies. Lee called Longstreet his "Old War Horse" and one of his most reliable commanders. In the fall of 1863, Longstreet and his corps of 15,000 men were sent to Gen. Braxton Bragg by railroad from Virginia to Georgia for the Battle of Chickamauga, only the second time that reinforcements had been brought in by railroad during a battle (the first was in Manassas), requiring a trip of nine days and 900 miles over 16 different railroads. On the first day, Sept. 19, Bragg was unable to break through. Longstreet arrived that evening and was put in charge of the left wing. The next day, Longstreet's troops crushed the Federal right wing in the largest battle of the Western Theater.

Gainesville's monument is the only Georgia county memorial whose soldier is "at ready."

General Longstreet Burial Site Park Hill Farm and Vineyards & Piedmont Hotel Site

 **CK CT GI**

Alta Vista Cemetery, Jessie Jewel Parkway, Gainesville
Farm and Vineyards: Park Hill Drive, Gainesville
Hotel Site: Main St. and Myrtle, Gainesville

I-985 to Gainesville. Jessie Jewel Parkway to Alta Vista Cemetery.

Longstreet, the son of a Gainesville farmer, was born on Jan. 8, 1821 in Edgefield District, South Carolina, at his grandmother's home. Until he was nine, he lived on the family farm near Gainesville, then moved to live with his aunt and uncle in Augusta in order to attend Richmond Academy. In 1838, he was appointed to West Point, and graduated 54th out of 56 in 1842. Classmates included eight future Union

generals and eight future Confederate generals. At his first command in Missouri, he introduced his cousin Julia Dent to U.S. Grant, and the two later married. He fought for the U.S. Army in Mexico with Zachary Taylor, and was with Winfield Scott when he marched on Mexico City and was wounded. He resigned his U.S. commission when the Civil War broke out and won fame as a Confederate general. He was still commanding forces when Lee surrendered at Appomattox. After the war, his criticism of Lee's strategy at Gettysburg, his Republican politics, and support of voting rights for blacks earned him scorn from many Southerners. His wife died in 1889, and he remarried in 1897 at 76 to 34-year-old Helen Dortch. He died on Jan. 2, 1904. His unique **gravestone** has the Confederate and U.S. flags crossed, and one says from "Palo Alto to Chapultepec"; the other "From Manassas to Appomattox."

After the War, Longstreet lived in Gainesville from 1875 until his death in 1904. Soon after his arrival, he bought a 45-acre farm one mile north of the town's center. At the property's highest point, he built a two-story house and planted a scuppernong grape vineyard, which local residents affectionately called "Little Gettysburg." He was proud of the wine fermented from his grapes. His house burned in 1889, destroying many of his mementos and his almost completed memoirs. Today, the **granite steps**, outlines of the **foundation**, and portions of the **terraces** still remain and one small arbor of Longstreet's grapes has been preserved by a devoted homeowner. The home is in a park maintained by the Longstreet Society.

In 1875, Gen. Longstreet purchased the **Piedmont Hotel**, which he owned and operated till

the end of his life. It served as his political base during his long career as an influential Republican Party leader, and here he played host to many Civil War era luminaries, including Gen. Joseph Johnston. Woodrow Wilson, then a lawyer in Atlanta, was a frequent guest in the 1880s, as his aunt lived one block away. One of Wilson's daughters was born in the hotel. The hotel was demolished in 1918, although the north wing's lower level still exists. The Longstreet Society has purchased and saved approximately 2,000 square-feet of the hotel and has plans to open it for tours. For information on the farm and vineyards or the hotel, contact the Longstreet Society at 770-531-0100.

Confederate Memorial

GI

Town Square, Gainesville

Square faces Washington, Spring, Bradford, and Main streets.

There are approximately 102 county monuments honoring Georgia's Confederate soldiers located across the state. Sixty-three have soldiers, but only one has a soldier "on guard" or "at ready": the **Confederate monument** in Gainesville. The Longstreet Chapter of the United Daughters of the Confederacy wanted to erect a memorial "at ready" as a memorial to the veterans of Hall County. The Chicago firm they contacted tried to sell them one "at rest," but the ladies would have none of it. After two years of discussion, they got what they wanted for $2,500, and dedicated it on June 7, 1909.

Touring Atlanta

THE ATLANTA REGION CIVIL War sites, out of all the regions in the book, have the greatest range of substance, style, and historic importance because of several factors. First, Atlanta was burned by Federal troops in 1864, destroying most historic structures. Second, Atlanta's civic leadership has generally been more focused on constructing new buildings instead of saving older ones. Third, thanks to this same leadership, the economic prosperity Atlanta has experienced — like a phoenix rising from the ashes — has obliterated many battlefields, as the railroad town of 10,000 has grown and developed into an urban area of more than 2 million.

The good news for Civil War buffs is that some sites are in great condition and available for touring. The **Kennesaw Mountain National Battlefield Park**, opened in 1935 and covering 2,884 acres, is a gem, and much can be experienced and learned by touring these historic grounds, where you can actually see trenches from the battle and learn the life-and-death importance of high ground. This park is in marked contrast to many of the battlefields near Atlanta, which consist mainly of state **historical markers** next to busy highways. Here, your imagination is needed. Although most of the historic homes of Atlanta were razed or destroyed in battle by Sherman, towns surrounding Atlanta — **Marietta, Roswell, Jonesboro,** and **Decatur** — have historic homes open to tours. There are excellent cemeteries to tour in the Atlanta area, including **Oakland Cemetery,** the **Confederate Cemetery** in Marietta, **Marietta National Cemetery,** the **Patrick R. Cleburne Memorial Cemetery** in Jonesboro, and **Westview Cemetery.** Good museums include the **Atlanta History Center,** the **Cyclorama, Kennesaw Civil War Museum,** and the **DeKalb Historical Society Museum.** And don't forget **Stone Mountain Park.** The North has the impressive Mount Rushmore, but the South has Stone Mountain, a carving of Confederate heroes Robert E. Lee, Thomas J. "Stonewall" Jackson, and Jefferson Davis. The South's is larger. If you can make it to one of the summer's nightly laser shows to hear Elvis sing Dixie, then you've experienced something uniquely southern.

Atlanta's History

ATLANTA WAS THE PRIZE sought by the Union and for good reason. Atlanta was second only to the Confederate capital of Richmond in importance to sustaining the Confederate government. Atlanta, the "Gate City of the South," had become the transportation hub of the Confederate war machine, with four railroads connecting here. Rail lines spoked out from Atlanta, going east to the Atlantic seaboard states and the Eastern Theater and Richmond. West, it was the backdoor to the blockaded Confederate seacoast states; north to Chattanooga and the mid-south states and Western Theater; and south to the Atlantic seaboard and port of Savannah. Atlanta served as a vital arsenal, and was a productive factory town manufacturing war materiel of all kinds, from cannon and rifles to rails and armor plate, to uniforms and even wooden coffins. Atlanta also was vital in supplying the Confederacy with food supplies, connecting the rich farmlands and breadbasket of the south — Georgia, Alabama, and Mississippi — with all other points of the Confederacy. Early in the War, Georgia and Atlanta's geographic position in the heart of the Confederacy insulated it from the more destructive ravages of war, except for the coast. Georgians had answered the call of their new government, and supplied approximately 112,000 men (some were among the best troops, generals, and officers in government), who fought in almost every battle of the Civil War. When Grant was commissioned General-in-Chief of the entire U.S. Army on March 10, 1864, he appointed his friend W.T. Sherman as commander of the Western Theater. At a meeting in Cincinnati, they agreed on a simple plan to end the War: The two main armies would move simultaneously against the two great armies of the Confederacy, with Grant pounding his way to Richmond and Sherman fighting his way 100 miles from his base in Chattanooga to strategically important Atlanta. This strategy would prevent the south from reinforcing either front, and either Grant would get to Richmond first, or Sherman would help split the Confederacy and strangle the Eastern Theater by destroying Atlanta. Thus the **Atlanta Campaign** was born, which led to the major Civil War events in the Atlanta area (after Sherman had fought his way through northwest Georgia) from June 15 to Sept. 2, 1864 when Atlanta surrendered, including battles at **Gilgal Church, Kolb's Farm, Kennesaw Mountain, Peachtree Creek, Atlanta or Bald Hill, Ezra Church, Utoy Creek,** and **Jonesboro.** Also in the Atlanta area was the beginning of one of the more famous stories of the Civil War, the **"Great Locomotive Chase,"** on April 12, 1862, and the start of Sherman's infamous **"March to the Sea"** on November 15, as Atlanta was in flames.

Left, a portion of the Cyclorama canvas illustrating The Battle of Atlanta.

A SERIES OF RUNNING BATTLES, sometimes called the "battles before Kennesaw," or the "Lost Mountain/Brush Mountain Line," took place before the major battle at Kennesaw Mountain. In this area, near the town of Kennesaw (formerly Big Shanty), the traveler will find many **historical markers**, one small **park**, and a **museum** dedicated to the "Great Locomotive Chase."

Gilgal Primitive Baptist Church Battlefield

HM ✕ 🚂 AC

GA 294, Kennesaw

Exit 125 off I-75, east on GA 20 to GA 294.

The **Battle of Gilgal Church**, from June 15-17, 1864, was a prelude to fighting at Kennesaw Mountain. U.S. Maj. Gen. Daniel Butterfield, composer of *Taps*, fought Confederate Maj. Gen. Patrick Cleburne here. To the northeast, some of the Union earthworks and an example of a Civil War entrenchment can be found. The original church, destroyed in the battle, stood several hundred yards from here at the crossroads.

Battle of Pine Mountain Monument

HM ✕ 🐾 AC

Beamont Rd., Kennesaw

From Kennesaw National Battlefield Park entrance take Stilesboro Rd. to Beamont Rd. to marker.

On top of this mountain on June 14, Confederate generals Joseph Johnston, William Hardee and Leonidas Polk — the "Fighting Bishop" — were reviewing the Lost Mountain line. They were spotted by Gen. W.T. Sherman, who personally ordered artillery fire on the mountain. When the shells started landing, the generals scrambled to take cover, but the fat, dignified churchman, Polk, was slow to move and took a shell through his body, mangling him terribly and killing him instantly. In his pocket, Johnston found three bloody books of spiritual guidance that were inscribed as gifts for Johnston, Hood, and Hardee. A **20-foot tall, marble shaft** marks the spot where Polk was killed on the summit of Pine Mountain, located on private property and not open to the public. For more information, contact Kennesaw Mountain National Battlefield Park at 770-427-4686.

Gilgal Church entrenchment display.

Kennesaw Civil War Museum

HM 🏠 🏛 AC GI GLC

2829 Cherokee St., Kennesaw 770-427-2117

Exit 118 off I-75, follow the signs.

This museum houses the *General*, the locomotive of the "Great Locomotive Chase," which was stolen less than 100 yards from this spot. The museum is housed in an authentic cotton gin, and it has many exhibits, a video explaining the raid, and a gift shop.

The Great Locomotive Chase

Early on the morning of April 12, 1862 in Big Shanty, 21 Federal soldiers dressed as Confederates and under the leadership of civilian spy James J. Andrews, stole the engine *General* and three boxcars and headed north with a plan to destroy the Western and Atlantic Railroad, so important to supplying Confederate armies. The crew and passengers were eating breakfast at a nearby hotel. Hearing the engine pull out of the station, conductor William A. Fuller and two others gave chase on foot for two miles. They found a railroad crew, and commandeered their platform car, which is propelled by pushing long poles or pushing off on railroad ties with one's feet. At the Etowah River, they picked up the steam-powered yard engine *Yonah*, belonging to Cooper's Iron Works. Meanwhile, the raiders had been delayed an hour in Kingston, where southbound train traffic had to be switched to the side to let them pass. Four minutes after they rolled north, the *Yonah* came puffing into Kingston. Delayed in Kingston, Fuller abandoned the *Yonah* and pursued on foot and quickly was able to commandeer the *William R. Smith*. Farther north, Andrew's raiders were vandalizing track, and gathering wood to help burn bridges to the north, which would stop their pursuer. At Adairsville, the *General* had to wait to let the southbound *Texas* get by, then

Top, W&A tracks near Kennesaw. Below, the *General*'s nameplate at Kennesaw Civil War Museum.

they steamed north. Behind them, Fuller had to abandon the *Smith* when he came to some destroyed track. Proceeding on foot three miles, Fuller and his men came upon the southbound *Texas*. When told of the situation, the engineer threw the *Texas* in reverse to pursue the *General* at more than 60 miles an hour. When the *Texas* closed on the *General* near Resaca, Andrews' men released a boxcar to slow him up, but the *Texas* just pushed the car along in front of it. Other attempts to slow the *Texas* were unsuccessful, and the *General* was running out of fuel as it roared through Tunnel Hill and Ringgold.

If the desperate raiders could get beyond Chattanooga, a few miles away, they would be safe behind Northern lines, but it was not to be, as the engine came to a stop. Andrews told his men to "Jump off and scatter! Every man for himself!" Soon they were all captured and imprisoned in Chattanooga. Eight escaped, six were exchanged, and eight — including Andrews — were hanged and buried in Atlanta. The Medal of Honor — the nation's highest award for valor — was established by the U.S. Congress and given to the raiders, except for Andrews himself, who was a civilian. Later the dead were reinterred in Chattanooga National Cemetery, their ultimate goal, and honored with a monument and commemorated by three movies, most recently being the popular Walt Disney film, *The Great Locomotive Chase*.

Kennesaw Mountain National Battlefield Park

HM 🏠 ⚔ 🚂 🗺 AC

U.S. 41, Marietta 770-427-4686

Exit 116 off I-75, west to U.S. 41. Follow signs to the park.

Start your tour at the **Visitors Center**, which has exhibits, maps, an audiovisual introduction to the June 27, 1864 battle, an excellent bookstore, and during the summer, living history demonstrations. Materials at the Center will guide you to the sites described here. Various trails are available for hiking over the 2,882-acre park, totalling two, five, 10, and 16 miles roundtrip. One, located behind the Visitors Center, takes you to the top of the mountain where weather permitting you can get a great view of the Kennesaw area battlefield and Atlanta. The battlefield has many interesting intact entrenchments from the battle. At **Cheatham Hill**, you can see the site of the fiercest fighting — called the "Dead Angle" — **Confederate and Union trenches**, the magnificent **Illinois monument**, and the **Tunnel monument** which marks where trapped Federal soldiers tried to blow up entrenched Confederates. Going down Cheat-ham Hill, you can follow a trail 600 yards to where the Federal attack began. Notice the granite monument to **Dan McCook**, one of the "Fighting McCooks" and former law partner of Gen. W.T. Sherman, who died during the assault. For a complete understanding of the battle, travel to **Pigeon Hill**, named for the extinct passenger pigeon, which rested here on its annual migrations. **Kolb's Farm**, located near the park, has been restored but is not open to the public. A pull-off area with markers and interpretive signs help the traveler understand this bloody battle, which occurred on June 22, 1864. U.S. Gen. Joseph Hooker used the 1836 cabin as his headquarters after the encounter. A **living history event** is held each year on the weekend closest to the anniversary of the battle (June 27).

Clockwise from top, the Illinois and Tunnel monuments at Cheatham Hill or the "Dead Angle," scene of the fiercest fighting at Kennesaw Mountain when Union forces attacked a Confederate salient using European heavy infantry tactics; Kolb's Farm; intact entrenchments and cannon found on the battlefield; living history reenactors at Kennesaw Mountain preparing for battle; and the rocky terrain of Pigeon Hill, the scene of bloody fighting on June 27, 1864.

Battle of Kennesaw Mountain

THE ATLANTA CAMPAIGN OF 1864, the Union's attempt to destroy the Army of Tennessee and capture Atlanta, had progressed steadily south from Chattanooga across northwest Georgia until late May, when Union Gen. William T. Sherman's men stalled with defeats near Dallas. Frustrated with attempts to swing south around Johnston, Sherman moved back north to Acworth near his rail line, and Johnston extended his line from Brush Mountain southwest to Lost Mountain to block Sherman's route to Atlanta. All along, Confederate Gen. Joseph Johnston's strategy had been to entrench his numerically inferior forces in superior defensive positions and hope Sherman would chew up his numerical advantage in futile attacks. Sherman had not cooperated, attempting flanking maneuvers which had resulted in Confederate retreats. Sherman extended his lines southward until June 19, when Johnston pulled back to Kennesaw Mountain. Probing southward, Sherman again tried to flank the Confederate left. Johnston responded by sending Gen. John Bell Hood and 11,000 men to Kolb's Farm, where on June 22, Hood's men savagely attacked Union generals Joe Hooker and John Schofield's troops unsuccessfully. Union batteries with more than 40 cannon fired solid shot into the Rebels, resulting

Little Kennesaw Mountain, where Union forces attacked entrenched Confederates and lost.

in more than 1,000 Southern casualties compared to 350 Yankees.

After the month-long deadlock, Sherman, frustrated with trying to flank Johnston, decided on a frontal assault for June 27, hoping for a decisive battle, possibly thinking Johnston was expecting another flanking move or perhaps worried that his troops were getting too used to going around rather than directly at the enemy. Sherman would demonstrate on both flanks, and send Gen. George Thomas' Army of the Cumberland at the center and farther north, Gen. James McPherson's Army of the Tennessee. Thomas' men were

mowed down attacking Cheatham Hill, defended by C.S. Maj. Gens. Patrick Cleburne and Benjamin Franklin Cheatham. McPherson's men did no better. At the end of day, the Union had lost 3,000 men and the Confederates 1,000. However, Schofield, demonstrating at the southern end of the line, had gotten around Johnston's left flank and made headway toward the Chattahoochee River, the last natural barrier before Atlanta, providing an opportunity for another Sherman flanking maneuver. It was only a matter of time. Johnston, on July 2, had to pull back from Kennesaw Mountain.

C.S. Gen. Joseph E. Johnston

Confederate General Joseph Eggleston Johnston was a complex military man who never lost a battle, but never won a major battle either. Born in 1807 in Prince Edward County, Virginia, to a Revolutionary War veteran, Johnston attended West Point, graduating 13th in the class of 1829. He served on the Black Hawk expedition, resigning to become a civil engineer. He was wounded five times in the Mexican War, where he fought at Cerro Gordo and led a charging column at Chapultepec. By the outbreak of the Civil War, Johnston had risen to brigadier general and chief quartermaster of the army. He resigned his U.S. commission and was promoted to full general after service at First Manassas or Bull Run, a Confederate victory. He took command of the main Confederate army protecting Richmond, but was ranked fourth in seniority among officers, which renewed a feud between Johnston and Confederate President Jefferson Davis, which would last the entire war. In May 1862, Johnston fought Union Gen. George McClellan to a draw at the Battle of Seven Pines or Fair Oaks, and was seriously

Confederate Gen. Joseph E. Johnston in a stained glass window at Rhodes Hall in Atlanta.

injured and replaced by Robert E. Lee. He was appointed to overall command in the Western Theater, but had little operational con-

trol, and Federal forces defeated Confederates at Vicksburg and pushed them out of Tennessee. In December 1863, he took command of the demoralized Army of Tennessee, and built it back into fighting shape. Ordered to go on the offensive against Sherman's army, Johnston instead fought defensive battles during the Atlanta Campaign, with the strategy that his outnumbered forces could even the odds by inflicting greater casualties on attacking Federals. Dissatisfied with Johnston's failure to stop Sherman before Atlanta, Davis replaced him with Gen. John Bell Hood on July 17, 1864. Johnston returned to the field in February 1865 with the remnants of the Army of Tennessee, now wrecked by Hood's command, to oppose Sherman's march through the Carolinas. Against Davis' wishes, he surrendered to Sherman on April 26, 1865 at Durham Station, North Carolina, 17 days after Lee had surrendered to Grant at Appomattox Court House, Virginia. After the War, he served one term in Congress and wrote his memoirs. He died in 1891, after catching pneumonia while standing bareheaded in the rain at the funeral of his respected battlefield opponent and old friend, William T. Sherman.

MARIETTA STARTED AS AN antebellum planter's retreat, and some of the **historic homes** remain from the Civil War period, despite the destruction Sherman brought to the area. Wealthy coastal planters had summer homes in Marietta, with its 1,100-foot elevation and springwaters, to escape the stifling heat and yellow fever epidemics. The injured were attended to here during the battles in the Kennesaw area, and two large **cemeteries** are found here. **The Georgia Military Institute**, which supplied many officers to the Confederate cause, was located here, but burned when Sherman moved on to the coast. Camp McDonald, was one of the three camps of instruction for volunteers in Georgia. The Andrews Raiders, of the "Great Locomotive Chase" made their plans at the **Kennesaw House**, located next to the **Visitors Center**.

Morning over Kennesaw Mountain, the defensive barrier between Marietta and the Yankees.

W & A Train Depot & Visitors Center

🏠 **AC GI**

No. 4 Depot St., Marietta 770-429-1115

I-75 to exit 113, go west to Marietta and turn left onto Mill St.

The **depot** is not from the Civil War, but it is built on the original site. Sherman's men burned the original. This one, built in 1898, houses the **Marietta Welcome Center**. Available here is a guide to a driving tour of 52 sites on the National Register of Historic Places, including homes used as generals' headquarters and churches used as hospitals.

Kennesaw House

🏠 **AC GI GLC**

No. 1 Depot St., Marietta 770-425-5566

One block west of city square.

Built in 1855 as a summer resort hotel and known as the **Fletcher House**, James Andrews and his raiders met here April 11, 1862 to finalize their plans to steal the *General* the next day. Civilian refugees from Tennessee and Kentucky stayed here, moving south as Federals drew near. It was used as a hospital during the War, and Gen. William T. Sherman briefly established his headquarters here, July 3, 1864, when Johnston retreated to his River Line in front of the Chattahoochee. Partially

burned by Union troops when Sherman left to go on his "March to the Sea," it was remodelled, and today it houses a restaurant and offices.

Cheney House Plantation

🏠 **AC**

Bankstone Dr., West Of Marietta

From Kennesaw Mt. Natl. Battlefield Park, travel west on Powder Springs Rd. After road splits, marker and house will be at the intersection of Powder Springs and Bankstone Dr.

U.S. Gen. John Schofield made his headquarters here from June 22-30, 1864 during the Atlanta Campaign. From here, he commanded troops in the Battle of Kolb's Farm nearby and made the "only advantage of the day," when he was able to get around Johnston's flank during the Battle of Kennesaw Mountain. The **house** was used by the Signal Corps, artillery, and as a hospital during this time. The house is privately owned and not open for tours.

Fair Oaks

🏠 **AC**

505 Kennesaw Ave., Marietta 770-427-3494

From the city square, travel north on Church St. and turn left on Kennesaw Ave.

Built in 1852, this was Confederate Gen. Joseph E. Johnston's headquarters during the Battle of Kennesaw Mountain. Today it serves as the **Marietta Educational Garden Center** and is open to the public.

To left in photo, the rebuilt Western and Atlantic railroad depot. To right, Kennesaw House where Andrews Raiders met before they stole the *General*.

1848 House

HM 🏠 ✕ AC

780 S. Cobb Dr., Marietta 770-428-1848

I-75 North to exit 111. Travel west on South Cobb Dr.

This **house** was built by Charleston planter and Marietta's first mayor, John H. Glover, and was located on a 3,000-acre plantation called Bushy Park. It took seven years to build. Sold to William King, he recorded in his diary a cavalry skirmish on the property during the Atlanta Campaign, July 3, 1864. A bullet from the battle rests embedded in a wooden door frame. Today, it is a restaurant.

Marietta National Cemetery

HM R.I.P. 🏛 AC BA CK CT GI

500 Washington Ave., Marietta 770-428-5631

From city square go east on Roswell St. Turn left onto Cole St.

This beautiful, 24-acre **cemetery**, established in 1866, contains the remains of more than 10,000 Union soldiers, 3,000 unknown, who lost their lives south of Resaca. The land was offered by Henry Green Cole as a joint Union and Confederate cemetery, hoping it would heal ill-feelings. When this effort failed, Cole offered it to the Federal Government for use as a Union cemetery. His offer was accepted. Monuments to various states are found in the cemetery, as are soldiers from five other wars.

Confederate Cemetery

HM R.I.P. 🏛 AC BA CK CT GI

Powder Springs and West Atlanta streets, Marietta

Go west on South Marietta Pkwy. Turn right onto Atlanta St. and travel until it becomes South Atlanta St. Bear right into the cemetery.

The largest Confederate **cemetery** in Georgia, with approximately 3,000 soldiers from 14

Top left, Marietta Confederate Cemetery. Above, Marietta National Cemetery.

states buried here, the first being a Confederate army physician, in early September, 1863, and the last being the black body servant of Thomas McCall Yopp. In 1866, a project was begun to remove the Confederate dead from Chickamauga and the Atlanta Campaign battlefields. A **statue** to the memory of these men and Cobb County veterans has been erected in the cemetery. A bronze **cannon**, used for training by the Georgia Military Institute (formerly located across Powder Springs Road, directly opposite the cemetery and burned by Sherman's men) and by cadets opposing Sherman's "March to the Sea," is located in the cemetery. Sherman seized the cannon in Savannah and sent it north as a trophy of war. It was returned in 1910.

U.S. Gen. William T. Sherman

William Tecumseh Sherman is one of the most famous generals in history, and one of the most hated in the South. The son of an Ohio Supreme Court Justice, Sherman was born in Lancaster, Ohio, orphaned at nine and raised by a wealthy friend of his father's, Sen. Thomas Ewing, Sr. (His younger brother, John, was also adopted and became a U.S. Senator.) He attended a local academy in preparation for West Point, where he graduated sixth in his class in 1840. He married his adoptive parents' daughter, Ellen, and served in Florida and California during the Mexican War, seeing limited action. Frustrated and bored in the U.S. Army, he resigned and became a banker in San Francisco in 1853. When his bank failed, he turned to law and lost his only case. Thanks to several Army friends, among them Confederate generals-to-be Braxton Bragg and P.G.T. Beauregard, he was appointed to superintendent of the newly established Louisiana Military Academy (now Louisiana State University) in 1859, where he was successful, if only briefly. Here he witnessed the secession movement first hand, which he viewed with dismay. He was offered a Confederate commission, which he refused, and at the outbreak of war he rejoined the U.S. Army. At First Manassas or Bull Run, Sherman had his first battle experience and commanded one of the few brigades that performed well that day. He was promoted to brigadier general and placed in charge of Union forces in Kentucky. Here he suffered a nervous breakdown and was sent home to rest. When newspapers published a story titled, "General William T. Sherman Insane," Sherman, ashamed and disgraced, considered suicide, but didn't out of consideration to his children. In February 1862, he was assigned to lead a division in the Army of the Tennessee, serving under Gen. U.S. Grant. Grant and Sherman would become best friends and the Army of the Tennessee would become the most successful on the Union side. Grant helped stabilize the brilliant and erratic Sherman, while Sherman helped Grant through rocky times as well. Sherman helped Grant capture Vicksburg and Chattanooga. After Chattanooga, Grant was promoted to the overall command of the entire Union Army and he promoted Sherman to command of the Western Theater. Sherman and Grant developed the strategy which would finish the War, with each simultaneously attacking one of the two main armies of their enemy. Sherman dueled with Confederate Gen. Joseph Johnston and then Confederate Gen. John Bell Hood during the Atlanta Campaign in a campaign of maneuvers, ending with the fall of Atlanta on Sept. 2, 1864. From here, his 60,000-man army went on its famous and controversial "March to the Sea," a punishing, destructive campaign through the heart of Georgia to Savannah, where Sherman could resupply his troops from the sea and march to help Grant with Lee. "I can make Georgia howl," Sherman wrote Grant. It took approximately a month to march from Atlanta and capture Savannah. After a six-week rest in Savannah, he conducted the Carolinas Campaign, a more difficult and destructive march through the heartland of the secession movement. On April 26, 1865, near Durham Station, North Carolina, Sherman received the Army of Tennessee's surrender from Johnston, effectively the end of the War. Ironically, the generous terms he granted to the surrendering Rebels outraged Federal politicians, who harshly censured him. In 1869, he was made commander-in-chief of the U.S. Army, where he oversaw the completion of the transcontinental railroad and the defeat of the Plains Indian tribes. He hated politics and rebuffed all attempts to draft him as a candidate for the Republican Party. "If nominated I will not accept. If elected I will not serve," he said. In 1891, he died of pneumonia at 71. His old adversary, Joe Johnston, helped carry his casket, and died of pneumonia not long after he had stood bareheaded in the rain at Sherman's funeral.

Union Gen. William Tecumseh Sherman's rough exterior matched his reputation for destruction in the South.

THE SMYRNA AREA WAS WHERE CONFEDERATE GEN. Joseph Johnston retreated after he was forced to abandon Kennesaw Mountain, when Sherman's forces under Gen. John Schofield threatened Johnston's southern flank July 3-9, 1864.

Johnston's River Line

🏛 🚋 AC

Oakdale Rd., Smyrna

I-285 to Bankhead Hwy. exit. Travel east apx. 3 miles to Oakdale Rd.

Little remains of Johnston's bold stand in front of the Chattahoochee River during the Atlanta Campaign, called by historians Johnston's River Line. Unique and innovative fortifications, called "Shoupades" after their designer C.S. Gen. Francis A. Shoup, were painstakingly built along a high ridge in front of the river. They were mostly misunderstood by the Confederates, who stood to gain from their use. Slaves were used to build these fortifications, which were designed to create interlocking fields of fire. Instead of digging in for protection, these fortifications were above grade to create both defensive and offensive opportunities. Some experts believe them to be the most formidable defensive position taken by an army during the entire War. Gen. Hood urged they be abandoned, but Cleburne believed them to be excellent. The River Line was abandoned when Union troops found river crossings elsewhere. The Shoupades and artillery forts have mostly been destroyed by development. Some remain on private property. One Shoupade and artillery fort are located on property deeded to Cobb County and may become a River Line Park. Drive along Oakdale Road, which follows the ridge of the river line, and you get a sense of Johnston's position.

Sope Creek

🏛 ⚙ AC GI

Paper Mill Rd., Smyrna

Exit 111 off I-75, travel east on Delk Rd. Turn right on Powers Ferry Rd., and turn left on Terrell Mill Rd. Travel to Paper Mill Rd. and Chattahoochee River National Recreation Area.

In the Atlanta Campaign, Confederate Gen. Joseph Johnston entrenched his army in front of the Chattahoochee River, called the River Line, hoping to prevent U.S. Gen. W. T. Sherman from crossing this last natural barrier before Atlanta. Sherman, as was his style, decided to go around Johnston, and sent cavalry under Gen. Kenner Garrard north to Roswell. A detachment from the cavalry burned the Marietta Paper Mill on Sope Creek on July 5, 1864, while guarding the Federal left flank which was preparing to cross the Chattahoochee River at Sope Creek. Union soldiers under Gen. Schofield crossed over a Cherokee fish dam on July 8 and secured the other side. Johnston was forced to abandon his River Line on July 9 and withdraw

Sope or Soap Creek mill ruins.

Shoals on the Chattahoochee River show where Union soldiers waded across.

over the Chattahoochee River. The impressive, stone papermill ruins are located on public grounds in the **Chattahoochee National Recreation Area**.

Ruff's Mill/Concord Covered Bridge

🏛 🏠 ✗ ⚙ AC GI

Concord Rd., Smyrna

I-285 to S. Cobb Dr., north to Concord Rd., then left.

Several structures here were involved in the Civil War, including **Ruff's Mill**, the **miller's house**, and the **Concord Woolen Mill**. Federal troops moved through here after Johnston pulled back from Kennesaw Mountain during the Atlanta Campaign. Confederates set up a double line of field works approximately along Concord and Smyrna/Roswell roads, and two skirmishes occurred here on July 4, 1864; one to the east 1-1/4 miles called the Battle of Ruff's Mill, and another two and 1/4 miles farther east along this road called the Battle of Smyrna. Look for **historical markers** along this route. Union soldiers burned the mills and **covered bridge**, which was later rebuilt in 1872 and is still in use. The mill ruins are on private property.

ANTEBELLUM ROSWELL WAS A New England-style village centered around the cotton and woolen mills of the **Roswell Manufacturing Company**. Founded in 1839, the town's mills played an important role in supplying goods such as the "Roswell Grays" to the Confederacy. When Union Gen. W. T. Sherman's 100,000-man army arrived in the general area during the Atlanta Campaign the first week of July 1864, his Confederate opponent Gen. Joseph Johnston entrenched his 65,000 men in front of the Chattahoochee River southwest of Roswell. Sherman decided to go around Johnston by looking for a river crossing north of his River Line. Sherman sent Gen. Kenner Garrard's 4,000 cavalry 12 miles north to Roswell to see if they could cross at a covered bridge there. On July 5, a skirmish erupted between the Union and Confederate soldiers at the bridge. Outnumbered Confederate soldiers under Capt. James R. King, burned the bridge and pulled back across the river. On July 9, Federal soldiers waded across the river at "**Shallowford**" and attacked Confederates on the other side, driving them back and securing the crossing, causing Johnston to pull back to the Atlanta side of the river. More than 36,000 Union troops occupied Roswell, and Sherman ordered the Roswell mills burned and the workers and managers deported to Indiana, but did not burn other private property. Two bridges were built by Dodge, and from July 13 to 17, Gen. James McPherson's corps crossed and marched to the Battle of Atlanta. At the **Roswell Historic Visitors Center,** a walking tour of Roswell's historic district is available, guiding you to more than 31 sites, some with Civil War significance, including **Roswell Presbyterian Church** on Mimosa Blvd., used as a hospital.

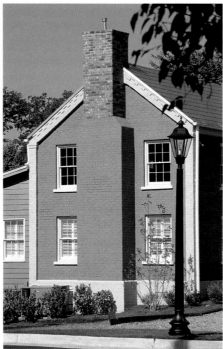

Top and right, Bulloch Hall. Lower left, factory apartments.

Bulloch Hall

🏛 🏠 **AC GI**

180 Bulloch Ave., Roswell 770-992-1731

One block west of historic town square.

Bulloch Hall, built in 1840, is one of the most significant houses in Georgia. Constructed from hard, heart of pine, this Greek Revival mansion was the home of Mittie Bulloch, the mother of 25th U.S. President Theodore R. Roosevelt, Jr. Her other son was the father of Eleanor Roosevelt, who married her fifth cousin and 31st President Franklin D. Roosevelt. Mittie's father, Maj. James S. Bulloch, was a naval agent for the Confederacy. The house was used as Federal barracks during the Union occupation of the town.

Factory Ruins & Apartments

🏛 🏠 ◎ **AC GI**

Mill St., Roswell

Travel north on GA 9 (Atlanta St.) and turn right on Sloan St. Turn right on Mill St.

Chattahoochee River water power caused Roswell King to establish a town here in 1837 called Roswell. By 1839, he had a cotton mill in operation. By 1853, two cotton mills, a woolen mill, flour mill, and tannery were in operation, employing 250 workers. In 1864, Union Gen. Sherman's cavalry entered the town and established law and order. The mill owners had fled the town the night before loaded down with gold, and millworkers and others were looting the stores, mansions, and mills. In an effort by owners to save the mills

from Sherman, owners deeded the mills to a defiant Frenchman named Theopholie Roche, who ran up a French flag and claimed the mills to be neutral French property. His claim irritated Sherman, who recognized it as a ploy, and he told his commanders to burn the mills and send the managers and workers to the North. Concerning Roche, he ordered, "Should you, under the impulse of anger, natural at contemplating such perfidy, hang the wretch, I approve the act beforehand." Roche avoided hanging, and in 1882 sued the U.S. for $125,000 claiming false arrest and damage of his property. He lost his suit. Mill workers lived at the Old Bricks, erected in 1839 and believed to be the first apartments in the South and the oldest in the U.S. They served briefly as a hospital for wounded Federal soldiers in 1864. The **mill ruins** are located nearby in the steep Vickery Creek gorge.

Atlanta History Center

🏠 🏛 GI

130 West Paces Ferry Rd. NW, Atlanta 404-814-4000

Travel north from downtown Atlanta on I-75 and take the West Paces Ferry Rd. exit. At the end of the exit ramp, turn left onto Northside Pkwy. At the next intersection, turn right onto West Paces Ferry Rd.

A good place to start your Civil War touring in Atlanta, this 33-acre complex includes the new **Atlanta History Museum** (30,000 square feet of exhibit space featuring the DuBose Civil War Collection), the **Tullie Smith farm house** (circa 1840), the **Swan House** (a 1928 mansion), and **McElreath Hall** which contains a research library and archives. In 1996, the museum will open a new, 9,200 square foot Civil War exhibit titled "Turning Point: The American Civil War." The Center, located close to the Peachtree Creek battlefield, has a wide variety of fine artifacts, not only from Georgia but from the rest of the Civil War field of operations as well. The History Center annually hosts a Civil War Encampment in July. Call the Center for details.

The Atlanta History Center has the largest collection of Civil War artifacts in Georgia and one of the five largest Civil War collections in the country, with approximately 7,500 objects of all types. Clockwise from top, reenactors at the Atlanta History Center's Civil War Encampment; surgeon's kit used for amputations; Spiller and Burr Revolver made in Atlanta during the War; and hat worn by Lt. George Young of the 149th New York Infantry who was wounded at the Battle of Peachtree Creek.

Battle of Peachtree Creek
Tanyard Creek Park

HM ⚔ ◎ 🏃 AC BA

Collier Road, Atlanta

From Piedmont Hospital on Peachtree St. turn onto Collier Rd. Park is on left.

As the Union army fought its way to the outskirts of Atlanta in 1864, Confederate President Jefferson Davis decided it was time to make a change of command, relieving his old rival Joseph Johnston with Gen. John Bell Hood on July 18, 1864. (A **monument** of stacked cannonballs at 950 W. Marietta Road marks the **Dexter Niles House site**, where Johnston was fired.) Davis was frustrated with the reticent Johnston's retreats, and now the enemy was at the door of Atlanta. Hood, who had already lost a leg and use of an arm in the Civil War, was a fierce fighter and loved to attack. Sherman was pleased that Johnston was replaced, regarding the wily Johnston as superior to the 33-year-old Hood. The first battle of the Army of Tennessee under Hood occurred near Peachtree Creek on July 20, 1864. Hood went against George "Rock of Chickamauga" Thomas' corps with a complicated battle plan which was poorly executed due to unfriendly terrain. The result was a Confederate loss, with more than 2,500 Confederate casualties compared to Thomas' 1,750. Twenty-third president-to-be Benjamin Harrison, grandson of President William Henry Harrison, led his 400 men from Indiana in a counterattack at Peachtree Creek where the line almost gave way to Confederate assaults. Today you can view portions of the battlefield at the City of Atlanta's **Tanyard Creek Park** located near the heart of Buckhead. (National park officials, wanting to establish a Civil War park to commemorate the Atlanta Campaign, came down to a decision between Kennesaw Mountain and Peachtree Creek. Kennesaw won out.) Many **plaques** and **Georgia Historical Markers** in the area explain the battle. South of Piedmont Hospital on Peachtree Street is a **WPA monument** marking the spot where Confederate troops opened the assault.

Clockwise from top, Peachtree Creek; the home-made frock coat worn by Private John Johnston when he was wounded at the Battle of Peachtree Creek (property of the Atlanta History Center); historical marker at Peachtree Creek; Peachtree Battle marker; officer's frock coat worn by Lt. George Young of the 149th New York Infantry when he was wounded at the Battle of Peachtree Creek (property of the Atlanta History Center).

The Battle of Atlanta

The Battle of Atlanta on July 22, 1864 was the largest, bloodiest and perhaps most closely fought battle of the Atlanta Campaign, with 3,700 Union and 7,000 Confederate casualties. Although Hood had suffered a defeat two days earlier at Peachtree Creek, he had not lost any of his ambition or aggressiveness. His battle plan was to lure Gen. James B. McPherson's army, the Army of the Tennessee, located east of Atlanta on the Georgia Central Railroad, closer to Atlanta, while he sent Gen. William Hardee's men on a 15-mile flanking maneuver to strike at McPherson from the rear or flank, and Wheeler's cavalry to Decatur to cut McPherson's supply lines. Once attacked, McPherson would turn to fight, and Maj. Gen. Benjamin Cheatham's men would attack McPherson's center. As luck would have it, McPherson, worried about his left flank, had placed reserves under Maj. Gen. Grenville Dodge squarely in the path of Hardee's surprise attack. When it came, the fighting was bloody and vicious, with Cleburne's Division making charge and countercharge against the Union line, finally breaking through, until a battery of 10 Federal artillery pieces beat back the assault. Cleburne lost 40 percent of his men and 30 of 60 officers in this battle. McPherson, checking on firing in this area, was shot from his horse and carried back to Sherman, who wept at the sight of his dead friend. Confederate Gen. William H.T. Walker was killed by a skirmisher near this area at the beginning of the battle and Georgia Gov. Joe Brown's brother was killed in this battle. Meanwhile, at the center of the Union line, Cheatham had broken through and was rolling up the line, routing four Union regiments which found themselves fighting in two directions. Sherman, his headquarters located dangerously close to the fighting, ordered 20 massed cannons to fire on the gap, turning the charging Confederates to pulp. A counterattack from the Yankees, under Gen. John "Black Jack"

Top, the Ponder House (sometimes erroneously referred to as the "Potter House"), blasted by Union artillery after Confederate sharpshooters nested in the upper story. Below, Sherman leans on cannon at Federal Fort No. 2. Photos by George N. Barnard, 1864.

Logan who replaced McPherson, returned the trenches to the Union and sealed the gap, thus decisively turning the battle in the Federals' favor. After eight hours of continuous fighting, the battle was over.

C.S. Gen. John Bell Hood

John Bell Hood was a gallant combat leader and one of the fiercest fighters in the Confederacy, whose brigade of Texans was generally considered by historians to be the best to serve the South. Born in 1831 in Owingsville, Kentucky, Hood graduated from West Point in 1853 near the bottom of his class. He served on the western frontier, and joined the Confederacy when the War began. He gallantly led a Texas brigade during the bloody Seven Days Battles, Second Manassas, and Antie-tam, where his heroism brought him command of a division under Lt. Gen. James Longstreet at Fredericksburg and Gettysburg. He led his men

in a nearly successful assault on Round Top in pivotal action on the second day of Gettysburg, and lost the use of his arm. He accompanied Longstreet with reinforcements to Georgia, where at Chickamauga he led the successful assault on the Union right flank, smashing the Federals and sending them retreating back into Chattanooga. During this battle, a .58-caliber lead Minie ball shattered his right leg, which was amputated leaving a 4-1/2 inch stump. His bravery earned him a promotion to lieutenant general, and he fought strapped into his saddle. During the Atlanta Campaign he served under Johnston, and wrote letters to Davis undermining Johnston's authority. When Johnston was replaced with Hood, he lost four bloody battles

and the city of Atlanta by launching aggressive attacks against Sherman's superior army, which destroyed much of his army's fighting strength and morale. Abandoning Georgia, he made a suicidal strike into Tennessee and met disaster at Franklin and Nashville. Relieved at his own request, he finished the war under P.G.T. Beauregard in Tennessee, and was captured in Mississippi in May 1865. After the War, he became a New Orleans merchant, but his business failed during the yellow fever epidemic of 1878. The next year he, his wife, and some of their children succumbed to the disease, leaving the surviving children to be divided among various foster homes.

State Capitol Building
Catholic Church
Underground Atlanta &
Original Lamppost

[HM] 🏠 🏛 🏞 AC BA GI MTS

Capitol: 431 State Capitol Ave., Atlanta 404-656-2844
Catholic Church: 48 Martin Luther King, Jr. Dr., SW, Atlanta 404-521-1866 Underground Atlanta: Peachtree St. at Alabama St., Atlanta 404-523-2311

I-75 North to Capitol Ave. exit (exit 90).

From 1853-1883, Atlanta's city hall and courthouse were located on the state capitol grounds. (During the Civil War, the state capitol was located in Milledgeville and temporarily moved to Macon.) During Sherman's occupation from Sept. 2 to Nov. 1864, the 2nd Mass. Regiment constituting the provost guard of Sherman's army camped on this site. From here came the order to Atlanta citizens to evacuate the city on Sept. 7th as Sherman prepared to burn the city and go on his "March to the Sea." The present State Capitol was begun in 1884 and completed in 1889, for the cost of $999,881.57. It doubles as the official museum of natural science and industry for Georgia. On the grounds is an excellent statue of Georgia native **Gen. John B. Gordon**, who organized the Raccoon Roughs in Georgia and led them to Virginia, where he rose to command half of Gen. Robert E. Lee's army by the end of the war. Returning home, the war hero served two terms as governor and three as senator. Another statue shows Georgia's Civil War governor **Joseph E. Brown** and his wife. Another interesting monument is **"Expelled Because of Color,"** honoring 33 black state legislators who were elected but expelled from the legislature in Reconstruction Georgia in 1868. Four Civil War plaques next to cannon on the grounds explain many of the events which occurred in Atlanta. Inside the Capitol are displays, battleflags, paintings and statues with Civil War significance. The statue of **Benjamin Harvey Hill**, an effective supporter of Jefferson Davis, was originally erected outdoors in 1886. At the dedication, Davis, making one of his last public appearances, was introduced by newspaperman Henry Grady. Also attending were Confederate gens. James Longstreet and John B. Gordon. Northwest of the State Capitol is the **Shrine of the Immaculate Conception** church, which is the oldest complete building standing in Atlanta, erected in 1869. During the occupation of Atlanta, the church's pastor Thomas O'Reilly, convinced General Henry Slocum to not burn five churches and City Hall. A few blocks north of here in Underground Atlanta, is the **Old Lamppost**. This 1855 gas lamppost was struck in the base by a shell during the Battle of Atlanta on July 22, 1864. The shell ricocheted and exploded, injuring Salomon Luckie, a freed slave and well-known barber, in the leg. He was carried into a doctor's office to have the leg amputated and died a few hours later. An Underground Atlanta historical plaque marks the location and tells the story of Atlanta's **Union Depot**, destroyed by Sherman. **Heritage Row** museum at Underground Atlanta (404-584-7879) tells Atlanta's history in six interactive exhibit halls. A short walk from the Capitol at 330 Capitol Avenue is the **Department of Archives and History** (404-656-2393), which preserves the state's official records and has a Civil War library.

Clockwise from top: state capitol, built in 1889, rests on the site of former Atlanta city hall; old lamppost in Underground Atlanta; Catholic Church; Civil War cannon and markers; John B. Gordon statue at Capitol grounds.

A stained glass window at Rhodes Hall depicts the firing on Fort Sumter and a Southern soldier saying goodbye as he goes off to fight in the War.

Rhodes Hall

🏠 🏛 🎨 GI

1516 Peachtree St., NW, Atlanta 404-881-9980

Exit off I-75/85 on the Tenth & Fourteenth St. exit. Go east to Peachtree St. Travel north on Peachtree. Rhodes Hall will be on the left.

Rhodes Hall, built 1902-04, is the home of the Georgia Trust for Historic Preservation, an important organization committed to preserving Georgia's history. An interesting feature of Rhodes Hall — and one of the most unique Civil War oriented attractions in the nation — are nine complex stained glass windows made up of 1,250 pieces of German glass honoring the South during the Civil War. Called **"The Rise and Fall of the Confederacy,"** the windows are set into three panels that range in height from 15 feet to nine feet as they follow a mahogany staircase. If you can identify all the individuals in the windows, you're an expert on the Civil War. The Georgia Trust is a good place to get answers on historic homes in Georgia.

Sherman's army destroyed Atlanta, including the Atlanta Round House. Photo by George N. Barnard, 1864.

THE BATTLE OF ATLANTA WAS bloody, hotly contested, perhaps the most significant battle on Georgia soil, and possibly one that saved the Lincoln presidency and Union. It is best understood by first going to the **Atlanta Cyclorama** in Grant Park. The battlefield, located in east Atlanta, has been significantly changed by mass transit lines, highways and commercial development. The area is very congested, but there are some monuments and **historical markers** which, with some imagination, can help you visualize the battlefield. Historic **Oakland Cemetery** is considered by some to be the most beautiful cemetery in Georgia.

Above, the Battle of Atlanta depicted by the Cyclorama. Below, Logan riding to save the Union on the painting he commissioned.

Cyclorama Museum & Fort Walker

🏛 🚂 🏛 **AC BA GI GLC**

Cyclorama: 800-C Cherokee Ave., SE, Atlanta 404-624-1071

Both the Cyclorama and Fort Walker are located in Grant Park. I-20 East to exit 26. Follow signs to the park.

The **Cyclorama** not only tells history, but it *is* history. Considered the world's largest, the 9,000-pound painting measures 358 feet by 42 feet, which is longer than a football field. It was painted by German artists in the 1880s, who came to Atlanta and viewed the battlefield and interviewed battle veterans. Set in the round with three-dimensional figures added in the 1930s, it tells with emotional impact the story of the Battle of Atlanta. Commissioned by U.S. Maj. Gen. John "Black Jack" Logan, it was a travelling attraction when it came to Atlanta in 1892 and exhibitors ran out of money. Bought by philanthropist George Gress and given to the city in 1898, it was given its own building in 1921. Notice the dead figure of Clark Gable, added after *Gone With The Wind* premiered in Atlanta.

The museum houses the famous *Texas*, the locomotive which captured the *General* in the "Great Locomotive Chase." Other interesting artifacts are on exhibit, and the museum has an excellent bookstore.

The Cyclorama is located in **Grant Park**, named for Col. Lemuel P. Grant, who helped design many of the 12 miles of fortifications circling and protecting Atlanta for 42 days during the Civil War, and donated the land making up Grant Park. All but a few fragments of this vast network of fortifications have disappeared. **Fort Walker**, an artillery bastion named for Georgian William H.T. Walker who died at the Battle of Atlanta, is located in the southeast corner of the park.

Oakland Cemetery

🏛️ 🏠 ⚰️ 🏞️ **AC BA GI GLC**

248 Oakland Ave., SE, Atlanta 404-688-2107

I-20 East to exit 26(Boulevard exit). Go north on Boulevard to cemetery.

Oakland Cemetery has five Confederate generals, a 65-foot tall memorial, 2,500 Confederate dead, the Lion of Atlanta, and to top it off, the grave of **Margaret Mitchell**, author of *Gone With The Wind*, the bestselling work of fiction of all time and for some the best expression of what it means to be Southern. Established in 1850, Atlanta's oldest cemetery is considered one of the finest Victorian cemeteries in America, with much elaborate statuary across its 88 acres. Confederate generals buried here are **John B. Gordon, Alfred Iverson, Jr., Clement A. Evans, William S. Walker,** and **Lucius J. Gartrell.** The vice president of the Confederacy, **A.H. Stephens,** was buried here until he was reinterred at his home in Crawfordville, Georgia. **Benjamin Harvey Hill,** another prominent Georgia politician in the Civil War, is buried here. Hanged and buried here until their reinterment in Chattanooga in 1866 were seven of the **Andrews Raiders** of the "Great Locomotive Chase." James Andrews was hanged at the corner of Juniper and Third and buried near there, his remains lost until they were found and moved to Chattanooga in 1887. **Capt. William**

Fuller, **Anthony Murphy,** and **Jeff Cain,** who chased Andrews, are all buried in Oakland. Lincoln grieved over his brother-in-law's death, **Benjamin H. Helm,** who was also interred here temporarily after suffering a mortal wound at Chickamauga. Civil War burials occurred here before Sherman got to Atlanta, with thousands of ill and wounded Confederate soldiers sent to Atlanta for treatment at nearby hospitals. Today they rest in eight sections of Oakland, one being unknown soldiers. One row in Section C has **20 Union soldiers,** who died in local hospitals. The **Confederate Obelisk,** made from Stone Mountain granite, is 65-feet high with a 20-foot base. It had its cornerstone placed on the day of Gen. Robert E. Lee's funeral. At the dedication on

The Lion of Atlanta honors the unknown Confederate dead in Oakland Cemetery.

Confederate Memorial Day, April 26, 1874, it was the tallest structure in Atlanta. The **Lion of Atlanta,** designed to honor the unknown Confederate dead, was inspired by the Lion of Lucerne, which was carved to honor the Swiss Guards who were killed defending Marie Antoinette in 1792. This monument, weighing 30,000 pounds, was carved from Georgia marble by T.M. Brady of Canton, Georgia. A plaque in the cemetery near the sexton's house marks the site of the house where Confederate Gen. John B. Hood watched the Battle of Atlanta, only a few blocks away. Union occupiers vandalized the cemetery, opening crypts and stealing silver nameplates, and burying Union dead in previously occupied coffins.

An upturned cannon honors the spot where Gen. W. H. T. Walker, an Augusta native, was killed by a Union sharpshooter.

Battle of Atlanta Markers:
Augustus Hurt House
Troup Hurt House
Leggett's Hill Marker
Gen. Walker Monument
Gen. McPherson Monument

🏛️ ⚔️ 🏞️ **AC BA**

Atlanta

I-20 East at exit 30 (Glenwood Ave. exit).

The **Augustus Hurt House site,** is located at the Carter Presidential Center, located at 1 Copenhill Avenue, NE. This was Gen. W.T. Sherman's headquarters during the Battle of Atlanta, where from less than half a mile away he saw the Confederate breakthrough and ordered Gen. John Schofield's artillery to direct their fire at the oncoming enemy. The unfinished brick **Troup Hurt House,** featured prominently in the Cyclorama painting as the site of Confederate Manigault's brigade's breakthrough, is marked by a **historical marker** on DeGress Avenue. The stone Primitive Baptist Church sits on the site

today. **Leggett's or Bald Hill,** site of the Confederate attack on the Union flank, is located where Memorial Drive, Moreland Ave., and Interstate 20 come together. Two **Georgia Historical Markers** mark the spot at Trenton Street at Moreland Ave. An upturned cannon marks the spot where Augusta-native Confederate **Gen. William H.T. Walker** was shot by a Union sharpshooter, one of the first casualties of the Battle of Atlanta. It is found at the intersection of Wilkinson and Glenwood Avenue. Another cannon at McPherson and Monument avenues marks the spot where Union **Gen. James B. McPherson** was killed, not long after Walker. The commander of the Union fighting forces that day was inspecting his lines when he encountered some of Patrick Cleburne's troops, who asked him to surrender. He tipped his hat, wheeled his horse, and raced away, only to be shot dead through the back. An officer who was with him also dashed off and hit a tree, breaking his watch and preserving the time of McPherson's death: 2:02. McPherson was the only Union army commander killed in the War, and according to Sherman and Grant, perhaps the most talented. Maj. Gen. John "Black Jack" Logan replaced him at the Battle of Atlanta.

Westview Cemetery has a large marble monument honoring Confederate dead.

Battle of Ezra Church
Westview Cemetery

🏛 ⚔ 🚂 R.I.P. 🏃 AC BA GI

Ezra Church: 1565 MLK Jr. Blvd. Mozley Park, Atlanta
Westview Cemetery: 1680 Ralph David Abernathy, SW, Atlanta

I-20 West to Martin Luther King Jr. exit. Turn left and drive under the bridge, and turn left again onto Ralph David Abernathy. Cemetery entrance will be on the right.

Not much remains of the **Ezra Church battlefield**, the scene of a lopsided, bloody Union victory on July 28, 1864. Union Gen. W.T. Sherman was determined to cut the last railroad supplying Confederate Gen. John Bell Hood's troops located inside Atlanta's fieldworks. He sent troops under Maj. Gen. O.O. Howard counterclockwise around Atlanta to destroy the Macon & Western Railroad at East Point, which served the town from the south. Hood sent four divisions, two commanded by newly arriving Stephen Dill Lee, and two others by A.P. Stewart. Lee was to block the Federals while Stewart was to circle and come up on their rear. On July 28, near Ezra Church, Gen. Lee, without orders and before Stewart had arrived, launched assaults on an entrenched Union army and was se-verely beaten back. When Stewart arrived, he led several unsuccessful assaults, and became a casualty. Four assaults and three hours of fighting produced what is considered by historians to be the most one-sided victory of the entire war, with 3-5,000 Confederate casualties compared to 600 Federals. Gen. William Hardee reported to Hood that this battle had broken the proud spirit of the Army of Tennessee. Ten days and three battles since taking command, Hood had lost one-third of his infantry attacking entrenchments. **Historical markers** are found in and around **Mozley Park**, the main part of the battlefield where the log chapel Ezra Church was located. Nearby **Westview Cemetery** is another protected part of the battlefield, where Confederates rushed up to charge the center of the Union line. The solitary grave of **Lt. Edward Clingman**, killed at Ezra Church, is marked with engravings of a saber, pistol and Confederate flag, and is located along the eastern outer drive. Behind the grave is a section of **Confederate trenches**. On a nearby hilltop, a **large marble soldier**, one of the few monuments ever erected by Confederate veterans, stands guard over fallen comrades. The inscription speaks of peace: "Nation shall not rise up against nation. They shall beat their swords into plough shares and their spears into pruning hooks. Neither shall they learn war anymore. Of Liberty born of a Patriots dream; of a storm cradled Nation that fell."

Utoy Church

🏛 🏠 ⚔ 🚂 R.I.P. AC BA

Cahaba Dr., SW, Atlanta

Turn right out of Westview Cemetery onto Ralph David Abernathy. Travel .8 mile and turn right onto Cascade (GA 154). Travel 1.6 miles and turn left onto Centra Villa. Travel .5 mile and turn left onto Venetian. Drive .3 mile and turn left onto Cahaba. On the corner is Utoy Church.

The Battles of Utoy Creek, Aug 5-7, 1864, were Confederate victories. During the Siege of Atlanta, Sherman again tried to work his men closer to the Macon & Western Railroad by flanking the Confederate defensive line. While two of Sherman's generals squabbled, Gen. William Hardee extended his lines and entrenched on a ridge to meet the threat near Utoy Creek. The Yankees attacked the Orphan Brigade, but were bloodily repulsed. The next day they tried again, with even worse results. The Union quit the field with several hundred Federal casualties. The Confederates lost several dozen. The battlefield today is in Cascade Springs Nature Preserve (Instead of turning onto Centra Villa, continue driving on Cascade, which was the front line of the battle. **Historical markers** will be on the right, the nature preserve on the left). **Utoy Church**, circa 1828, is located two miles east of the battlefield at Venetian and Cahaba drives. The oldest Baptist church in present Fulton County, today Utoy Church is the Temple of Christ Pentecostal Church, Inc. This church served as a Confederate hospital, and apx. 25 Confederate graves from the Battle of Utoy Creek and the Battle of Atlanta are located in the northwestern **cemetery**, as is a portion of the Rebel defensive line a few feet north. In Adams Park, also located off Cascade, is a **historical marker** at the top of the 17th tee, marking the location of some of the few remaining Confederate **entrenchments** from the Siege of Atlanta.

Surrender Marker
Fort Hood
Change of Command Marker

HM AC BA

Northside Dr. & Marietta St., Atlanta

Not much remains at this location from the Civil War, but the historic event that took place here changed the nation. Lincoln's presidency and the Union were saved — and the Confederacy was doomed — after the fall of Atlanta. This is probably the most important Civil War event in Georgia. A **historical marker**, titled "**Surrender of Atlanta**," tells the story: *Gen. Hood, in person with Stewart's A.C. and the Georgia Militia abandoned the city, Sept 1, as a result of Hardee's defeat at Jonesboro, August 31, and marched S. to Lovejoy's Station. Federal forces at Chattahoochee River Crossings, since Aug. 25, suspecting the evacuation of the city on hearing loud explosions, sent forward a reconnaissance to investigate. At this point it met Mayor James M. Calhoun with a committee, who tendered the surrender of the city, asking protection for citizens and property. Col. John Coburn, vice Maj. Gen. Henry W. Slocum, com'd'g 20th A.C. received the surrender.* A short distance southeast from here at 793 Marietta St., a **plaque** on the Wells Fargo building and a **street** named Fort Hood Place mark the site of **Fort Hood**, which stood on the city's northwest fortifications. A stack of **cannon balls**, on 950 West Marietta Rd., marks the location of the **Dexter Niles House site**, where Confederate Gen. Joseph Johnston learned he was replaced by Gen. John Bell Hood.

Above, the view from Ft. Hood of the Ponder House (sometimes erroneously referred to as the "Potter House,") and Confederate defense works which Sherman found too strong to assault, photographed by George N. Barnard, 1864; right is surrender marker; left opposite page is Change of Command monument.

DECATUR, A RAILROAD TOWN and county seat of DeKalb County, was on many Georgia maps before Atlanta grew into a larger city. Unlike their neighbors in Fulton County, a majority of DeKalb citizens voted not to secede in the election of Jan. 2, 1861. But their Union sympathies wouldn't spare them the ravages of war. During July 1864 of the Atlanta Campaign, Sherman found Atlanta's fortifications "too strong to assault and too extensive to invest," so he switched to a strategy of destroying the railroads which kept the town supplied. His first target was the Central of Georgia Railroad, which connected Atlanta with Augusta and the Eastern Theater. Destroying this transportation line would prevent supplies and reinforcements from coming to Hood's support. Cavalry raids and McPherson's army came through Decatur, occupying the town and tearing up tracks and burning bridges east and west. During the Battle of Atlanta on July 22, 1864, Confederate cavalry under Maj. Gen. Joseph Wheeler attacked Union Gen. McPherson's wagon train near the Decatur courthouse, driving the Union troops and the Chicago Board of Trade & Michigan batteries back up the North Decatur road. From here, Wheeler left to join the Battle of Atlanta raging west of Decatur down the rail line. An **engraved stone** on the loop in front of Main Hall on the Agnes Scott College campus indicates the site of the Decatur engagement.

DeKalb History Museum

HM 🏛 👤 AC GI

Old Courthouse on the Square, Decatur 404-373-1088 (DeKalb Historical Society)

I-85 North to Clairmont Rd. Turn right and follow Clairmont until it deadends at the courthouse.

DeKalb County history is the main focus of this museum, but it contains an interesting permanent exhibit, "Johnny Reb and Billy Yank: The Life of the Common Soldier" with various artifacts including Confederate surgical tools which contain traces of blood.

Mary Gay House
Swanton House

HM 🏠 AC BA GI

Gay House: 716 West Trinity Place, Decatur 404-378-2162
Swanton House: 720 West Trinity Place, Decatur 404-373-1088 (DeKalb Historical Society headquarters)

Travel east from Atlanta toward Decatur on Ponce de Leon Ave., and turn right on Trinity Place.

The **Swanton House**, circa 1825, is the oldest building in Decatur, and was the headquarters of Union Brig. Gen. Thomas W. Sweeny during the Civil War. Bullets are embedded in the wall. Visitors must call the DeKalb Historical Society in advance to arrange a tour of the home. Located next door is the **Mary Gay House**, where Mary Ann Harris Gay lived from 1850 to 1914. Her personal account of the War, *Life in Dixie During the War*, vividly describes the events of those years and was a major source for Margaret Mitchell's *Gone With The Wind*. The house is open for self-guided tours.

Top, Mary Gay House. Right, spinning wheel at Swanton House. At left, the Swanton House.

Stone Mountain, the world's largest carving, commemorates Confederate heroes Jefferson Davis, Robert E. Lee, and Stonewall Jackson.

Stone Mountain Park

HM R.I.P. AC GI

Hwy. 78, Stone Mountain 770-498-5702

Located east of Atlanta on Hwy. 78, follow signs.

The 3,200-acre **Stone Mountain State Park** features the world's largest carving, a memorial to three heroes of the Confederacy, Confederate President Jefferson Davis, and Generals Robert E. Lee and Thomas J. "Stonewall" Jackson. The carving, larger than Mount Rushmore, took more than 57 years and three main carvers to complete, from conception to finishing touches, due to delays and lack of funds. Started by Gutzon Borglum, the carver of Rushmore, disputes between him and the monument association ended his commission. In 1958, the state took over the project which was eventually completed in 1972. The carving is much larger than it appears: sculptors could stand inside a horse's mouth to escape a sudden shower. Also at the Park is **Memorial Hall museum**, which contains one of the largest Civil War exhibits in the state. At **Confederate Hall** is a huge diorama explaining Civil War events in Georgia and **statues** of famous Confederates. You can walk to the top of the mountain from Confederate Hall or take a tram near Memorial Hall. Also found at the park is an old grist mill and an authentic antebellum plantation complex consisting of 19 restored buildings. The Park offers golfing, lodging, conference center, camping, fishing, swimming, and watersliding. Stone Mountain's Antebellum Festival, held each year on the last weekend in March, features a Civil War encampment and reenactment. In nearby Stone Mountain Village is **Stone Mountain Confederate Cemetery** with the graves of approximately 150 Confederate soldiers, who died in nearby hospitals or were killed in a skirmish with Federal raiders under Gen. Kenner Garrard who destroyed the railroad here on July 18-19, 1864.

JONESBORO WITNESSED THE LAST battles of the Atlanta Campaign, desperate affairs that sealed the fate of Atlanta on Aug. 31-Sept. 1, 1864. Sherman had laid siege to Atlanta and sent cavalry raiders in an unsuccessful campaign to tear up the railroads feeding Atlanta. Gen. Judson Kilpatrick destroyed track, stores and depots in Jonesboro on Aug. 19, 1864, and returned to Atlanta reporting success. But within 24 hours of his raid, the rails had been fixed by the Confederates. So after a month-long stalemate outside the fortifications of the city, Sherman decided on Aug. 25 to silence his artillery — which had been pounding Atlanta for six weeks — and to evacuate his trenches, and send almost his entire army in a sweep west and south to do what smaller forces could not: destroy at three different places the remaining railroad serving the city. (Some in Atlanta, believing a frustrated Sherman had been defeated and was heading north, planned victory parties.) Confederate Gen. John Bell Hood in Atlanta, who had sent his cavalry north and lacked good reconnaissance information, learned Union troops were marching south to the railroads, and thinking it was a small raiding party, sent Gen. William Hardee and Gen. Stephen Lee's corps to protect the railroads. The Confederate soldiers found themselves against a much larger force, and in an uncoordinated attack on entrenched Federal troops in Jonesboro on Aug. 31, suffered a defeat. Meanwhile, Gen. John Schofield's men north of Jonesboro had cut the railroad, and Hood ordered Lee's men north from Jonesboro to Atlanta. In Jonesboro on Sept. 1, Hardee's depleted men, now being attacked by Union forces, fought valiantly under Gen. Patrick Cleburne until the Federals withdrew. Hardee withdrew his Confederates south to Lovejoy, where Hood and his remaining forces met him, having abandoned Atlanta. Sherman had won Atlanta, but he missed his chance to destroy the Confederate Army of Tennessee. Hood would move north to fight again, and Sherman would march to Savannah in November. The battlefield is more or less obliterated from the time of the battles, but nine **historical markers** in the area of Jonesboro's **Historic District** help tell the story. Don't miss the **Patrick Cleburne Cemetery**. Some interesting antebellum homes can be found in Jonesboro, some which claim to be the inspiration for Margaret Mitchell's Tara in *Gone With The Wind*, and a driving tour map with 32 attractions is available at the **Clayton County Visitors Center** at 8712 Tara Boulevard. Mitchell's great grandfather, Philip Fitzgerald, was a well-to-do planter in Clayton County, and the stories he told to Mitchell about the War, many believe, became *Gone With The Wind*. On the second weekend in October, Jonesboro hosts its annual Fall Festival and Battle of Jonesboro Reenactment.

Top, reenactors at Jonesboro. Lower right, the Warren House, which was a battlefield landmark; on left is Patrick R. Cleburne Cemetery.

Warren House
Crawford-Talmadge Plantation
Johnson-Blalock House
Stately Oaks Mansion
Patrick R. Cleburne Cemetery

⌂ ⛺ ⚔ 🏚 R.I.P. **AC BA GI**

Jonesboro & Lovejoy
South of Atlanta on U.S. 41.

The privately owned **Warren House** (102 W. Mimosa), built in 1860, was the most prominent landmark on the Jonesboro battlefield, and it was used as a headquarters and hospital by Confederate forces and then by Union forces. Signatures of convalescing Union soldiers still appear on the walls in an upstairs room. The **Crawford-Talmadge Plantation** (Talmadge Road in Lovejoy) is where Hood's defeated army gathered after the fall of Atlanta. It is thought to be the inspiration for Twelve Oaks in *Gone With The Wind*. It is open to tour for groups of 30 or more. The privately owned **Johnson-Blalock House,** (155 N. Main Street) built in 1859 by Col. J.F. Johnson, a signer of the Secession Ordinance, was used as a hospital and commissary. **Stately Oaks Mansion** (100 Carriage Lane 770-473-0197) is an 1839 planta-

tion home open for tours. It was located four miles north of Jonesboro, where Union soldiers camped on its grounds, until it was moved to its present location. The **Patrick R. Cleburne Cemetery,** (Johnson & McDonough streets) established in 1872, holds the remains of 600 to 1,000 unidentified Confederate soldiers who died during the Battle of Jonesboro. The unmarked headstones are laid out in the shape of the Confederate battle flag, with a memorial in the center, and 12 cannon balls embedded in the entrance archway. The cemetery is found in historic downtown Jonesboro near the railroad tracks.

PALMETTO

ON SEPT. 19, 1864 IN PALMETTO, Gen. John Bell Hood gathered his 40,000 troops after the fall of Atlanta. He planned his northward move to attack Sherman's supply lines and started his disastrous Tennessee Campaign. On Sept 25-26, Jefferson Davis visited Hood, reviewed the troops, gave a speech, and left for Richmond. Gen. Joseph Hardee was relieved of his command here. A **monument, historical marker,** and **two cannons** are found near the railroad tracks in downtown Palmetto. Near Palmetto in Sharpsburg is the privately owned **Windemere Plantation.**

Presidential Pathways, named for the two U.S. presidents, Franklin D. Roosevelt and Jimmy Carter, who made homes here, was an important area for the Confederacy during the Civil War. Here the terrain changes from the wooded, hilly piedmont in the north, to the agricultural plains in the south. The beautiful Chattahoochee and Flint rivers wind through this area to the Gulf of Mexico. Columbus was the second most important industrial town for the Confederacy, producing everything from fifes to cannon to Confederate battleships. **The Confederate Naval Museum** here, with the salvaged remains of two Confederate warships, is a highlight. The most successful Union cavalry raid made during the Civil War happened in this area under Gen. James H. Wilson and the last important land battle occurred in Columbus when Wilson attacked the town on April 16, 1865. Cavalry battles also occurred at West Point, Newnan, and other smaller towns. The most notorious Civil War prison camp was located at **Andersonville**, today a National Historic Site. In this region, you find towns which served as hospital centers because of their location on strategic rail lines. Many of these retain much of their antebellum character and have Civil War markers, monuments, cemeteries and historic homes to tour.

Columbus Confederate Naval Iron Works.

NEWNAN, DURING THE CIVIL War, was known as the "hospital city of the Confederacy," having seven field hospitals. It was located on the Atlanta and West Point Railroad during the War. A cavalry battle, the Battle of Brown's Mill, was fought near here on July 30, 1864, between Union Brig. Gen. E.M. McCook's 3,600 men and Confederate Maj. Gen. "Fighting" Joe Wheeler's 1,400 men. Wheeler routed the Union forces, capturing 2,000, a full battery, and releasing 500 Confederate prisoners who had been captured days earlier by Gen. Edward McCook in Fayetteville. Wheeler's message to Gen. John Bell Hood in Atlanta about the battle was, "We have just completed the killing, capturing and breaking up the entire raiding party under General McCook." McCook was participating in the Great Cavalry Raid or Stoneman-McCook Raid, Sherman's plan to destroy the railroads south of Atlanta. In a great pincer movement, McCook was to swing around the west side of Atlanta and Stoneman around the east, where they would meet in Lovejoy south of Atlanta and proceed to tear up track to Macon.

McCook got to Lovejoy, but Stoneman was not there. When Wheeler's men drew near, McCook turned back west toward Newnan. Wheeler's success meant the town was spared capture and possible destruction. So today, Newnan is known as the City of Homes because of its outstanding examples of period and contemporary architecture. More than 22 antebellum homes are found here in five National Register Historic Districts. A driving tour is available at the Male Academy Museum. A **Battle of Brown's Mill Reenactment** is held at Catalpa Plantation. Call the Museum for details.

Male Academy Museum

 AC GI

30 Temple Ave., Newnan 770-251-0207

I-85 South from Atlanta to Newnan exit (exit 9). Turn right off the exit ramp onto Bullsboro Dr. Bullsboro becomes Jackson St.

Turn right onto Temple Ave.

This converted 1840 male seminary building, run by the Newnan-Coweta Historical Society, serves as a **local history museum** with an excellent collection of Civil War memorabilia, including a war-scarred battle flag, gun collection, period photographs, surgical tools, amputation instructions, and a Civil War artificial leg.

Oak Hill Cemetery

[HM] [R.I.P.] **AC BA GI**

Jackson St., Newnan

I-85 south to exit 9. Turn right off of the exit ramp onto Bullsboro Dr. Bullsboro becomes Jackson St. Cemetery on both sides of Jackson.

A large **Confederate cemetery** with 268 soldiers, many of whom died in the hospitals located here and some who died at the Battle of Brown's Mill. All but two are identified, a testament to the efficiency of local hospitals.

LAGRANGE IS A BEAUTIFUL railroad town located on the Atlanta and West Point Railroad, which was the location of Confederate hospitals during the Civil War. It is most famous, however, for being the only place in the Confederacy to organize its own female military company, the Nancy Harts. Most of LaGrange's men had gone to fight for the Confederacy, but thanks to the Nancy Harts, it was spared some of the ravages of the War that befell other towns in Sherman's path. Three historic districts are featured in LaGrange's driving tour, with 13 homes on the National Register.

Bellevue

[HM] 🏠 **GI**

204 Ben Hill St., LaGrange 706-884-1832

From I-85 North take exit 4 and travel west on Hwy. 109. Turn right on Hwy. 27 and travel north. Turn left on Broad St. and right onto Ben Hill St.

The **home** of U.S. Senator Benjamin Harvey Hill is an excellent example of Greek Revival architecture popular in the Old South. Built around 1854, it is open to tours. Hill was one of the more amazing figures of the Civil War. He graduated first in his class at the University of Georgia and moved to LaGrange to practice law. His practice was quickly successful, and soon he was serving in the Georgia legislature. He opposed secession but became one of the foremost champions of the Confederacy's cause and was regarded as the ablest supporter of the policies of Jefferson Davis, who was a frequent visitor at Bellevue. Arrested but paroled at the end of the War, Hill resumed his activities in politics and as Georgia's foremost orator and champion of the South, vigorously opposing the Reconstruction Acts of Congress. At the urging of Senator Hill during Reconstruction, President Hayes removed Federal troops occupying the South. Hill is buried in Oakland Cemetery in Atlanta. Bellevue was purchased in 1942 by the Fuller E. Callaway Foundation and presented to the LaGrange Woman's Club, which maintains it today. A grant in 1975 by the Callaway Foundation helped restore the magnificent mansion.

Nancy Harts Marker

[HM]  **GI WR**

Ridley Ave., County Courthouse, LaGrange

On the courthouse lawn.

This **historical marker** commemorates the Nancy Harts, a company of women soldiers who saved LaGrange from destruction in April of 1865. Legend states that all the men in town had enlisted in the War, leaving LaGrange undefended. In 1863, Mrs. J.

Brown Morgan organized the Nancy Harts, named in honor of Georgia's Revolutionary War heroine, and soon they were holding drill and target practice and "became proficient at each," according to a Georgia historian. On April 17, 1865, a column of Union cavalry under Col. O.H. LaGrange, had crossed the Chattahoochee from Alabama 18 miles down the rail line, captured Fort Tyler after a tough battle, and destroyed the bridges, rail facilities, 19 locomotives, and 340 cars loaded with Confederate army supplies. As they destroyed the track en route to LaGrange, they were met by the Nancy Harts on the edge of town. The **historical marker** finishes the story: "*Seeing the charmingly militant array formed to meet him, Colonel LaGrange complimented them upon their fearless spirit and fine martial air and, after a brief delay, marched on toward Macon leaving no scar other than the broken railroad to deface this gracious Georgia town whose name he chanced to bear.*"

Confederate Cemetery

[HM] [R.I.P.] **AC BA GI**

Miller St., LaGrange

Travel west on Broad St., turn left and go south on South Greenwood St. Turn right onto Miller St., cross the railroad tracks and find the cemetery on the left.

This **cemetery** holds the remains of 300 Confederate soldiers, most serving in the Army of Tennessee, who died at one of the four hospitals in LaGrange. The Nancy Harts assisted in nursing the sick and wounded in these hospitals.

Home of Benjamin Harvey Hill, a brilliant orator and friend of Jefferson Davis. At left, LaGrange Confederate Cemetery.

FAYETTEVILLE

Fayette County Historical Society

🏛 **AC**

195 Lee St., Fayetteville

One block south of the courthouse.

This facility houses extensive research material on Georgia and Fayette County, including complete sets of *The War of the Rebellion* and *The Confederate Veterans*. Resources in-clude material on those who served in the Georgia Infantry, and many other books, publications and articles on the War as it pertained to Fayette County and Georgia. Fayetteville was the scene of a Union cavalry raid on July 27, when Gen. Edward McCook's 3,600 men captured a long Confederate supply train with 300 guards and wagoners and 500 wagons. The wagons were burned, more than 500 mules and horses slaughtered on the spot, and the Confederates taken prisoner. They were freed three days later by Confederate cavalryman Joe Wheeler at the Battle of Brown's Mill near Newnan.

Stonewall Cemetery

🏛️ ⚰️ 🧍 AC BA GI MTS WR

845 Memorial Dr., Griffin

U.S. 41 to Griffin. U.S. 41 curves into Taylor and becomes Memorial Dr.

Griffin's story of its Civil War years is a mixed collection of events. Most of the Georgians who fought in the Confederate army were mobilized in Griffin, with cavalry going to **Camp Milner** north of Griffin on the McIntosh Road, now Municipal Park, and infantry going to **Camp Stephens**, named for Georgian and Vice President of the Confederacy A.H. Stephens. Griffin, located on the Macon & Western Railroad, was also a hospital town and target of Union raiders. Griffin has one of the older Confederate cemeteries, **Stonewall Cemetery**, where more than 500 Confederate soldiers and one Union soldier are buried. Many were casualties of the battles of Atlanta and Jonesboro and died while patients at the many hospitals located in Griffin. Also buried in the cemetery is John McIntosh Kell, a Confederate naval commander who served on the famed C.S.S. *Alabama*, which sank or captured more than 60 Federal ships. One of

the first **Confederate Memorial Days** in the South was held in Griffin in 1866, and one of the first monuments to Confederate dead was erected here in 1869. Time has worn most of the inscription away, but legible are the words "Rest! Soldiers! Rest!" At the edge of the cemetery, a boulder marks the site of **Gen. Wheeler's headquarters** during Sherman's occupation of Atlanta. Griffin was where the famed **Orphan Brigade** of Kentucky became a cavalry unit, using horses captured from Union Gen. George Stoneman. The Orphan Brigade served under Wheeler, actively opposing Gen. Sherman's destructive "March to the Sea" and the Carolinas. When Sherman moved out of Atlanta, his armies divided into two wings with each following the general course of a railroad, one to Augusta and the other toward Macon. Sherman's right wing appeared to be closing on Griffin, so 2,800 members of the **Georgia Militia** prepared to oppose him in entrenchments at Griffin, but Sherman veered east toward Locust Grove and Indian Springs.

On April 19, 1865, a detachment of cavalry under Union Gen. James Wilson rode into Griffin and burned the railroad facilities, and distributed Confederate stores to poor whites and blacks.

Above and below, Stonewall Cemetery.

First Cannon Ball Fired Confederate Memorials

HM GI WR

Courthouse Square, Thomaston

U.S. 19 to Thomaston. U.S. 19 turns into Church St. and runs in front of the courthouse.

Perhaps the most unique artifact of the Civil War is found, not in any museum, but out in the open, braving the elements, on a courthouse lawn attached to a marble base, the "First Cannon Ball Fired at Outbreak of the War Between the States at Fort Sumter, April 12, 1861." An engraving on the base tells the story of the cannon ball: It was "*Presented to the UDC by Mrs. Sallie White to whom it was given in 1861 by P.W. Alexander, leading Confederate war correspondent who was present when the ball was fired and knew it to be the first. The first marker stating these facts was erected on this square in 1919.*" The courthouse has several **other memorials** to the Civil War, including a marker noting Upson County as the birthplace of famed Gen. John B. Gordon; A Woodmen of the World memorial to the Upson County men who were missing in action in the Civil War; and an Upson County Confederate monument. On April 17, Union cavalry, Wilson's Raiders, surprised 50 Confederates guarding Double Bridges over the Flint in Upson County, and marched to Thomaston where they destroyed three textile factories and a train filled with Confederate stores. Late on the 19th, a train unwittingly arrived from Macon, only to be seized by the Raiders. On the train were newspapers whose news sent cheers roaring through the Yankees. Lee had surrendered to Grant!

Confederate Cemeteries

HM R.I.P. AC BA GI

Glenwood Cemetery: Off E. Lee St., Thomaston
The Rock Confederate Cemetery: The Rock Rd., The Rock

Thomaston, a cotton mill town on the Flint River located on a spur off the Macon and Western Railroad, was the location of two Confederate hospitals, the Newsom and Frank Ramsey, and several temporary hospitals. A Confederate **cemetery** holds 54 soldiers, six unknown, who died in these hospitals. The **grave** of Dr. Edward A. Flewellen, a noted Confederate surgeon and Medical Director for the Army of Tennessee, is near this spot. The Rock also has a Confederate Cemetery.

Top, the "First Cannon Ball Fired" at Upson Co. Courthouse. On bottom, Confederate cemetery and the flag adopted in March 1865.

Fort Tyler & Fort Tyler Cemetery

🏛️ ⚔️ 🏚️ R.I.P. 🏴 AC GI WR

Fort: Sixth Ave., West Point
Cemetery: U.S. 29 in eastern edge of town, West Point

Fort: Cross over the river into downtown. Turn right at Main St. (Third Ave.), left at Tenth St., right at Sixth Ave.

You can visit **Fort Tyler** and see the remains of the earthworks in a park established by the Fort Tyler Association. Interpretive signs tell the story of Tyler, Wilson's Raiders, and the fort. A path leads to the summit. In **Fort Tyler Cemetery**, part of Pine Hill Cemetery, 76 casualties, 19 marked with names or initials, are buried from the Battle of West Point. At West Point after the War, Gen. John B. Gordon, when introducing Winnie Davis, the daughter of Jefferson Davis, used the term "Daugh-

ters of the Confederacy," which then became the name of the organization. A **marker** on the lawn of Hawkes Library (100 W. Eighth St.) honors the site. For information on visiting these sites, contact the West Point Downtown Development Authority at 706-645-1440.

The Battle of Fort Tyler

Fort Tyler and Fort Tyler Cemetery are located in West Point, which was an important railroad town in Georgia during the Civil War. Because the gauges of the rails were different between Alabama and Georgia, train cargo had to be transferred between cars here, which necessitated a large railroad yard. The town had been the scene of raids by Union cavalry,

with the most significant resulting in a battle at Fort Tyler on Easter Sunday, April 16, 1865, a full week after Confederate Gen. Robert E. Lee had surrendered to U.S. Gen. Ulysses S. Grant at Appomattox, Virginia, and two days after Lincoln had been assassinated. Word hadn't reached these parts, as Confederate Gen. Robert C. Tyler, and his 120 men held off 3,500 cavalrymen of Wilson's Raiders under Col. O.H. LaGrange, for a full day at Fort Tyler, before surrendering when they ran out of ammunition at dusk.

Fort Tyler, built in the fall of 1863 to protect vital transportation bridges at the Chattahoochee River, was an earthenwork fort approximately 35 feet square. It had three artillery pieces, a stockade on the rear or south and a ditch 10 feet deep and 15 feet wide in front. Tyler, called by some historians the most enigmatic Confederate general of the Civil War, was a veteran of Walker's expedition to Nicaragua; Shiloh; Chickamauga; and had lost his left leg at Missionary Ridge at Chattanooga. The disabled Tyler was posted at West Point, where he was in command of Fort Tyler and 128 men, made up of convalescents from Confederate hospitals, young boys in the town, and a garrison of old men from LaGrange. He was given a flag by the community, and he pledged to die beneath it rather than surrender it to the enemy.

On the morning of April 16, Union cavalry moved on West Point, placing a battery on a nearby hill and opening fire on the fort, which returned the same. Union cavalry worked their way closer, taking cover at some homes in close range to the Fort. Gen. Tyler had been urged to burn them to prevent their use as cover by Union sharpshooters, but he refused, not wanting to destroy the homes of people he had befriended in the past year of his convalescence. After a few hours of battle, Tyler, who was on crutches, hobbled outside the fort to get a better view of the Union positions. A sharpshooter — located in one of the homes Tyler refused to burn — shot him in the chest. He was borne back inside the fort and placed under the flag staff, where he died an hour later under the flag he swore to defend, and became the last Confederate general to die in the Civil War. The men in the fort, under assault by Union soldiers on foot and out numbered 10 to 1, surrendered just before dusk, making the fort the last to fall in the Civil War. Eighteen Confederates were killed along with seven Federals and 29 wounded. In a cemetery in West Point, Tyler was buried in a **joint grave** with his second in command, Captain C. Gonzales, who was also killed during the battle. From West Point, Wilson's Raiders destroyed 19 locomotives and burned 340 cars, and moved east up the tracks to LaGrange and eventually to Macon. A **living history event** is held annually in mid-April to commemorate the anniversary of the Battle of West Point.

Top, the path to Fort Tyler. Left, the grave of Gen. Robert C. Tyler, killed at his fort on April 16, 1865.

Columbus Confederate Naval Iron Works is now the Columbus Iron Works Convention & Trade Center.

DURING THE CIVIL WAR, Columbus was an important industrial town, second only to Richmond in the amount of goods it provided to the Confederacy. Located at the northernmost navigable point on the Chattahoochee River, this prosperous industrial town of 15,000 at the time of the War had cannon, munitions, and sword factories; many textile mills which produced uniforms; and the second-largest iron works in the Confederacy. A 1,500-bed hospital was located here as well. The energy of falling water powered textile, grist, saw, and paper mills. Its access to the Gulf through the river and proximity to Deep South cotton plantations, made Columbus a major railroad and shipping center. When Sherman marched on Atlanta in 1864, the Atlanta arsenal was moved to Columbus. All these reasons made Columbus a target of the Union, and on Easter Sunday, April 16, 1865, forces under Gen. James H. Wilson attacked from the west in a rare night engagement. It was the last significant land battle of the Civil War, occurring a full week after Lee had surrendered to Grant, and after Lincoln was dead at an assassin's hands.

Wilson's Raiders were sweeping through the previously untouched industrial belt of the Deep South, located along the fall line through Alabama and Georgia, and looking for a place to cross the Chattahoochee. Wilson sent a brigade to West Point to capture the river crossing there and sent his main force of 11,000 against Columbus. In an engagement lasting a few hours, the town was defended by a hastily gathered force of less than a few thousand, consisting of old men and boys, but by 1 a.m. on April 17, the town had fallen, with approximately a dozen casualties on each side, and 600 Confederate troops escaping toward Macon, then the capital of Georgia. The next day, Columbus suffered the same fate as Atlanta six months earlier, when Union troopers burned all the property of what was considered the last great Confederate storehouse, including more than 100,000 bales of cotton, the Arsenal, Confederate Naval Iron Works, Confederate Quartermaster Depot, Haiman Sword factory, 15 locomotives and 200 cars, 5,000 rounds of ammunition and 74 cannon, and the gunboat *Jackson*, also known as the *Muscogee*.

In the **26-block, National Register Historic District of Columbus**, the traveler finds historic homes, cobblestone streets, and many old brick buildings along the river which capture the feel of an antebellum industrial center. On Broadway in the historic District, Dr. John S. Pemberton, a captain in the Confederate Army and the druggist who invented Coca-Cola in 1866, operated a pharmacy before the Civil War. His country home was moved to this district. Many **plaques and monuments** around Columbus mark its rich industrial history. The unique **Confederate Naval Museum** is a must visit for the Civil War buff, and the **Columbus Museum** has excellent displays. The historic **Linwood Cemetery** has two Confederate sections, and Fort Benning has the **National Infantry Museum**, with many fascinating exhibits from all American wars, including the Civil War. Columbus was the home of Gen. Alfred Iverson, Jr., Gen. Henry L. Benning, and Gen. Paul J. Semmes, two of whom are buried in Linwood Cemetery.

Confederate Naval Museum

⌂ ⚓ 🏛 GI

202 4th St., Columbus 706-327-9798

Columbus-Manchester Rd. becomes 4th Ave. Travel on 4th Ave. until it deadends into 4th St. Turn right on 4th St. and find the museum on the left.

The James W. Woodruff, Jr. **Confederate Naval Museum** is the national and international clearinghouse of information on the Confederate Navy, in which was the genesis of modern naval warfare. At the start of the Civil War, the South, with few shipyards, naval engineers, sailors, or heavy industries, had to improvise to compete with the organized and well-supplied Union Navy.

Museum displays illustrate the development and operation of the naval mine, submarine, and battleship, all of which trace their first practical deployment to the Confederate Navy. Two exterior exhibits display the salvaged remains of two entirely different Confederate warships: The 225-foot long ironclad ram C.S.S. *Jackson*, and the 130-foot long steam/sail powered gunboat C.S.S. *Chattahoochee*. Both were sunk in the Chattahoochee River near the War's end. The *Chattahoochee*, built in 1861-62 at Saffold, Early County, Georgia, was first captained by Cmdr. Catesby ap R. Jones, who is famous for commanding the C.S.S. *Virginia*, known as the *Merrimack*, during its famous duel with the U.S.S. *Monitor*, known as the first battle between ironclad warships and the beginning of modern naval warfare. The *Chattahoochee* operated on the upper Appalachicola until it suffered a boiler explosion and sunk on May 27, 1863, near Blountstown, Florida. Those killed were buried in Linwood Cemetery in Columbus. The *Chattahoochee* was raised and taken to Columbus for repairs, and later scuttled on April 16, 1865 to prevent capture by Union forces under Gen. James H. Wilson. The *Jackson* was built in Columbus, but after the center paddlewheel-powered ironclad's failed launch in early 1864, the vessel was redesigned to a

The C.S.S. *Chattahoochee* was scuttled by Confederates to prevent capture by Wilson's Raiders.

twin-screw arrangement and relaunched on Dec. 22, 1864. The powerful *Jackson* featured 4-inch thick iron plating backed by two feet of wood, with six large Brooke rifles. Shortly before the ship was finished, it was captured in Columbus by Wilson's Raiders, torched and set adrift, where it floated 30 miles downstream before beaching on a sandbar and burning to the waterline. Both the *Jackson* and the *Chattahoochee* were salvaged in the early 1960s.

Columbus Naval Iron Works

⌂ 🏠 ⚓ ◎ 🏛 GI WR

801 Front Avenue, Columbus 706-327-4522

I-185 to exit 5. Travel on the Columbus-Manchester Exp./Alt. 27 into the historic district. Front Ave. faces the Chattahoochee River.

Built in 1853, originally the Columbus Iron Works and then Confederate Naval Iron Works, this factory was the second largest iron producer in the Confederacy. This factory supplied steam engines, iron cladding, and other parts to all the Confederate shipyards in the South, along with cannon and a wide variety of cast iron products. Today, the restored building, with its old brick walls and huge timbers representing the best of 19th century crafts-manship, is on the National Register of Historic Places and serves as Columbus' convention center, named the Columbus Iron Works Convention & Trade Center. The building is open to the public and has exhibits of machinery, products, casting and armor from the C.S.S. *Chattahoochee* and C.S.S. *Jackson*, and the "Ladies Defender," a cannon manufactured from brass cooking utensils donated by the ladies of Columbus.

Linwood Cemetery

 ⚓ R.I.P. GI

Linwood Blvd. west of 10th Ave., Columbus

Linwood Cemetery has two Confederate sections — Naval and Army — with the graves of more than 200 soldiers from the Civil War, many of whom died in the several Confederate hospitals located in Columbus from 1862-65. Some buried in the cemetery are casualties from the Battle of Columbus. Others died in a boiler explosion on the C.S.S. *Chattahoochee* and are buried in the Naval Section, with their graves guarded by one of the rifled guns from the ironclad *Jackson*. **Maj. Gen. Paul Jones Semmes**, a Columbus banker and planter who won glory fighting in the Eastern Theater with Gen. Robert E. Lee, died from a wound to the thigh suffered at Gettysburg while leading his men across "the wheatfield" and is buried here. So is **Brig. Gen. Henry L. "The**

A big gun from the ironclad *Jackson* guards the Naval section of Linwood Cemetery.

Rock" Benning, a Columbus lawyer and politician who gained respect from his troops for his coolness and bravery during many battles in the Eastern Theater throughout the Civil War. Fort Benning is named for him. Also buried in the cemetery is **Brig. Gen. Pleasant J. Philips**, who commanded troops at the Battle of Griswoldville, Georgia, one of the few actions opposing Union Gen. W.T. Sherman's "March to the Sea."

National Infantry Museum

🏛 GI

Building 396, Baltzell Ave., Ft. Benning 706-545-2958

Victory Dr. south to Ft. Benning Rd. Follow signs to museum.

The **National Infantry Museum** is considered the finest military museum in the country and is one of the larger museums in the state, displaying more than two centuries worth of artifacts in 30,000 feet of exhibit space on three floors. Its collections run from the 1600s to the present day. From the Civil War, the museum has on display Gen. Ulysses S. Grant's traveling liquor cabinet, Union and Confederate uniforms, a set of Civil War dominoes, playing cards, a painted eagle drum, bugle, numerous Confederate flags, a re-creation of Confederate Gen. Henry L. Benning's drawing room, a rare regimental flag from the Union's 2nd Regiment of Colored Troops, and more.

Columbus Museum

🏛 GI

1251 Wynnton Rd., Columbus 706-649-0713

Tenth Ave. to Wynnton Rd. Travel east. Museum will be on the left.

The **museum**, with its focus on the Chattahoochee River Valley, has many fine exhibits, including one on the significance of the Civil War in Columbus history and a collection of Confederate and Union weapons.

Columbus Museum Union/Confederate gun collection.

ANDERSONVILLE IS A MUST-SEE for anyone interested in the Civil War. A National Historic Site, nothing in Georgia delivers the full impact of the cost of the Civil War as do the thousands of graves tightly lined together at Andersonville. The **park** does a great job of telling the story of all Civil War prison camps. The town of Andersonville proudly calls itself a Civil War village, and features museums and shops worth a look, as well as the **Wirz Monument**, erected to the memory of Henry Wirz, the commandant of the prison camp at Andersonville.

The town sponsors two annual living history events, which include encampments: the Andersonville Historic Fair on the first weekend of October and the Andersonville Spring Antiques, Crafts and Civil War Collectibles Fair on Memorial Day weekend. At **Andersonville National Historic Site**, living history events include Andersonville Revisited on the last weekend in February and on the first weekend in October, a recreation of the Union Occupation of Camp Sumter.

Americus was home to **two hospitals** during the Civil War, the Foard and Bragg hospitals. In the **Confederate section** of Oak Grove City Cemetery (East Church and Reese St.) 129 soldiers, 45 of them unknown, are buried. Most of them died in local hospitals. West of Americus in **Preston** on U.S. 280 is where the first Confederate flag raising in Georgia took place. The ceremony was held on March 31, 1861. When the War ended, Union troops cut down and destroyed the historic flagpole.

POW Camp Sumter, Andersonville

No visit to Georgia's Civil War sites is complete without a trip to Andersonville, the site of Confederate prisoner-of-war **Camp Sumter**. This national park tells the tragic story of Civil War prisons in general, and what happened at Camp Sumter, the most deadly Civil War prison. On Oct. 27, 1863, U.S. Secretary of War Edwin Stanton, at Gen. U.S. Grant's urging, halted the customary exchange of prisoners. Grant stopped exchanges because they helped the South, which was short on manpower. The numerically superior North could afford attrition. Neither side was prepared to house, feed and care for the growing population of prisoners, and this led to the building of Camp Sumter in early 1864 by the Confederacy to more securely house the growing number of Federal prisoners in and around Richmond, Virginia, which was close to the front lines. Camp Sumter confined more than 45,000 Union prisoners, of which more than 13,000 died from disease, poor sanitation, malnutrition, overcrowding, or exposure to the elements over the 14 months it was in operation. In the Federal prisons, the conditions were not much better, and by the end of the war, approximately 30,000 Union prisoners had died in Confederate camps and 25,000 Confederates had died in Union prisons.

Camp Sumter was a stockade fort, built roughly in the shape of a parallelogram, covering 26 and 1/2 acres. A 15-foot high fence of hewn pine logs, embedded six to eight feet in the ground, surrounded the prisoners, with sentry boxes, or "pigeon roosts" as prisoners called them, at 30-yard intervals. Approximately 19 feet inside the fence was the deadline, which the prisoners were forbidden to cross at the penalty of instant death. A muddy, shallow branch of Sweetwater Creek flowed through the yard, insufficiently supplying the water needs of the prisoners, and it was the source of much disease, as the Confederate latrine was located nearby outside the fence. Two gates were on the west side of the fort, and eight earthen forts with artillery sur-

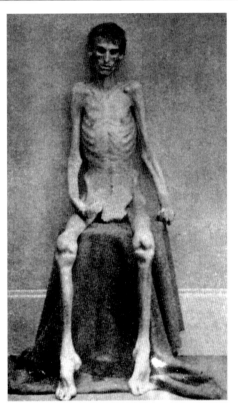

Disease and malnutrition killed many Civil War prisoners of war. Facing page: mass graves.

rounded the prison for the purpose of putting down uprisings on the inside or cavalry attacks from the outside.

Designed to hold 10,000 prisoners, the camp received its first shipment in February 1864. Prisoners continued to arrive by train at the Andersonville Depot, from where they would march 1/4 mile to the prison. During the next few months, approximately 400 prisoners arrived daily, swelling the population to more than 26,000 by the end of June and to more than 32,000 by August. Overcrowding was so severe that each man had less than four square yards of living space. Every tree was felled except two, leaving the prisoners with no protection from the elements, except for their rude shanty tents. The men were issued no clothing, so with freezing winter temperatures and hot summer temperatures, the men's clothing rotted away, leaving some men naked to the elements.

Worst was the lack of sanitation. The men were served by a small, muddy creek which became "a mass of liquid excrement" as it was used as a latrine outside the stockade by guards and inside the stockade by prisoners, who were more and more stricken with dysentery. Flies and maggots swarmed over the entire area, spreading disease which claimed the lives of up to 127 men a day. As the War produced deteriorating conditions in the South, prison officials had difficulty getting food to the camp due to transportation difficulties and a lack of resources. They often served unbolted corn, which acted like broken glass on the prisoners' deteriorated digestive systems. "Since the day I was born," said one prisoner, "I've never seen such misery." Wrote Father Hamilton of Macon, "I found the stockade extremely filthy; the men all huddled together and covered with vermin ... I found the Hospital almost as crowded as the stockade. The men were dying there very rapidly from scurvy ... diarrhea and dysentery ... they were not only covered with the ordinary vermin but also maggots ... they had nothing under them at all except the ground." Wrote Eliza Andrews of Washington, Georgia: "It is dreadful. My heart aches for the poor wretches, Yankees though they are, and I am afraid God will suffer some terrible retribution to fall upon us for letting such things happen. If the Yankees ever should come to southwest Georgia and go to Andersonville and see the graves there, God have mercy on the land!"

When Union Gen. W.T. Sherman captured Atlanta on Sept. 2, 1864, his cavalry troops were within easy striking distance, threatening Camp Sumter. This started the period of decline in importance of the camp, as prisoners were shipped out to South Carolina and coastal Georgia. The prison ceased to exist at the end of the war in May of 1865, and the camp's commandant Capt. Henry Wirz, was arrested and charged with conspiring with high Confederate officials to "impair and injure the health and destroy the lives ... of Federal prisoners" and "murder, in violation of the laws of war." A conspiracy never existed, but public anger in the North demanded retribution. Wirz was tried and found guilty by a military tribunal in Washington, D.C., and hanged. His arrest, trial, conviction and execution at the first war crimes trial remains controversial to this day.

In July and August of 1865, Clara Barton, founder of the American Red Cross, along with a detachment of laborers and soldiers and Dorence Atwater, came to Andersonville to identify and mark the graves of the Union dead. In one of the more extraordinary acts of the war, Atwater, while prisoner, was assigned to record the names of deceased prisoners for Confederate officials. Fearing the loss of the records at the end of the war, Atwater secretly made a duplicate copy of his list and hid it in his coat lining, hoping to notify the relatives of the more than 12,000 dead. Thanks to Atwater's daring act, only 460 of the 12,912 Andersonville graves had to be marked "unknown U.S. soldier." On August 17, 1865, an American flag was raised over the newly established Andersonville National Cemetery.

PP — ANDERSONVILLE

Andersonville National Historic Site

🏛️ 🏠 🚂 ⚰️ 🏛️ 🏛️ 🧍 GI

GA 49, Andersonville 912-924-0343

Located 1 mile east of Andersonville on GA 49.

The **Visitors Center** has a 12-minute slide show to introduce the 475-acre park, an excellent bookstore with material on the prison camp and the Civil War in general, and an audiotape one can rent to play on a driving tour of the park. From the center one goes to the **National Cemetery** and reconstructed **Camp Sumter Stockade** and **monuments,** and **National Prisoner of War Museum.** The nearby town of Andersonville has a Civil War theme and is worth visiting.

Clockwise from top: more than 16,000 graves are packed into the National Cemetery; Clara Barton, the founder of the Red Cross, came to Andersonville to help with the cemetery; the bodies were buried in trenches; a monument to the suffering of the prisoners of war.

Andersonville National Cemetery

🏛️ ⚰️ 🧍 GI

Andersonville National Historic Site, Andersonville 912-924-0343

Located at Andersonville National Historic Site in Andersonville.

Touring the hauntingly beautiful **National Cemetery**, with its seemingly endless rows of white headstones packed tightly together, is an emotionally moving experience. The cemetery is the final resting place of the 13,000 Camp Sumter dead and 3,000 others, including 700 additional Union soldiers, approximately **2,300 veterans** from other American wars, and many former prisoners of war. Twenty-two headstones are engraved U.S.C.T. for **United States Colored Troops**, marking the graves of black Americans who were captured at the Battle of Olustee, Florida. Union burial trenches are located in the cemetery. Eleven distinctive **monuments** honor the dead. A mystery surrounds the headstone of **Lewis S. Tuttle**, which is the only one of the identical marble headstones in the Cemetery to have a dove on top.

Buried off to the side from the general group near section J are the **Raiders' graves**, six ringleaders of a gang of Union prisoners who preyed on other prisoners inside the stockade for food, money, and clothes. In July of 1864, a group of prisoners calling themselves the Regulators banded together to oppose the Raiders, and rounded them up, and held them in the south gate area of the prison with the camp commandant's permission. The Raiders were put on trial for their deeds and judged by a jury of 24 Union sergeants. Six who were considered ringleaders were hanged and buried dishonorably in a separate plot in the prison cemetery, and the minor gang members were flogged by a gauntlet of inmates.

National Prisoner Of War Museum

🏛️ GI

Andersonville National Historic Site, Andersonville 912-924-0343

Located at Andersonville National Historic Site in Andersonville.

The **National Prisoner of War Museum** is fittingly found at Andersonville. Exhibits and a slide show depict the plight of American prisoners of war from the Revolution to the Persian Gulf War. An effort is under way to build a larger museum.

Camp Sumter Stockade & Monuments

[HM] [icons] GI

Andersonville National Historic Site, Andersonville 912-924-0343

Located at Andersonville National Historic Site in Andersonville.

Nothing replaces the actual experience of touring the grounds of **Camp Sumter** where so many men suffered so much. Here you can view the actual muddy creek called **Stockade Branch**, which served as their water supply and sewer; visit **Providence Springhouse**, the spot where lightning struck within the stockade, releasing a natural spring of potable water. The prisoners believed it was the work of Divine Providence and after the war built a lovely stone memorial on the spot; view **escape tunnels and wells** and the reconstructed **stockade fence and sentry boxes** while you imagine 32,000 men crowded inside the inner stockade. There are earthwork forts surrounding the prison; many state monuments; a monument to Clara Barton, honoring the founder of the American Red Cross; and markers placing other significant sites of the prison.

Clockwise from top right: Stockade Branch, cause of much disease; the stockade; Providence Springhouse; prisoner's house.

Wirz Monument

⚑ GI

Church St., Andersonville

Downtown Andersonville.

This **monument**, erected in the center of town in 1909 by the Daughters of the Confederacy, honors the memory of Captain Henry R. Wirz, the Confederate commandant of Camp Sumter and the only person hanged for war crimes during the Civil War. His trial and execution remain controversial to this day, as some believe the truly guilty parties were his supervising officers, and that he was made a scapegoat for their incompetency. In a famous trial in Washington, D.C., before a miliary tribunal at the first War Crimes trial, Wirz refused a pardon if he implicated President Jefferson Davis. He was hanged on Nov. 10, 1865, on the same scaffold which executed the Booth conspirators. Inscriptions on the base of the **obelisk** give the southern point of view on the character of Wirz and Union Gen. U.S. Grant, who is credited with ending the exchange system.

Top left, the Wirz monument; above, Henry Wirz.

Andersonville Farm Museum
Civil War Village Depot
Drummer Boy Museum

⌂ 🏛 GI

Downtown Andersonville, Andersonville 912-924-2558 (Welcome Center)

On Church St., downtown Andersonville.

This **seven-acre pioneer farm complex** includes a log barn, a log cabin, farm animals, a mule-powered sugar cane mill, a water-powered grist mill, a blacksmith shop with working blacksmith, and a country store. It is located behind the post office which is across the street from a restored, turn-of-the-century **depot**. The depot houses a **visitors center,** which is the first stop on a **15-site walking tour**, and includes a local history museum with civil war artifacts. Across the street is the **Drummer Boy Civil War Museum**, featuring memorabilia from both the North and South including uniforms, guns, documents, flags, and a diorama. Other **stores** nearby have Civil War-related merchandise and memorabilia.

The Historic Heartland was an important political, agricultural and industrial support center of the Confederacy. The capital of Georgia was located in Milledgeville, and Macon was an important manufacturing center which produced vital war materials for the Confederacy. The area was the scene of cavalry raids during the Atlanta Campaign during the summer of 1864. Many of the towns in this area were located on rail lines, making them hospital centers. When Sherman went on his famous "March to the Sea," on Nov. 15, 1864, his 60,000 men divided in four columns and traveled right through this area toward Savannah. The only significant large battle during the March was fought on Nov. 22, 1864, at Griswoldville, a town that no longer exists due to Sherman's "carelessness with matches." There is no main Civil War park to tour here, but much history spread out through the region in the form of Civil War markers, monuments, cemeteries and historic homes. The Historic Heartland, due to a long-running historic preservation ethic, has the most towns with architectural and cultural treasures, many open to tour.

Cannonball House, Macon, Georgia.

Sherman's March To The Sea

Union Gen. William Tecumseh Sherman's "March to the Sea" is one of the most famous events in the annals of war. Much has been written about his Savannah Campaign, some acclaiming his brilliant military strategy, others denouncing his ruthless tactics. Sherman wanted to bring the war home to Georgians in harsh terms, proving that the Confederacy couldn't protect its citizens. He also thought that pressure on the home front might lead to desertions on the front lines of the Confederacy, as soldiers learned that their loved ones and property were threatened. Sherman's treatment of defenseless civilians and their private property is legendary, and his "March to the Sea" is frequently described as a "60-mile wide path of utter destruction" in history books, which is somewhat exaggerated if one has seen the beautiful antebellum homes in Madison, Covington, Milledgeville, and other towns on the route. Popularized in song and verse, an abundance of material exists on the March, written mostly from the Northern point of view. Northerners believe it was bold and effective stroke against the Southern foe; Southerners believed his destruction of private property was unnecessary and cruel; and that the March was successful only due to a lack of or-

ganized opposition. For Sherman — the man who said, "War is all Hell" — his style of warfare was a military issue, not a moral one: "This may seem a hard species of warfare, but it brings the sad realities of war home to those who have been directly or indirectly instrumental in involving us in its attendant calamities," he said. For Sherman it was a type of rear attack, not on the army of the enemy but the people of the enemy. Some historians believe the most important military advances from the Civil War came from Sherman, saying he invented modern warfare. Confederate Col. Charles Colcock Jones, who opposed Sherman under Lt. Gen. William J. Hardee, summed up the feelings of many Southerners when he wrote: "The conduct of Sherman's army and particularly of Kilpatrick's cavalry and the numerous parties swarming through the country in advance and on the flanks of the main columns during the march from Atlanta to the coast, is reprehensible in the extreme ... the Federals on every hand and at all points indulged in unwanton pillage, wasting and destroying what could not be used. Defenseless women and children and weak old men were not infrequently driven from their homes, their dwellings fired, and these noncombatants subjected to insult and privation. The inhabitants, white and black, were often

robbed of their personal effects, were intimidated by threats — and occasionally were even hanged to the verge of strangulation to compel revelation of the places where money, plate and jewelry were buried, or plantation animals concealed, — horses, mules, cattle and hogs were either driven off, or were shot in the fields, or uselessly butchered in the pens." Today, it is not hard to find Georgians who have ugly family stories to tell from the days of Sherman's March, and still hold hard feelings.

If a traveler wanted to exactly follow Sherman's "March to the Sea," they would need an army tank and a lot of time, because Sherman's armies didn't take the interstate or travel together on the same single route. Splitting his army into four main columns, Sherman's men traveled on many different roads and bridges which don't exist today. They went through towns that are neither found on a map or on the ground. And towns have sprung up on his March route which didn't exist when his troops came through. The best you can do is approximate his journey and cover most of the ground over several trips. Compared to touring the Atlanta Campaign route, you get a lot fewer Civil War sites per mile on this tour, but you will get a feel for an older, original Georgia, which was an agrarian state consisting of small towns.

ATHENS POLITICALLY AND MA-terially was a Rebel stronghold during the Civil War, supplying many men and supplies to the Confederacy. Factories located on the Oconee River produced goods for those fighting for the Southern cause in Athens, which was located at the end of a railroad spur.

Clarke County was also the scene of a cavalry engagement during the Atlanta Campaign. Sherman attempted to cut railroads supplying besieged Atlanta during the Atlanta Campaign by launching the Great Raid or Stoneman-McCook Cavalry Raid, which he intended to sweep around Atlanta from both sides and meet at the southern railroad link to the city. Gen. Edward McCook was routed near Newnan, and Gen. George Stoneman was captured outside Macon. Two brigades of Stoneman's cavalry escaped northeast from Macon, and decided to raid Athens in order to resupply their commands and to "destroy the armory and other government works." Four miles southwest of Athens at the Middle Oconee bridge, they were met and repulsed by the Mitchell Thunderbolts, the Athens Home Guards consisting of ineligibles of the C.S.A. A **historical marker** marks the spot at Highway 441 southwest of Athens at the Middle Oconee Bridge. From here the two Union cavalry brigades eventually split up, with Lt. Col. Silas Adams working his way back to Federal lines at Marietta, and Col. Horace Capron camping out near Winder, then called Jug Tavern. On Aug. 3, 1864, Confederates under Col. William C.P. Breckinridge who had been pursuing Capron's men since Sunshine Church pounced on Capron's men in the Battle of King's Tanyard, capturing 430 and sending them to Andersonville. Capron escaped back to Federal lines. A **historical marker** on GA 211, five miles northwest of Winder marks the spot.

In Athens on East Broad Street is a **marker** telling the story of the Cook and Brother Confederate Armory at Chicopee Building, said to be the most efficient private armory in the Confederacy, producing a rifle which was considered "superior to any that I have seen of Southern manufacture," according to one ordnance officer. The armory was under contract to supply 30,000 Enfield rifles to Confederate forces until the Cook brothers, recent English immigrants, organized their workers into a reserve battalion and fought at Griswoldville and Savannah, opposing Sherman's "March to the Sea." Major Ferdinand W.C. Cook was killed in these actions. A one-of-a-kind artillery piece was invented by a private in the Athens Home Guards and is on display on the county courthouse grounds.

Athens' unique double barreled cannon is a relic of Confederate ingenuity.

Double Barreled Cannon

College & Hancock Avenues, Clarke County Courthouse, Athens

Travel into Athens on U.S. 129. This road will turn into Prince Ave. and run into downtown. Turn right on College Ave.

Athens' **Double Barreled Cannon**, the only one of its kind in the world, is among the most unusual Civil War relics. It was designed by John Gilleland of Athens, a private in the "Mitchell Thunderbolts," a home guard unit composed of business and professional men who were ineligible for service in the C.S.A. because of age or disability. Unlike the home guards, the cannon never saw service because of its inability to function properly. Cast in the Athens foundry in 1862, it was designed to fire simultaneously two balls connected by a chain, which would "mow down the enemy somewhat as a scythe cuts wheat." It failed due to its inability to fire both barrels at the exact instant, and the cannon has been the butt of jokes by UGA's instate rival, Georgia Institute of Technology's students and alumni ever since. The double barreled cannon was tested in a field on the Newton's Bridge Road against a target of upright poles. With both balls rammed home and the eight-foot chain dangling from twin muzzles, the cannon was fired. But the lack of simultaneous firing caused an uneven explosion of charges, snapping the chain and giving each ball an erratic and unpredictable trajectory. One contemporary at the first firing reported that the projectile "had

a kind of circular motion, plowed up an acre of ground, tore up a cornfield, mowed down saplings, and the chain broke, the two balls going in opposite directions. One of the balls killed a cow in a distant field, while the other knocked down the chimney from a log cabin." The observers "scattered as though the entire Yankee army had been turned loose in the vicinity." The cannon was donated to the City of Athens, where for more than a century it has been a curiosity and has "performed sturdy service for many years in celebrating political victories," according to a **historical marker**.

UGA Campus
Old College
Chapel
Robert Toombs Oak
Confederate Monument

Broad St., University of Georgia, Athens

U.S. 78 comes into Athens and turns into Broad St. UGA's old north campus is on Broad St., across from downtown.

Athens is the site of the University of Georgia, first known as Franklin College, the oldest state land-grant university in the United States. The University closed in 1864 when most of its students had joined the Confederate Army, and it reopened in January 1866. Many Confederate veterans became students after the war. Union troops camped on the college grounds and used the front columns of the **Chapel** for target practice. The Vice President of the Confederacy, Alexander H. Stephens, and Benjamin H. Hill, considered the ablest supporter of the Davis regime, went to school here. A plaque on **Old College** commemorates Stephens and Crawford W. Long, the inventor of anesthesia, who were roommates and represent Georgia in the Hall of Fame at the U.S. Capitol in Washington, D.C. Robert Toombs, Secretary of State of the Confederacy and a brigadier general in the C.S.A., was expelled from the University in 1828. Toombs returned and spoke on the next commencement day, outside under a magnificent oak tree, causing the entire audience in the Chapel to leave their seats to hear him. The day Toombs died in 1885, lightening struck the tree, now known as the **Robert Toombs Oak**. When the tree died in 1908, it was cut into mementos that have been handed down by UGA alumni ever since. A **historical marker** is near the spot where the tree stood. Not far from here, on Broad Street, on a traffic island across from the UGA Arch, is the **Clarke County Confederate Memorial**, one of the oldest monuments in the state. Fund-raising was begun by Ladies Memorial Association president, Mrs. Laura Cobb Rutherford in 1866, and after raising the needed $4,444.44, the marble shaft totalling 32 feet in height and resembling a church spire with a finial on a stepped base of Elbert County granite, was unveiled in June 1872. It is the first of the large general county monuments in the state. Inscribed on the monument are the names of the Clarke County dead with an inscription by the Rev. A.A. Lipscomb, chancellor of the University of Georgia, 1860-74.

Taylor-Grady House
Howell Cobb House
Oconee Hill Cemetery

HM 🏠 **R.I.P** 🗡 **GI**

Taylor-Grady House: 634 Prince Ave., Athens 706-549-8688
Cobb House: 698 Pope St., Athens
Cemetery: Off E. Campus Rd. on Cemetery St., across from the UGA Stadium, Athens 706-543-6262

Behind UGA Stadium

The **Taylor-Grady House**, built in 1845 by Gen. Robert Taylor, was the home of Henry Grady while he was a student at the University of Georgia from 1865 to 1868. Grady was credited with helping to establish a New South image after the Civil War, when he became editor of the Atlanta Constitution and a famous journalist and orator. The home's 13 Doric columns symbolize the original 13 colonies. It is open to tours.

Howell Cobb was one of the major figures of Georgia's Civil War history, and one of his homes is found in Athens. It is not available to tour. He graduated from the University of Georgia in 1834 and married a woman from Athens. He served in the U.S. Congress from 1843-51 and as Speaker of the House from 1849-51. A moderate on Southern rights, he was elected governor of Georgia from 51-53 and returned to Congress in 1854. Appointed Secretary of the Treasury in 1857 under U.S. President James Buchanan, he served in this capacity until the election of Lincoln. He then resigned his appointment and became a secessionist. A contender for the presidency of the Confederacy, Cobb was the presiding officer of the Confederate Congress held at Montgomery, Alabama, but Jefferson Davis was elected president. As a Confederate brigadier general, he fought at Shiloh, Seven Pines, the Seven Days Battles, Second Bull Run and

Above, the Howell Cobb House. Cobb is buried in Oconee Hill Cemetery. Below left, the columns of the University of Georgia Chapel, used by Union troops for target practice.

Antietam. He later became major general of the Georgia District, commanding Georgia's reserves. His troops accepted the surrender of George Stoneman at Round Oak, Georgia July 31, 1864, during Sherman's Great Cavalry Raid.

Cobb's great plantation near Milledgeville was destroyed during Sherman's "March to the Sea," when Sherman, who was travelling with the XIV Corps, personally visited the plantation and ordered its total destruction except for the slave quarters. On April 20, 1865, Cobb surrendered at Macon to Gen. James H. Wilson. As one of the five men that the Federal government most wanted captured, Cobb was arrested but paroled by President Andrew Johnson. Cobb finished his legal career in Macon, where he died on Oct. 9, 1868, and he was buried in **Oconee Hill Cemetery** in Athens, his grave marked with an impressive obelisk. Cobb's brother, T.R.R. Cobb, was colonel in Cobb's Legion, Howell Cobb commanding. T.R.R. Cobb distinguished himself and was eventually made brigadier general in the Confederate Army. He bled to death after receiving wounds at Fredericksburg. T.R.R. Cobb, who graduated from the University of Georgia with the highest marks ever received there, is also buried in Oconee Hill Cemetery. The cemetery also has the graves of two other Confederate Generals, Martin L. Smith and William M. Browne, 11 unknown Confederate graves, and a memorial near the entrance of the cemetery.

WATKINSVILLE

Eagle Tavern Structure

HM 🏠 🏛 **AC**

Main St., Watkinsville 706-769-5197

Located near downtown Watkinsville on U.S. 441/129.

Eagle Tavern was built in the late 1700s, and served as a stopping place on a stagecoach line before the advent of railroads. Watkinsville was a frontier town on the edge of Creek and Cherokee territories then, and travelers would stop here for food and drink and a place to sleep. Gen. George Stoneman's fleeing brigades came through here, before being turned back four miles short of the their goal of Athens by the Mitchell Thunderbolts at the Middle Oconee Bridge. A Confederate soldier remained concealed for weeks in a loft hiding place behind the huge chimney, kept alive by slaves who handed up food and buckets of hot coals. Today, the building serves as a Welcome Center and Museum for Oconee County.

MADISON IS THE TOWN Sherman thought too pretty to burn, so the locals will tell you. Actually, the general himself never came through Madison, but the Left Wing of Sherman's "March to the Sea" consisting of two army corps under Maj. Gen. Henry Slocum did, and lucky for us today, they did not burn the town, only the industrial and railroad facilities which supported the Confederacy. A depot, cloth factory, cotton gin and 200 bales of cotton were burned. The stragglers or bummers who followed Sherman's army on its march looted stores in town, but the residences were left alone. A communion service was stolen from the **Presbyterian Church**, built in 1842, but Gen. Slocum ordered it returned. (The church is located at 383 South Main Street. Notice the Tiffany stained glass windows. The service is found at the Madison/Morgan Cultural Museum.)

Madison was located on the Georgia Railroad connecting Atlanta with Augusta and the Eastern Theater. Some say the pro-Union sympathies of Madison Mayor Joshua Hill saved the town from the utter destruction suffered by other Georgia towns in the path of Sherman's men. Hill had recently lost his son Legare at Cassville and had met with Sherman when he went to pick up the body in Atlanta.

Madison had been previously visited by Union cavalry under Col. Horace Capron, who was fleeing with his brigade from the ill-fated Stoneman-McCook Raid. Here Capron stopped to burn commissary and quartermaster stores on Aug. 1, 1864, before being surprised and losing his entire command near Winder on Aug. 3 at the Battle of King's Tanyard. Madison was also the site of Confederate hospitals. Today, the town is a popular tourist site with more than 50 antebellum homes and structures, lovingly built by the planter aristocracy here in Georgia's cotton belt. A tour of homes is sponsored in May and December by local groups, and some homes are open to the general public year round. C.S. Gen. Clement A. Evans spoke at the dedication of the county Confederate monument in 1909, now located in Hill Park, with the soldier at the top looking resolutely north.

Madison/Morgan Cultural Museum
Joshua Hill Home
🏛 🏠 🏛 **GI MTS**
Museum: 434 South Main St., Madison 706-342-4743
Home: 485 Old Post Rd., Madison
I-20 East from Atlanta. Take exit 51 (U.S. 441/129) into historic downtown.

Located in a large, brick Romanesque school built in 1895, the **cultural museum** is an excellent place to start your tour of Madison, with guides to the area's architecture and heritage available here. Also located here is a history museum which contains some interesting Civil War artifacts.

The **Joshua Hill Home**, privately owned, was built in the 1830s and is located at 485 Old Post Road. A **historical marker** concerning Hill is at South Main Street and Hill Street. Hill was a pro-Unionist and Whig, but he was drawn into the American or Know Nothing party when the Whig party collapsed in Georgia and was elected to Congress in 1856, beating Linton Stephens. An outspoken opponent of secession, Hill resigned his seat in 1861 rather than withdraw Georgia from the Union with the other members of the Georgia delegation. In 1863, he made an unsuccessful bid for the governorship, losing to Gov. Joe Brown. After the War, he joined the Republican Party, participated in the work of Reconstruction, and was elected to the U.S. Senate, defeating Brown, where he served until 1873. Despite his politics, Hill remained popular with the people of Georgia. His daughter Belle married Captain Gazaway Knight, Commander of the Panola Guards, a Confederate brigade that was organized in Madison.

Above, the uniform of Confederate Capt. Charles Sanders, and stolen communion service, found at the Madison/Morgan Cultural Museum. The communion service dates back to 1840, and is still used once a month by the Madison Presbyterian Church. Right, the grave of a "Colored Hosp. Attend" stands at the Madison Confederate cemetery.

Confederate Cemetery
🏛 R.I.P. **GI MTS**
Old City Cemetery, Central Ave., Madison
From South Main St., turn left onto Central Ave. and cross the railroad tracks.

The dead in the Confederate section, located near the railroad tracks, consist of 51 unknown and one known Confederate soldier and one black hospital attendant. These men died of wounds or disease in the Confederate hospitals located in Madison, known as Stout, Blackie, Asylum, Turnbull and others, which operated from late 1862 to early 1865. Note the Confederate headstone marked "Unknown Colored Hosp. Attend." Closeby, a headstone marks the grave of a member of the Clinch Rifles, a Georgia regiment which lost every original recruit except the drummer boy, which states: "Handsome, magnetic, intellectual, his friends were many and his life so early sacrificed, was full of promise." Elsewhere in the cemetery find Joshua Hill's grave, where he's buried near his son Legare.

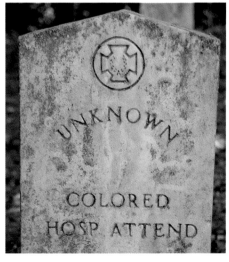

COVINGTON, WEST OF MADISON ON THE GEORgia Railroad, was a town similar to its neighbor. Its prosperity was based on cotton, and the beautiful antebellum homes found here reflected the wealth and taste of the planter aristocracy from that period. Mills powered by the Alcovy River near Covington made it an industrial target of Sherman's army as well, and Union Brig. Gen. Kenner Garrard's cavalry forces raided the area from July 22-24, 1864, while the Battle of Atlanta raged west of him down the railroad line. The raid was successful, as Garrard burned the railroad depot, hospital center of 30 unoccupied buildings, cotton, commissary supplies, trains, bridges, and six miles of track. Doing so prevented Confederate Gen. John Bell Hood's army in Atlanta from receiving reinforcements from the Eastern Theater, as they had during Chickamauga. Garrard returned to Atlanta with 200 prisoners, leaving Covington to pick up the pieces.

On the 27th, Stoneman camped near Covington on his way toward Macon, where he would be turned back, defeated, and captured by Gen. Alfred Iverson, Jr.'s cavalry near Sunshine Church at Round Oak.

On Nov. 18 of the same year, Gen. W.T. Sherman, traveling with the XIV Corps, moved through Covington on his "March to the Sea." His troops looted the town and residences but did not burn it. Wrote Sherman about Covington, "the soldiers closed up their ranks, the color-bearers unfurling their flags, and the bands striking up patriotic airs. The white people came out of their houses to behold the sight, in spite of their deep hatred of the invaders, and the negroes were simply frantic with joy." It took from 9 a.m. to late in the evening for the entire column to march through the town, pausing between Covington and east of the town to camp for the night.

A driving tour is available at the Newton County Chamber of Commerce designed to lead you to many of the fine homes in Covington. Don't miss **Swanscombe**, built in 1828 and the former home of C.S. Gen. Robert J. Henderson; the **First United Methodist Church**, 1854, and the "**Old Church**," 1841, which were used as Civil War hospitals. In excellent shape is the granite **Newton County Confederate Memorial** near the county courthouse, one of the first to honor Southern women and include an anchor honoring Confederate seamen.

The Newton County courthouse in Covington.

Soldier's Cemetery
Confederate Cemetery

AC BA GI MTS

Oxford Cemetery: Oxford College at Emory St. and W. Collingsworth, Oxford
Confederate Cemetery: Covington City Cemetery, Off Conyers St., Covington

Oxford College, established in 1836, is the birthplace of Emory University, which later moved to Atlanta. Oxford closed during the war, and the literary society buildings (Few and Phi Gamma) were used as Confederate hospitals. Down a wooded path behind the college gym is a secluded, quiet **cemetery** containing 25 Confederate graves and a Confederate **memorial**. The Oxford community has thirty structures built in the 1800s, including the home where Confederate spy Zora Fair hid, at 1005 Asbury St. She disguised herself as a black while spying on the Union army in Atlanta.

Covington was another important hospital town of the Confederacy, treating more than 20,000 soldiers from 1862-64 at the Hill, Hood, Lumpkin, and other hospitals, under the immediate supervision of Samuel H. Stout, Medical Director Confederate Army of Tennessee. Not everyone survived at these hospitals, and 67 known and unknown Confederates who died of wounds or disease are buried in the **Covington City Cemetery**, honored by a stone platform, **historical marker**, and three flags. Confederate generals James P. Simms and Robert J. Henderson are buried close to each other in this cemetery. Simms fought in Virginia, and Henderson led his men in the Army of Tennessee and was wounded at Resaca. Henderson survived and fought on, eventually surrendering at Greensboro, N.C. April 26, 1865.

Near the county courthouse stands the Newton County Confederate Memorial.

THROUGH THIS GENERAL AREA marched the Right Wing of Sherman's army, the 15th and 17th corps, as it made its way to the sea in late 1864. In **Stockbridge**, Sherman's army met its first resistance when it clashed with the Orphan Brigade, approximately 1,000 men who had become mounted infantry assigned to C.S. Gen. Joe Wheeler. Almost all of the battles during the "March to the Sea" would be running cavalry fights between Wheeler's cavalry and U.S. Gen. Judson Kilpatrick's cavalry. In general, it would be impossible for Wheeler's much smaller force to halt the flow of 60,000 Union troops to Savannah, but Wheeler, the native Georgian famous for fighting with reckless abandon, would harass them nonetheless.

In **McDonough**, the Right Wing burned two churches, slaughtered animals in another, and camped near town on Nov. 16, 1864. The **Old Globe Hotel** on Jonesboro Street, constructed in 1833, remains from this period. To the west, Georgia Militia, with 2,800 men under Maj. Gen. Gustavus W. Smith, prepared for anticipated attacks at Lovejoy's Station, then Griffin, then Forsyth, and eventually Macon, keeping pace with the Right Wing but not engaging it. The Right Wing was protected by Kilpatrick's cavalry, whose mission was to protect the western flank of the marching column. Federal cavalrymen feigned at Griffin, Forsyth, and Macon, deceiving the Rebels into thinking these were the targets of the Federal forces. On Nov. 17, the Right Wing marched to Jackson in Butts County, where they did an estimated $1 million worth of damage, destroying everything on the courthouse square except the Masonic Hall, and camped for the night. At **High Falls State Park**, mill ruins can be found by an old bridge over the Towaliga River. Factories were once located here, until Wheeler burned them as he retreated toward Forsyth. The Right Wing, consisting of approximately 30,000 men, invariably had to split up taking different routes as it worked its way southeastward. One part of the Right Wing camped at Indian Springs on Nov. 18, 1864. They visited the **Indian Springs Hotel**, located on Highway 42 near Jackson, which was built in 1823 by Creek Indian Chief William McIntosh. The hotel is open to tours. The entire Right Wing crossed the Ocmulgee River at Planters Factory and continued its march through the **Monticello** area, which today is the site of many beautiful historic homes. A tour guide is available from the Chamber of Commerce.

Farther to the east, part of the Left Wing went through Eatonton and the surrounding area. Eatonton was briefly looted by the fleeing Lt. Col. Silas Adams brigade from the Stoneman-McCook Cavalry Raid on July 31, 1864, and on Nov. 20, 1864 Sherman's men returned, tearing up track and destroying the nearby Eatonton Factory. Today, Eatonton has some fine antebellum homes worth touring, but it is best known as the home of Brer Rabbit and the Uncle Remus Tales. Joel Chandler Harris was born in Eatonton in 1848, and growing up he heard wonderful tales spun by slaves. Harris later became a newspaperman in Atlanta, and he wrote down the stories which became classics of literature and popular Walt Disney movies. His home, the **Wrens Nest**, is open to tour in Atlanta at 1050 Ralph David Abernathy Blvd. 404-753-8535. In Eatonton you find the **Uncle Remus Museum**, a log cabin museum formed from two original slave cabins, representing the home of Uncle Remus. The real Uncle Remus is believed to be "Uncle" George Terrell, a Putnam County slave who regaled local youth with his stories brought over on slave ships from Africa.

"Sherman and His Generals," a photograph by George N. Barnard. Standing from left to right are Oliver Howard, William Hazen, Jefferson C. Davis, and Joseph Mower. Seated from left to right are John Logan, W.T. Sherman, and Henry Slocum.

BARNESVILLE

Greenwood Confederate Cemetery

 R.I.P. GI MTS WR

Adams St., Barnesville

I-75 South from Atlanta to exit 66. Go right on Hwy. 36 and travel 14 miles to downtown Barnesville. Turn right on Rose Ave., cross the railroad tracks, and turn right on Adams St.

Barnesville was an important railroad town on the Macon and Western Railroad. A western spur to Thomaston off the main line connected this factory town with the main line. Because of its location on a transportation line, it also was a Confederate hospital town with the following hospitals: Kingsville; Kingston, moved from Kingston; Medical College Hospital, moved from Atlanta; Flewellen Hospital, named for Surgeon Edward A. Flewellen who was medical director of the Army of Tennessee and lived at The Rock and is buried in Thomaston; and Erwin Hospital. One hundred and fifteen Confederate and two Union dead (84 unknown) reportedly from local hospitals and the Battle of Atlanta are buried in the Confederate section of **Greenwood Cemetery**. (Locals wrote that they could hear the boom of Sherman's cannons during the siege of Atlanta, 60 miles away.) One of the worst train wrecks of the Civil War occurred near Barnesville when a train carrying sick and wounded collided head-on with a supply train. Twenty-two were killed and many were wounded. The dead were buried in unmarked graves next to the tracks. A 15-foot marble shaft stands on a small mound in the center of the cemetery, erected in 1889, with the plain inscription "To Our Confederate Dead."

On April 19, 1865, a skirmish occurred on the edge of Barnesville when a 2,000-man detachment of Union cavalry called Wilson's Raiders attacked a small local militia unit called the Dixie Rangers. The Rangers "fought with gallantry, gradually withdrawing from the field," according to local accounts. The Union cavalry burned some storehouses before moving on to Forsyth. Federal troopers came back through Barnesville on May 5, 1865 in pursuit of Jefferson Davis.

An 1889 **monument** to the women of the Confederacy is located east of the courthouse in a parking island. Gordon College is named for Thomaston native and military legend C.S. Gen. John B. Gordon. The library has

Downtown Barnesville.

an autographed, framed photo of Gordon, his governor's desk, and furniture belonging to him.

MILNER

Confederate Cemetery

 R.I.P. GI

Old Alabama Rd., Milner

Located on Old Alabama Rd. 100 yards south of intersection with Liberty Hill Rd., one mile from Milner.

A **historical marker** tells the story: *"In this lonely spot lie the mortal remains of more than 100 unknown soldiers of the Confederacy. Most of them were wounded while heroically defending the City of Atlanta against the overwhelming forces of General Sherman, and died in an improvised hospital at nearby Milner."*

Another **historical marker** places the spot of one of Milner's temporary hospitals for Confederate soldiers wounded in the Battles of Atlanta and Jonesboro in 1864, who were cared for by townspeople; Dr. John F. Hunt, a local physician; and doctors from nearby communities.

FORSYTH

Forsyth Soldiers Cemetery

 R.I.P. GI MTS

City Cemetery, Newton Memorial Dr., Forsyth

I-75 to exit 62. Take N. Lee St. into Forsyth. At courthouse square, N. Lee St. turns into S. Lee St. Turn left on Newton Memorial Dr.

Forsyth was the location of many hospitals, where approximately 20,000 wounded and sick Confederate soldiers were treated. In a **Confederate cemetery** located near the town square lie 299 unknown and one known Con-

federate soldier. Also buried here is Honora Sweeny, a "gallant Confederate girl" who died while serving as a nurse in one of the Confederate hospitals. Gen. Gilbert J. Wright, who commanded troops in the Eastern Theater, is buried here. The hospitals located in Forsyth were the Hardee, Clayton, Female College (now Tift College) and many other temporary ones. The Georgia Militia came to Forsyth from Griffin on the night of Nov. 16, 1864, in a move to protect the hospitals here from Sherman's army, which was marching east of the rail line in a feigned attack on Macon.

The **Monroe County Confederate Memorial** on the courthouse lawn is one of the finest in the state, featuring a seven-foot bronze statue of a Confederate soldier hurrying north to battle, on a base of Elbert County granite. In **Culloden** southwest of Forsyth, there was a two-hour battle between a part of the Union cavalry called Wilson's Raiders and the Confederate Worrill Grays on April 19, 1865. The Grays were greatly outnumbered but fought fiercely to delay the Federal move on Macon at the end of the War. Two Union soldiers were awarded Medals of Honor for their efforts here which resulted in capturing the Gray's flag. A **historical marker** establishes the location of the battle at the Culloden cemetery.

Jarrell Plantation State Historic Site

 🏠 ◉ 🏛 GI MTS

Jarrell Plantation Rd., Juliette 912-986-5172

Located southeast of Juliette, 18 miles from I-75 Forsyth exit 60.

This **state historic site** is an original middle Georgia plantation consisting of 200 historic buildings dating between 1847 and 1945. The site has one of the largest and most complete collections of original family artifacts of this time period in Georgia, with a mill complex, carpenter shop, blacksmith shop, machines and tools from this period. The farm was raided during Sherman's "March to the Sea."

MACON WAS AN IMPORTANT quartermaster center for the Confederacy, distributing supplies, ordnances and munitions to armies in the field. Located on the Macon and Western Rail Road and the Ocmulgee River, its industries manufactured cannon, weapons and ammunition here, along with other goods needed by the Confederacy. Train tracks went north to Atlanta, southwest to Columbus, and east to Savannah from here. Macon was also the site of Camp Oglethorpe, an officers prison which held 1,400 Union men originally kept at Libby Prison in Richmond, Virginia. This prison camp occupied three acres and was closed when Federal cavalry threatened it in July 1864. Because of the fighting in the Atlanta area, Macon became an important hospital and refugee center, swelling in population when Atlanta fell to Sherman. When C.S. Gen. Joe Johnston was relieved of command of the Army of Tennessee, he went to Macon. The state government relocated to Macon when Milledgeville fell to Sherman's army in November of 1864. Macon twice repelled Yankee cavalry attacks in 1864 — first Stoneman on July 30, then Kilpatrick on Nov. 20 — only to surrender to Wilson's Raiders on April 20, 1865. Macon today boasts five historic districts, with many historically significant structures, some which are open to tour. South of Macon in **Fort Valley** were the Buckner and Gamble hospitals as well as several temporary ones. A **historical marker** in the city cemetery, Oaklawn Cemetery (Hwy. 49 south of town), marks the site where more than 20 unknown Confederate soldiers are buried.

Rose Hill Cemetery

🏛 ⚰ R.I.P. GI MTS

1071 Riverside Dr., Macon, 912-751-9119

I-75 South to I-16. Take the Spring St. exit and take a right onto Spring St. Turn right onto Riverside Dr.

Rose Hill, designed by Macon City Councilman Simri Rose in 1839, remains an outstanding example of 19th century picturesque landscape design, and is one of the oldest surviving public cemetery/parks in the U.S. Many rare and exotic specimens were planted here with native species, including oriental cypress, balm of Gilead, Norway and silver firs, hemlock, arbor vitae, cedar, juniper, wild olive, broom, furze and thorn grown alongside poplar, oak, beech and sycamore. **Confederate Square** is the final resting place of approximately 600 Confederate and Union soldiers, some from the Battle of Griswoldville, others reinterred from various plots around hospitals located in Macon. Three Confederate generals are buried in Rose Hill: Philip Cook, Alfred Colquitt, and Edward Dorr Tracy. Tracy, a Macon native and lawyer, was killed leading his 1,500 men into battle at Port Gibson, Mississippi on May 1, 1863. Cook fought in the Eastern Theater and was wounded at Chancellorsville and Petersburg. He was captured in a hospital in Richmond on April 3, 1865. After the war, Cook was appointed Secretary of State for Georgia by Gov. John B. Gordon, and he served in this capacity until his death in Atlanta on May 21, 1894. Cook County is named for him. Colquitt was the son of a Georgia senator and secessionist. He graduated from Princeton College and settled in Monroe, Georgia, as a lawyer, planter and states' rights politician. He was a staff officer during the Mexican War. Colquitt led the Confederate army's 6th Georgia in the Peninsular Campaign, was promoted to brigadier general in September 1862, and led Colquitt's brigade at Antietam, Fredericksburg, Chancellorsville, The Wilderness, Spotsylvania and Petersburg.

He and his command surrendered at Greensboro N.C. on April 26, 1865. His greatest victory was at Olustee, in February 1864, where he stopped the Union incursion into Florida. He served as Georgia's governor from 1876-82 and U.S. senator from 1882-94, when he died. In adjacent **Riverside Cemetery** are the remains of a Confederate battery. Rose Hill was the scene of the first Confederate Memorial Day celebration in Macon, on April 26, 1866.

The Confederate section in Rose Hill Cemetery.

Woodruff House

🏛 🏠 GI WR

988 Bond St., Macon

Spring St. will become Georgia Ave. Turn right off of Georgia Ave. onto Bond St.

Built in 1836 for a railroad financier and banker, this Greek Revival **plantation** mansion was later owned by Col. Joseph Bond, one of the South's wealthiest cotton planters, who in 1857 made the world record setting cotton sale of 2,200 bales for $100,000. Bond was the state's largest cotton grower and most successful planter, but he was killed at age 44 by a former overseer fired for mistreating a Bond slave. Bond is buried in Rose Hill Cemetery, his plot marked by a large monument carved in Italy from Carrara marble. During his occupation of Macon in 1865, Union Gen. James Wilson resided here, and Confederate President Jefferson Davis and his family were entertained here in 1887, when Davis' daughter Winnie was given a 16th birthday ball. Today the home is owned by Mercer University and is only open to tour during the Christmas season and during the Cherry Blossom Festival in March.

Hay House

HM 🏠 GI

934 Georgia Ave., Macon 912-742-8155

I-75 South to I-16. Take the Spring St. exit and take a right onto Spring St. Follow Spring up the hill.

The **Hay House** is one of the finest antebellum homes in America, and a must see if you visit Macon. Open to tours, this unique, elegant Italian Renaissance Revival Villa mansion contains 18,000 square feet on four levels in 24 rooms, crowned by a three-story cupola. When it was finished in 1859 after five years of hard labor, it was declared "The Palace of the South." A sophisticated water system allowed the house's three indoor bathrooms to have hot and cold running water. Gas lighting illuminated the interior, and an ingenious ventilation system kept the house cool in the summer, while a central heating system, along with 19 fireplaces, warmed the house in the winter. The house also had an elevator and intercom system. Furnished with many treasures of fine art, furnishings, and antiques, the house features some of the finest decorations of the day with stained glass windows, exquisite plasterwork, gold leafing, grained woodwork and some of the country's finest examples of marbleized and trompe l'oeil finishes. The builder of the house, William Butler Johnston, was a successful banker. He is buried in Rose Hill Cemetery.

In 1862, the Confederate Treasury established a major depository at Macon, and Johnston was the receiver of Confederate deposits. Macon became the most important depository in the South, second only to Richmond. Legend states that a hidden room in a staircase in the house stored the Confederate gold. When Stoneman fired on Macon, he aimed at the prominent cupola on the Hay House. The shot instead hit the Holt House, now known as the Cannonball House. The Hay House is open to tours and has a bookstore and gift shop.

City Hall/Capitol
Women of the Confederacy & Confederate Monuments

HM 🏠 🏷 GI WR

City Hall: 511 First St., Macon
Women's Monument: Avenue of Flags, Macon
Confederate Monument: Cotton Ave. and 2nd St., Macon

Take Mulberry to Second St., and take Second St. into the historic district.

Built in 1836, the current Macon **City Hall** first served as a bank, then a fireproof cotton warehouse, the capitol of Georgia, a Confederate Hospital, and then City Hall. It was the temporary capitol of Georgia from Nov. 18, 1864 until March 11, 1865, when the last session of the Confederate general assembly of Georgia was held. The capitol came to Macon when Sherman's army threatened Milledgeville on his "March to the Sea." A picket on guard in the portico of the capitol was shot when Gen. James Wilson entered the city on April 20, 1865. Considered to have the tallest soldier on a county confederate memorial in the state, the 37- foot tall **monument** was dedicated on October 29, 1879. The soldier alone stands ten and a half feet tall, and is placed on a stepped Stone Mountain granite base. More than 35,000 citizens turned out to hear Gov. Alfred H. Colquitt, the hero of Olustee, introduce the speaker, Col. Thomas Hardeman, a Macon citizen and notable orator. Confederate veterans reportedly cried at Hardeman's moving speech. A sealed copper box in the cornerstone of the monument contains a letter from Jefferson Davis and Confederate, U.S. and foreign currency. The beautiful **women's monument** erected in 1911 has the inscription "Erected to the memory of the women of the south by their husbands, fathers, sons and daughters." It displays women nursing the sick and spinning thread for the Confederacy. A bas relief on one side shows a peaceful, bucolic farm, the other side shows the farm in flames. This was the second memorial to the women of the Confederacy in the state, with the first erected in Rome.

Above, the Confederate monument in downtown Macon. At left, the columns of Macon City Hall, which served as the temporary Georgia State Capitol during the Civil War.

Lanier Cottage

HM 🏠 🏛 GI

935 High St., Macon 912-743-3851

From I-75 South take exit 52. Turn left onto Forsyth St. At Orange St. turn left, and at High St. turn right. Cottage is on the left.

Great American Poet Sidney Lanier, author of "The Marshes of Glynn" and "Song of the Chattahoochee," was born in this Victorian cottage in 1842. Lanier was a private in the Confederate Army, was captured while commanding a blockade runner, and was imprisoned in Point Lookout, Maryland. There he contracted tuberculosis, which eventually killed the brilliant linguist, musician, mathematician and lawyer, at the age of 39. Lake Lanier is named in his honor. The cottage, the headquarters of the Middle Georgia Historical Society, is open to tour and has a bookstore and gift shop.

Old Cannonball House & Confederate Museum

🏛 🏠 🏛 **AC GI MTS**

856 Mulberry St., Macon 912-745-5982

I-75 South to I-16. Take the Spring St. exit and take a right onto Spring St. Follow Spring up the hill, and turn left onto Mulberry.

Built in 1853 by Judge Asa Holt, this beautiful antebellum **house** is considered an outstanding example of Greek Revival architecture of the Old South. It became known as the **Cannonball House** after it was struck by a cannon ball fired by Union cavalry forces under Gen. George Stoneman during the Battle of Dunlap Hill on July 30, 1864. Stoneman, located approximately 3 miles east on the Clinton Road, fired the shot which "struck the sand sidewalk, passed through the second column from the left on the gallery and entered the parlor over a window, landing unexploded in the hall. Its course may be traced by the mended column, a patch in the parlor plaster, and the dent in the hall floor." Stoneman was later captured 25 miles north of Macon on August 3.

The unlucky Holts thought they could avoid the Yankees by fleeing to their plantation in Jefferson County, but they were right in the path of Sherman's "March to the Sea." Their plantation home, used by Union officers, was spared, but all their livestock was slaughtered, their granary and cotton gin house and warehouse were burned with 200 bales of cotton, all their household goods stolen, food confiscated and well ropes and buckets destroyed. Worse, Asa Holt was hanged three times, as Union troops tortured him to learned where they thought he had hidden gold. He survived each time, revived by servants, although the third time he was described as being "barely alive."

The home was bought in 1863 by the Sidney Lanier Chapter, United Daughters of the Confederacy, and is managed by them today. Two rooms honor the founding of the first two sororities in the United States — Alpha Delta Pi and Phi Mu — at nearby Wesleyan College. The servants quarters and kitchen behind the house serve as the **Macon Confederate Museum** and have many interesting and rare relics. The house and museum are open to the public.

Above, the cannon, made in Macon, which stands in front of the Cannonball House. At left, a cannon ball sits in the spot where it came to rest inside the Cannonball House. Below right, the First Presbyterian Church in Macon.

First Presbyterian Church

🏛 🏠 **GI WR**

682 Mulberry St., Macon

I-16 to Spring St. exit. Turn right onto Spring St. and follow it up the hill. Turn left onto Mulberry.

Built in 1858 with a 185-foot steeple, poet Sidney Lanier was a member of this **church**. Local legend tells the story that when U.S. Gen. James Wilson occupied the city shortly after Appomattox, he ordered that the U.S. flag be hung over the front door. The minister refused to hold the service and was replaced by a colleague who read a Psalm: "For they that carried us away captive required of us a song and they that waste us required of us mirth." The congregation left by the back door to avoid the stars and stripes.

THE GRISWOLDVILLE AREA WAS the scene of several significant events during the Civil War. Not much remains to be seen, compared to Chickamauga or Fort Pulaski, but armed with your imagination you may be able to envision the events which took place here. This area witnessed the destruction by U.S. Gen. George Stoneman's cavalry until they were stopped at Round Oak by Confederate cavalry under Gen. Alfred Iverson, Jr. When Sherman's Right Wing moved through the area during his "March to the Sea," it was attacked by much inferior Georgia Militia forces, resulting in a tragic and unnecessary slaughter at Griswoldville. At Clinton, the tourist can find a historic community which retains its pre-Greek Revival quality.

Griswoldville

HM ✕ ◉ AC GI MTS

Apx. 10 miles east of Macon, Old Griswoldville

From Macon take U.S. Hwy. 80 East. After crossing the Ocmulgee River, proceed 2.5 miles and take the left fork onto GA Hwy. 57. Travel 3.5 miles and turn left onto an unmarked paved road. Travel 1.4 miles north to the railroad.

The only significant battle opposing Sherman's "March to the Sea" occurred unintentionally at **Griswoldville**, when vastly outnumbered Georgia Militia, made up mostly of inexperienced old men and boys, made a futile attack on part of the Right Wing of Sherman's army. Some call this the Gettysburg of Georgia.

Griswoldville was named for the brilliant entrepreneur Samuel Griswold, who came to the town of Clinton from Connecticut in 1820. Griswold established the first iron foundry in Georgia and a factory for making cotton gins. After the Georgia Central railroad was built between Savannah and Macon in the 1840s, Griswold purchased 4,000 acres and moved his operation two miles south to Griswoldville, located 10 miles east of Macon, so that he could be on the railroad. Here he had an enormous factory that produced cotton gins, a saw mill, a grist mill, and factories that produced bricks, soap, furniture, and candles. He built a three-story, 24-room mansion for himself, a church, and 60 cottages for his slaves and workers. In 1862, Griswold converted his gin factory into a pistol factory, where he manufactured more than 3,500 Colt's Navy Repeaters or Brass-frame Confederate Colts, prized weapons in the Confederacy.

Top, Duncan's Ridge at Griswoldville. Bottom, the railroad that runs through the site of Griswoldville.

On Nov. 21, 1864, Union Gen. Judson Kilpatrick's cavalry, operating on the Federal right flank during the "March to the Sea," destroyed the town, burning everything except Griswold's home, the slave cottages, and a worker's residence. The Confederate commander in charge of defending Georgia, William J. Hardee, realized that Macon was not a target, and assumed that Augusta, with its arsenal, foundry, and other facilities, was Sherman's real objective. Hardee ordered the local militia in Macon to reinforce Augusta. On Nov. 22, 1864, these troops, made up of 4,350 inexperienced troops and artillery under the command of Gen. Pleasant J. Philips, marched eastward on the Georgia Central railroad and ran smack into smaller detachments of the advancing Federal Army, just past the smoldering ruins of Griswoldville. Philips found a battle-hardened Federal brigade, under Brig. Gen. Charles C. Walcutt, numbering 1,513. The Yankees were armed with Spencer repeating rifles and cannon, and located on the crest of Duncan Ridge with flanks on a swamp and railroad embankment. Without orders from superiors, Philips formed his lines for battle and attacked across an open field, trying to cross a swampy creek and charge up a

hill. His men made seven assaults, coming within 50 yards of the Yankees before being repulsed by blistering fire. The Confederates reported losses of 422 wounded and 51 killed, and the Union reported 79 wounded — including Gen. Walcutt — and 13 killed. Union Col. Charles Wills later wrote of the battle, "Old gray haired men and weakly looking men and little boys, not over 15 years old, lay dead or writhing in pain," he wrote. "I pity those boys. I hope I never have to shoot at such men again. They knew nothing at all about fighting, and I think their officers knew as little, or else certainly knew nothing of our being there." In one spot, Federals found a 14-year-old boy, with a broken arm and leg. Next to him, "cold in death, lay his father, two brothers, and an uncle. It was a harvest of death," wrote a Union soldier. Today, the **battlefield** is in private ownership, but historical preservation groups have the goal of preserving it. One can go to the site of Griswoldville, located at a crossroads next to the train tracks, read state **historical markers**, and get a general sense of what occurred here.

Round Oak

🏛 ⚔ AC

U.S. 129/GA 11, Round Oak

Located on GA 11 apx. 10 miles north of Gray.

A single **historical marker** marks the location of the Battle of Sunshine Church, July 31, 1864, where Confederate cavalry under Gen. Alfred Iverson, Jr. deceived U.S. Maj. Gen. George Stoneman into surrendering 600 men, artillery, and a train to a smaller force. Stoneman was part of Sherman's Great Cavalry Raid, designed to destroy the railroad south of Atlanta in a great pincer move, with Edward McCook's forces sweeping from the west, and Stoneman's from the east.

Stoneman's 2,112 men were working their way toward Andersonville hoping to free Union prisoners at Camp Sumter, and had torn up tracks in Gordon, McIntyre, Toomsboro, and Griswoldville. Approaching Macon, Stoneman encountered entrenched Georgia Militia under Gen. Howell Cobb. He briefly shelled Macon before retreating northward, abandoning his plans. The next day, his cavalry ran full stride into 1,300 Confederate cavalry under Iverson sent to intercept him. Iverson, a native of nearby Clinton, was familiar with the terrain and organized his men appropriately. Stoneman, believing himself surrounded, surrendered on a hill which today bears his name. His black guide, Minor, was immediately hanged from a nearby tree, and the Confederates were preparing to do the same with Stoneman when Confederate officers halted the execution. It is reported that when Stoneman learned he had been captured by a force half his size, he openly wept. Stoneman was imprisoned in Macon, many of his soldiers were sent to Andersonville, and his horses helped turn the Kentucky Orphan Brigade into mounted cavalry. Two of Stoneman's brigades, Col. Horace Capron and Lt. Col. Silas Adams', escaped east then north from Sunshine Church, working their way to Athens and Winder. Capron's brigade was destroyed at King's Tanyard near Winder by Confederate cavalry under Col. William Breckinridge, which pursued Capron from Sunshine Church; and Adams' made it back to Federal lines. Approximately 1/2 mile south of the **historical marker** titled "The Stoneman Raid" on the east side of the tracks is Stoneman Hill.

The McCarthy-Pope House stands in Old Clinton.

Clinton/Gordon

🏛 🏠 AC MTS

Clinton: U.S. 129/GA 11
Gordon: GA 18

The historic town of **Clinton**, then the county seat of Jones County, was visited by Stoneman and Kilpatrick's cavalry and Sherman's Right Wing in 1864. Stoneman's 2,000 cavalry pillaged and looted the county and town of more than half a million dollars worth of property in late July 1864 on their way to Macon. On their way back to Atlanta, they stopped again and burned the jail. On Nov. 19, Kilpatrick's 5,000-man cavalry force occupied the town, only to be followed by Sherman's Right Wing consisting of 15,000 men, hundreds of wagons, and 4,000 head of cattle. C.S. Cavalry Gen. Joe Wheeler harassed the Union troops over a four-day period, causing the Federals to fortify the town. When they departed, one third of the town had been destroyed, including residences, a school house, churches, a tannery, and many fences and outbuildings. What remains is considered the best-preserved example of a southern county seat from the 1830s era, with **13 historic homes** and churches built in a pre-Greek Revival style called Plantation Plain. During **Clinton War Days** on the first weekend in May, living history reenactments are held, and the local historical society displays Civil War memorabilia at the McCarthy-Pope House, the oldest remaining structure in town from 1809. Approximately 10 miles southeast at **Gordon**, you find a rebuilt town which was obliterated by

Sherman's Right Wing as it worked its way east on the Georgia Central railroad. Gordon was the location of a northern railroad spur to Eatonton, and is the present location of a favorite **historical marker**, titled "He Wouldn't Run," which tells the story of Rufus Kelly. Kelly, who fought with Lee's Army of Northern Virginia, had been discharged and sent home to Gordon after losing a leg. But Kelly wasn't finished fighting. Back home on crutches, he voluntarily spied on the Yankees. Riding in from Macon on horseback, he warned Adjutant Gen. H.C. Wayne that the Federals were approaching. Wayne told Kelly that he was abandoning the town and retreating with his 700 cadets and paroled convicts to a bridge over the Oconee. Kelly, incredulous and upset, cursed the General "for a white-livered cur with not a drop of red blood in his veins" and added "Well, you damned band of tuck-tails, if you have no manhood left in you, I will defend the women and children of Gordon!" As Union skirmishers began to enter the town, the one-legged Kelly and one other man, Bragg, unlimbered their Winchesters and fired on the Federals, killing one and scattering the others. The two men were left alone in town for an hour and then, according to Kelly, "the whole world turned to Yankees." Bragg got away but Kelly was captured and sentenced to death by firing squad. He escaped into the swamps several days later by diving out of a wagon as it crossed the Ogeechee River. He survived the war and returned to Gordon, where he taught for 50 years. Gordon has four **historical markers** and a **stone memorial** near the depot saluting Kelly's bravery.

MILLEDGEVILLE'S CIVIL WAR history falls into two categories: the political activities which occurred here when it was Georgia's Civil War capital, and the occupation Nov. 22-25, 1864 by Gen. W.T. Sherman's split Left Wing, which came together here briefly from Eatonton and Shady Dale to cross the Oconee River. Milledgeville, a planned town inspired by Savannah and Washington, D.C., was the state capital from 1803-68. When the capital was moved to Atlanta in 1868 during Reconstruction, the town experienced economic decline but later rebounded in the early 20th century. Today, Georgia's antebellum capital boasts a wealth of well-preserved Federal-style architecture, enhanced by Greek Revival, Victorian, and Classic Revival houses. Easy to tour on foot and beautiful in the spring, a map and guide to 37 significant sites is available from the **Welcome Center** at 200 W. Hancock Street, 912-452-4687.

Old Governor's Mansion

 GI MTS

120 S. Clark St., Milledgeville 912-453-4545

Located at the corner of GA 49 (Hancock St.) and Clark St., across from Georgia College.

This Greek Revival **mansion**, built in 1838, was home to the governors of Georgia from 1838 to 1868. When Sherman occupied the town, he slept in his bedroll on the floor of this historic home, from which the furnishings had been evacuated to Macon along with Gov. Joe Brown. Brown was later arrested at this site in May 1865. This national historic landmark has been restored and furnished in period antiques and is open to tours.

Memory Hill Cemetery

HM R.I.P. GI

Liberty and Franklin Streets, Milledgeville

Located at the southern end of Liberty St.

This large, historic **cemetery** has a plot containing the remains of over 20 unknown Confederate soldiers, three Union soldiers in a separate plot, one of the earliest Confederate memorials in the state, and the grave of Gen. George P. Doles. Brig. Gen. Doles was a Milledgeville native who lead the Doles Brigade in the battles of Fredricksburg, Chancellorsville, The Wilderness, and Spotsylvania. Considered a great leader, he was killed

The old Governor's Mansion in Milledgeville, where Sherman spent the night.

at Bethesda Church near the entrenchments at Petersburg on June 2, 1864, and replaced by Philip Cook.

The cemetery was originally one of the four public squares of 20 acres each in the town plan of 1803, but it later became known as cemetery square. The **Confederate memorial,** erected early in 1868, is believed to be Georgia's first permanent, general county monument. It is a small, plain obelisk marked "Unknown Confederates," which cost its sponsors $300, a large sum in the Reconstruction South.

St. Stephens Episcopal Church
HM GI MTS
220 S. Wayne St., Milledgeville
GA 49 to Wayne St. Go south on Wayne St.

This unusual Carpenter Gothic **church**, consecrated in 1843, was damaged by Union soldiers, their horses, and a nearby explosion when the Yankees occupied Milledgeville. Federal troops stabled their horses in the building (hoofprints are still visible) and poured sorghum molasses down the pipe organ to "sweeten the sound." When Federals exploded a nearby arsenal, it damaged the roof which was originally flat. In 1909, a new organ was presented by George W. Perkins of New York, who had heard about the damage wreaked by Sherman's troops.

Old State Capitol Building
State House Square
Confederate Memorial
HM GI MTS

Located at Jefferson and Greene Streets on the campus of Georgia Military College.

The **old state capitol**, the site of the famous Secession Convention, is considered the oldest public building in the U.S. built in Gothic Style. It served as the seat of Government of the State of Georgia from 1803-63, and was twice partially destroyed by fire. Restored in 1943, the exterior of the present building is a replica of the original. The beautiful Gothic **gates** at the north and south entrances to the square were constructed in the 1860s, after the Civil War, of bricks from the arsenal and magazine destroyed by Sherman's soldiers. Today the old state capitol is used by Georgia Military College.

The Secession Convention convened here Jan. 16, 1861, and three days later passed the Secession Act by a vote of 208-89. Two **plaques** on the wall next to the entrance mention this historic event, with one describing the meeting as "the most brilliant convocation ever held in the commonwealth of Georgia." Elected delegates from all over the state came to Milledgeville, many were among the most able men the state has ever produced. Howell and Thomas R.R. Cobb, Francis Bartow, and Robert Toombs all favored immediate secession, whereas Alexander H. Stephens, Benjamin Hill, and Herschel V. Johnson all favored a delay. The secessionists obviously won out. However, three years later, visiting Yankees repealed the secession ordinance in a mock legislative session, featuring drunken and rowdy soldiers. Gen. W.T. Sherman's men did less damage to the town than what was probably expected by Georgians at the time. His provost guard, which camped out on the statehouse square, burned the brick State Arsenal on the North side, and exploded the brick magazine on the opposite side. Churches were damaged, as was the interior of the statehouse and the state library. Sherman burned the State Penitentiary where Georgia College is located today, but spared two large cotton warehouses, a textile factory, a flour mill and a foundry reportedly because they were owned by Northerners or foreigners.

Across the street from the entrance of the old capitol building is the second Confederate county **memorial**, unveiled in 1912. It is a 20 foot granite shaft, flanked by two marble statues of young Confederate soldiers.

Controversial Civil War Gov. Joe Brown worked his politics here, for which another book is needed to describe.

At top left, the old state capitol, the site of the famous Secession Convention and the Yankees' mock legislative session of 1864. Directly above, St. Stephens Episcopal Church.

Above, the Oconee River at Ball's Ferry. At right, the Ball's Ferry monument.

Ball's Ferry/Toomsboro

[HM] ✕ [⚑] MTS

GA 57, Toomsboro

Go left on GA 57 from Toomsboro for 7.8 miles to picnic area on left.

This area saw a series of fights on Nov. 22-25, 1864 between the Blue and Gray over the crossing of the Oconee River, one of the natural obstacles to Sherman's "March to the Sea." C.S. Maj. Gen. Henry C. Wayne, with six guns and a mixed force of 1,200 men consisting of Georgia Military Institute cadets and paroled prison inmates, retreated from Gordon to Oconee, a railroad stop just east of the Oconee River railroad bridge, to prevent the Right Wing from crossing there. When he learned on Nov. 23 that the Right Wing was attempting to cross 10 miles south of his position at Ball's Ferry, he sent two companies to drive

the Yankees back across the river. Meanwhile, the part of the Right Wing of Sherman's Army under Blair had marched down the railroad line from Gordon to Toomsboro, then marched east to the Oconee River to cross at Jackson's Ferry. There, they fought with Wayne's men at the railroad bridge and Jackson's Ferry, but decided it was impassible due to swamps, and his men moved farther south to meet the other half of the Right Wing under Osterhaus at **Ball's Ferry**. Here, Union troops on pontoons were decimated by Confederates on the eastern bank, slowing up the Right Wing. A series of flanking moves resulted in the withdrawal of Confederate troops eastward to Tennille.

A county park, with boat ramps and picnic tables, is found today at Ball's Ferry, located down a dirt road north of the Oconee River bridge crossing at GA 57. A stone **monument** to the historic ferry and battle are found by the road next to two **historical markers**.

The Classic South, the heart of King Cotton, is similar to the Historic Heartland, with its beautiful plantation homes and rich Civil War history. There is much to see in Augusta, a major Confederate city, with the **Confederate Powder Works** and many factories supplying goods to the South during the War. Located in the northern part of the region were important, rich merchant towns devoted to the cotton trade, such as Washington, the location of the **Robert Toombs House State Historic Site** and where Jefferson Davis held the last meeting of the Confederate cabinet, before fleeing south. At Crawfordville is **Alexander H. Stephens State Historic Park**, which features Vice President of the Confederacy's home and museum. In the southern part of the region are towns which experienced Sherman's "March to the Sea" in late 1864, including Sandersville, Louisville, Waynesboro, Wrightsville, and Millen. During the March, this region saw many cavalry skirmishes, between Confederate Gen. Joe Wheeler and Union Gen. Judson Kilpatrick. The world's largest prisoner-of-war camp was located near Millen. Today, it is a lush vacation land with large recreational lakes and rivers and abundant forests.

The Robert Toombs House in Washington.

A.H. Stephens State Historic Park

[HM] 🏠 [R.I.P.] 🏛 [🐾] GI

Alexander St., Crawfordville 706-456-2602

Exit 55 off I-20, go north on Hwy. 22 for 2 miles. Go east on U.S. 278 1 mile to Crawfordville. Follow signs to the Park.

Alexander Hamilton Stephens, a native Georgian, was a major figure of the Civil War, serving the Confederacy as vice president. **A.H. Stephens State Historic Park** features his home **Liberty Hall**, his **gravesite**, and an excellent **Confederate Museum** housing one of the finest collections of Civil War artifacts in the state. Stephens was born in a log cabin near Crawfordville and orphaned by his parents. Nicknamed "Little Aleck" or "the Little Giant," Stephens was 5 feet, 7 inches tall and seldom weighed over 90 pounds, and usually in frail health. He was raised and educated by an uncle, Brig. Gen. A.W. Grier, a distinguished soldier in the Indian and Mexican wars. Stephens graduated in 1832 at the head of his class at Franklin College (now the University of Georgia) and taught school for two years before returning to Liberty Hall to study law. From 1836-50, he was a member of the Georgia State House of Representatives, and in 1842 he was elected to the state senate. From 1843 to 1859, he served as a member of the U.S. House of Representatives, helping to pass the Kansas-Nebraska Act, and in 1860 was Presidential Elector on the Democratic ticket of Douglas and Johnson. In 1861, Stephens opposed secession at the Georgia Secession Convention in Milledgeville, but supported his state's decision once it passed, and he was elected vice-president of the Confederacy in Montgomery, Alabama. He helped draft a moderate Confederate constitution, worked for prisoner exchanges, and opposed Davis' centralization of power and suspension of civil rights. He was Commissioner of the Confederacy at the Hampton Roads Conference in February of 1865, where he met with Lincoln to negotiate for peace.

Stephens was arrested at Crawfordville and imprisoned at Fort Warren in Boston Harbor, Massachusetts for half a year. After the war, he was again member of the U.S. House of Representatives from 1873-82, then served as governor of Georgia briefly until he died at the age of 71 in Atlanta on March 4, 1883. Briefly interred at Oakland Cemetery, his body was reinterred at his beloved **Liberty Hall** property in 1884. He wrote *Constitutional View of the Late War Between the States*, as well as other books on U.S. history. His home has been restored to excellent condition, and many of Stephens' effects and furniture are found in the house, including his complete bedroom furnishings. Notice all of his medi-

cine bottles. In the backyard is a grave and monument to a favorite family pet, Rio. In front of Liberty Hall is a flattering **statue** of Stephens and some interesting inscriptions. The museum has more than 300 fascinating items relating to the Confederacy and A.H. Stephens.

During the Civil War, a factory which produced Leech and Rigdon pistols operated in **Greensboro**, west of Crawfordville. From 1863-1865, the town was also the home of several Confederate hospitals. In the **Greensboro City Cemetery** (off the Penfield Road) are buried approximately 45 Confederate soldiers, men who died locally of wounds or disease.

On GA 47 between Sharon and Raytown

is the gravesite of Gen. Aaron W. Grier. Two miles northeast of Sharon on GA 47 is a **historical marker** titled "Ray's Place — Now Raytown." The parents and grandparents of Jefferson Davis owned plantations near Rayton in the early 1800s. Mrs. Davis, fleeing Federal forces in 1865, spent a night in Raytown.

At left, a statue of Stephens, vice president of the Confederacy. Insets: top, Stephens' bedroom; bottom, Stephens' medicine bottles. Above, Stephens' home, his beloved Liberty Hall.

WASHINGTON IS ONE OF Georgia's historic gems, a town filled with many architectural treasures which capture the feel of antebellum Georgia. It was one of Georgia's original counties, and the first successful cotton gin was perfected and set up by Eli Whitney in Wilkes County in 1795 at Mount Pleasant Plantation, altering the history of the South, which became the home of King Cotton, plantations and slaves. (The first cotton mill in Georgia was erected in Wilkes County in 1811.) Washington was the terminus of a spur off the Georgia Railroad between Augusta and Atlanta, connecting it to the rest of the South. During the Civil War, a fleeing Jefferson Davis had his last cabinet meeting here, and Washington is the home of "Unreconstructed Rebel" and Confederate secretary of state Robert Toombs. The mystery of the Confederate treasure has its roots here, and treasure hunters continue to search the countryside for the buried treasure which was last sheltered in the town of Washington. Brig. Gen. Edward Porter Alexander, commander of Alexander's Battalion of Artillery, was born here on May 26, 1835. At Gettysburg, his 75 guns prepared the way for Pickett's Charge. This was the home-

Above, the Campbell Home. Below, Robert Toombs' house, with Toombs' portrait.

town of Eliza Francis Andrews, author of *The War-Time Journal of a Georgia Girl*, one of the best memoirs of the period. Two Confederate generals, Dudley M. DuBose and Toombs, are buried in **Rest Haven Cemetery** located on GA 44 east of town. Washington claims to be the first city in the nation to be incorporated in the name of George Washington in 1780.

Robert Toombs State Historic Site

HM 🏠 🏛 GI JDR

216 East Robert Toombs Ave., Washington 706-678-2226

Hwy. 44 to East Robert Toombs Ave.

Robert Augustus Toombs was one of the most colorful figures of the Civil War and one of the South's most impassioned and daring orators. Born in Wilkes County on July 2, 1810, Toombs attended Franklin College (now the University of Georgia) but was expelled because of a college prank. (See Robert Toombs Oak pg. 72.) He eventually finished school at the University of Virginia, was admitted to the bar, and returned to Washington to practice law. Elected to the state legislature from 1837 to 1844, he then served in the U.S. House of Representatives from 1845 to 1853, and then was elected to the U.S. Senate from 1853 to 1861, resigning at the outbreak of the War. Early in his Washington, D.C. career, Toombs was a moderate, consistently supporting compromise measures, but he turned into a "fire-eating" secessionist when the Crittenden Compromise in 1860 failed. Toombs ran for the presidency of the Confederacy, narrowly losing to Davis, and served briefly and unhappily as secretary of state until he resigned this position to join the C.S. Army in July 1861 as brigadier general. Toombs' brigade served in the Peninsular Campaign in Virginia, where he was injured at Sharpsburg, Maryland when a portion of his brigade stopped two charges of the Union Ninth Corps at the famed Burnside Bridge over Antietam Creek. Unhappy with the South's defensive strategy, Toombs resigned his command in March 1863, and returned to Georgia to serve as adjutant and inspector general under Gen. G.W. Smith in the Georgia State Militia and in the defenses of Atlanta and Savannah. Toombs was one of the five men that the Federal government wanted punished after the War, so to avoid capture by Union troops in 1865, he fled to Cuba, France, England and Canada, returning to Georgia two years later in 1867. He refused to take the hated "Oath of Allegiance" to the U.S. and declared himself an "Unreconstructed Rebel." Said Toombs in 1880, "I am not loyal to the existing government of the United States and do not wish to be suspected of loyalty." He was a power in Georgia politics but never held political office due to his refusal to take the oath. He died in Washington on Dec. 15, 1885 and is buried in **Rest Haven Cemetery**. The **Robert Toombs State Historic Site** features Toombs' antebellum home with period furnishings and Civil War artifacts.

The Mystery Of The Confederate Treasure

One might say Georgia is a state rich in Civil War history — literally rich that is, considering that private Virginia bank funds worth an estimated $250,000 in 1865 were stolen in Lincoln County and never fully recovered. These bank funds had traveled by train and wagons with the official Confederate treasure and President Davis on his flight from Richmond, Virginia at the end of the Civil War.

Along the way, the official Confederate treasure, valued at approximately $500,000 when it left Richmond, was spent supplying fighting Confederate troops and paying off Confederate troops returning home from the war. Under an elm tree near Washington, James A. Semple, "a trusted naval officer," was given gold coin and bullion worth $86,000 and ordered to conceal it in the false bottom of a carriage and take it to Charleston or Savannah. Semple never reached his destination — he and the money disappeared into private hands. Davis himself carried $35,000, until in the woods near Sandersville, he abandoned everything in hopes of escaping capture. He gave the money to C.S. Capt. Micajah Clark, whose party distributed $10,000 and made it south to Florida with $25,000. Realizing the War was over, Clark's party decided to divide the money among themselves, leaving a por-

President Jefferson E. Davis.

tion of it for Mrs. Davis.

Back in Washington, Georgia, the funds of the Virginia banks were placed temporarily in a local bank, but the bank tellers were eager to move the funds to a safer place. They obtained permission from U.S. Army Captain Lot Abraham to secretly ship the funds back to Richmond, and on May 24, 1865, they loaded five wagons with the money to begin

their journey. Word of the shipment spread quickly among Confederate veterans who believed the money belonged to the Confederate treasure.

When the wagon train stopped for the night in the horse lot of a Methodist minister, Dionysius Chenault, in Lincoln County near the Savannah River, a band of Confederate riders, which included Tennessee and Kentucky cavalrymen and probably citizens of Wilkes County, Georgia as well, hijacked the wagons. Coins spilled "ankle deep" on the ground, and Confederates rode away with bags, pockets, and saddle bags full of gold.

When C.S. Brig. Gen. Alexander heard news of the raid, he rounded up former members of a Washington Confederate battery and seized approximately $110,000 from the culprits who remained in the Washington and Lincoln County area. Federal soldiers stationed nearby embarked on a spree of pillaging and vandalism aimed at reclaiming the gold. However, most of the Virginia bank funds were never recovered, leading treasure hunters to search the locality even today. Chenault's daughter, Mary Anne had her own story about the fate of the gold: "The Yankees got a good deal of it, but there were oceans more of it scattered all over Wilkes and Lincoln counties, besides what was carried off. Some of it was hid about in swamps and woods, some was buried in the ground, and there is no telling how much has been forgotten and not found again."

Washington/Wilkes Historical Museum

🏛 🏠 🏛 GI JDR

308 East Robert Toombs Ave., Washington
706-678-2105

Hwy. 44 to East Robert Toombs Ave.

This is the best place to start your Civil War tour of Washington/Wilkes County. Exhibits in this Federal style house, built circa 1835, feature the Confederacy and Reconstruction as well as local history. Valuable Confederate relics, including the camp chest of Jefferson Davis, original photos, signed documents, and Gen. Robert Toomb's uniform, are found here. Material on the last cabinet meeting of the Confederacy is available, and the house has one floor furnished with furniture of the grade period, circa 1830.

A visitor's guide to Washington/Wilkes County is available at the **museum**, and it will lead you to more than 50 sites worth visiting, including the following historic homes with

Civil War significance: **Holly Court**, a combination of two homes, one built in 1807 and the other in the 1840s, located at 301 S. Alexander Ave., was where Mrs. Jefferson Davis and her two children spent a few days awaiting the arrival of Jefferson Davis after the fall of Richmond; the **Campbell-Jordan House**, East Liberty St., was the home of two distinguished Georgians, one Duncan G. Campbell who drafted the treaty resulting in the removal of the Cherokee Indians from Georgia on the Trail of Tears, and his son John Archibald Campbell, who was an Associate Justice of the U.S. Supreme Court from 1853 to 1861, when he resigned to become assistant secretary of war for the Confederacy; the **Gilbert-Alexander House**, circa 1808, on Alexander Drive, is one of the oldest brick structures north of Augusta and where C.S. Brig. Gen. E.P. Alexander lived; and the **County Courthouse**, U.S. 78, was built on the site of the Heard House, the scene of the last cabinet meeting of the Confederate government. A **historical marker** tells the story of Jefferson Davis' desire to continue fighting the War. A piece of the Heard House's wrought

iron balcony is incorporated into the design of the **Osborne Bounds-Barnett House** on Spring Street.

Holly Court in Washington.

AUGUSTA, LIKE COLUMBUS AND Macon, played an important role as a fall line industrial, transportation, and trade center for the Confederacy during the Civil War. Augusta was the location of the Confederacy's **Powder Works Factory**, which supplied the Southern states with badly needed explosive powder. Cotton is what shaped and supported Augusta in the antebellum and post Civil War years, giving its citizens wealth and importance.

Although no battle was fought here and Gen. W.T. Sherman's men didn't march through its streets on their way to the sea, much Civil War history is to be found in the Garden City. Augusta, the birthplace of "Fighting" Joe Wheeler, supplied many fighting men to the cause. Five hospitals were located here. Augusta is the second oldest city in Georgia, established in 1736 by Gen. James E. Oglethorpe as an Indian trading post on the Savannah River. It was the state's capital from 1785-95, and many of Georgia's historical "firsts" happened in Augusta. The oldest railroad in Georgia continuously operating under its original charter, the Georgia Railroad and Banking Company, carried more than 100,000 Confederate soldiers to their homes without charge after the War.

Augusta Canal
Confederate Powder Works

Canal: Near the Savannah River, Augusta
Powder Works: 1717 Goodrich St. at the Canal, Augusta

An excellent self-guided tour to the historic canal is available from the historic **Augusta Cotton Exchange Welcome Center**. This is the best way to tour the canal, which can be done on foot, by bike, or by canoe. Built in various stages starting in 1845, the canal was finished in the 1850s and is nine miles long and seven feet deep. This industrial improvement brought to Augusta needed power and water, vital to its manufacturing facilities, giving Augusta the nickname of the "Lowell of the South." Augusta's canal, water power, railroad facilities, and central location safe from attack made the city the ideal location for the Confederacy's **Powder Works**. A 168-foot obelisk chimney is all that remains from the Confederate Powder Works, which is the only permanent structure begun and completed by the Confederate government. The Powder Works Factory was the second largest munitions factory in the world during the Civil War, consisting of 26 buildings which

The chimney of the Confederate Powder Works Factory.

stretched two miles down the first level of the Augusta Canal.

In July 1861, President Jefferson Davis ordered West Point-trained engineer, Col. George Washington Rains to select a place for a gunpowder plant, and Rains selected Augusta. The munitions factory operated under Rains from 1862 until April 18, 1865, manufacturing 2,750,000 pounds of gunpowder of the highest quality then made from saltpeter smuggled through the Federal blockade from India via England. Rains was known to boast

that no battle was lost for want of gunpowder. The factory also produced cannons, cartridges, percussion caps, grenades, and signal rockets. Churches donated their bells, and local women donated their lead window weights to be melted into bullets. Other war industries along the canal produced pistols, uniforms, shoes, bedding, hospital supplies, baked goods, and gun and horse harnesses.

The city bought the dilapidated powder works from the U.S. government in 1872 and tore down the mills to make way for new industries. Col. Rains, then a professor of chemistry and pharmacy at the Medical College of Georgia, appeared before the city council requesting that "at least the noble obelisk be allowed to remain forever as a fitting monument to the dead heroes who sleep on the unnumbered battlefields of the South." Large stone tablets on the base of the chimney pay tribute to the fallen Confederacy and Rains, who "under almost insuperable difficulties erected, and successfully operated these powder works — a bulwark of the beleaguered Confederacy."

Historic Cotton Exchange and Welcome Center

32 8th St. at Riverwalk and Reynolds, Augusta 706-724-4067

I-20 East to exit 66 (Riverwatch Pkwy.).

The **Cotton Exchange** building, built in 1886, serves as a museum for King Cotton and a Welcome Center. At the height of the cotton boom, Augusta was second only to Memphis in the volume of cotton trade. This is a good place to begin your tour of Augusta, with tour brochures and maps available. Notice the 45-foot long wooden blackboard, discovered behind a wall during renovation, still chalked with cotton, currency, and commodities prices dating back to the early 1900s.

Augusta Arsenal

2500 Walton Way, Augusta

West of town in the historic district of Summerville.

Now the Augusta College Campus, this land served as an U.S. **arsenal** for more than 128 years. First commissioned by President George Washington in 1793, the first arsenal was located near the river in 1816, near where the future Confederate Powderworks was to be located. It moved to its current location in 1826 to escape the Black Fever which struck the garrison. During the Civil War, the arsenal manufactured a variety of ordnance for the Confederate Army. The **original barracks, jail house, cannons**, and **headquarters building** remain on campus. Notice the headquarters sign with two crossed cannons at Payne Hall and the gun ports in nearby walls. The commandant's house was the boyhood home of poet and novelist Stephen Vincent Benet,

Augusta College now stands on the site of the old Augusta Arsenal.

best known for *John Brown's Body*, 1928, which won a Pulitzer Prize for poetry. Over 300 pages, the poem covers the Civil War from John Brown's raid at Harpers Ferry, W.Va., to peace at Appomattox. The arsenal, with its garrison of 80 men commanded by Captain Arnold Elzey, was surrendered to Georgia troops on Jan. 24, 1861, five days after the Secession convention in Milledgeville. It was abandoned in 1955.

Nearby on the Augusta College grounds, on the east side of Arsenal Ave., is the private family **cemetery** containing the grave of Augusta native **Maj. Gen. William H.T. Walker**, who was killed by a sharpshooter at the Battle of Atlanta on July 22, 1864. Walker had served in the Indian and Mexican wars, taught cadets at West Point, and as a general saw action in a wide variety of locations, including Virginia, Florida, Vicksburg, Chickamauga, and all the battles in Georgia during the Atlanta Campaign until his death.

Confederate Memorial

⊞ 🏃 GI

700 block Broad St., Augusta

One block south of Reynolds St.

This is the tallest, one of the oldest, and one of best Confederate county monuments in the state. The 76-foot tall **monument** features a private at the top and generals at the bottom. The private is modeled on the likeness of Sgt. Berry Benson, who leans on his rifle, wears a kepi, and faces east from his perch of Italian Carrara marble. Benson was a Georgia scout and sharpshooter, who was captured more than once but escaped every time, and lived until New Year's Day 1923. On the bottom are fine sculptures of generals Robert E. Lee, Thomas "Stonewall" Jackson, T.R.R. Cobb, and William H.T. Walker. The monument rests on a stepped 22-feet square base of Georgia granite. Dedicated on Oct. 31, 1878, the monument cost $17,313.35, a very large sum in those days. Alexander Stephens was in Augusta for the ceremony, but was too sick to attend. A grand parade was held with many battle-scarred regiments and dignitaries, including Stonewall Jackson's widow and then governor, Gen. Alfred Colquitt. Gen. Clement A. Evans spoke, the first recorded appear-

Above, Augusta's Confederate Memorial. Below, General's Walk at Magnolia Cemetery.

ance of the "Reverend General" who would be speaking at monument dedications in Georgia for the next 30 years. On one side is perhaps the most common inscription on Georgia's Confederate monuments, first used here in Augusta: "No Nation Rose so White and Fair: None Fell So Pure of Crime."

The first monument in Richmond County to Confederate soldiers is in Green Street Park, a **20-foot obelisk** erected in 1873 to memorialize 24 Sunday School members killed in the War. On the shaft and on its base are an additional 290 names of Richmond County war dead.

Magnolia Cemetery

⊞ R.I.P. 🏃 GI

702 Third St., Augusta

East of the city in Olde Town.

Established in 1816, this 60-acre **cemetery** contains the remains of 337 Confederates buried near a fountain, who are believed to have died of battle wounds or disease in the five

hospitals located in Augusta. To the middle left of the fountain are the graves of four unknown soldiers. Directly behind this section are the graves of Capt. G.W. Rus and Lt. N.E. Levy, both who died at the Crater at Petersburg, Virginia. The **General's Walk**, located to the right of the Confederate Cemetery, has seven headstones and a plaque which memorializes seven Confederate generals whose graves are interspersed throughout the cemetery, which is tied with Oakland in Atlanta

and second to Laurel Grove in Savannah for most generals. The generals buried in Magnolia Cemetery are Edward P. Alexander, Goode Bryan, V.J.B. Girardey, J.K. Jackson, William D. Smith, Marcellus A. Stovall, and Ambrose R. Wright. To the left of the General's Walk are the graves of 13 Union soldiers. The fortified east wall of the cemetery has patches where cannon were once placed.

Richmond Academy
Presbyterian Church
Woodrow Wilson House
Springfield Baptist Church

ⓗ 🏠 GI

Academy: 540 Telfair St., Augusta
Presbyterian Church: 642 Telfair St., Augusta
House: 419 7th St., Augusta 706-724-0436
Springfield Baptist Church: 114 12th St. at Reynolds, Augusta 706-823-1056

The **Richmond Academy** is a Gothic Revival style structure completed in 1801, which served as the oldest chartered school south of Virginia. Lt. Gen. James Longstreet attended school here to prepare for West Point. The Academy was used as a Confederate hospital after Chickamauga in 1863 and was occupied by Federal troops until 1868. From 1930-95, it served as the Richmond County Museum. Beautiful **Presbyterian Church** was built in 1809, as designed by Robert Mills, the creator of the Washington Monument and U.S. Treasury Building in Washington, D.C. The church was used as a hospital and temporary prisoner of war camp during the Civil War, and its pastor from 1858-70, an ardent secessionist, was the Rev. Joseph R. Wilson, the father of President Woodrow Wilson. The future president's boyhood home is under renovation and is available for tour. As a boy, Wilson saw Confederate President Jefferson Davis and his retinue taken through Augusta en route to prison at the end of the War. **Springfield Baptist Church**, founded in 1787, is believed to be the oldest independent black church on its original site in the U.S. The church was formed for blacks, by blacks, and was a place of worship for "free slaves." In 1866, the Georgia Equal Rights Association was founded at Springfield, as was Morehouse College in 1867.

At top right, First Presbyterian Church, Augusta. Above, Gen. William H.T. Walker on the Augusta Confederate Memorial.

Richmond County Museum &
Morris Museum of Art

ⓜ GI

Richmond Co. Museum: 560 Reynolds St., Augusta 706-722-8454
Morris Museum: No. 1 Tenth St. at Riverwalk, Augusta 706-724-7501

The new history **museum**, scheduled to open in Feb., 1996, has displays on Augusta's Civil War history, including uniforms, weaponry, photos, paintings and a mural depicting Sherman's "March to the Sea." The new art museum has a gallery featuring Civil War art.

Old Medical College

ⓗ 🏠 GI

598 Telfair St., Augusta 706-721-7238 (Alumni Center)
Olde Town.

This Greek Revival building, designed by nationally renowned Georgia architect, Charles B. Cluskey, was the first medical school in Georgia, completed by 1835. It was used as a Confederate hospital during the War. Tours by appointment.

Fort Gordon Army Signal Corps
Museum

ⓜ GI

Ave. of the States and 36th St., Building 36301, Fort Gordon 706-791-2818
Off U.S. 1 near Augusta.

The U.S. **Army Signal Museum** offers one of the most complete and comprehensive collections of communications material in existence in the U.S. The U.S. Signal Corps, a separate branch of the army born of necessity during the Civil War on March 3, 1863, played a key role in the conflict through the use of wig-wag flags, signal balloons, and telegraphs. The Battle of Kennesaw Mountain is reportedly the first time an army used telegraphs to communicate between generals for the movement of troops. Civil War exhibits include the personal items of Albert J. Myer, the father of the Signal Corps and inventor of the wig-wag system of communication, a beardslee Magneto, Confederate Signal Corp items, and other artifacts and displays.

Harper's Weekly

Museum of Washington County
The Brown House

🏛 🏠 ✕ 🪦 🏚 🖼 GI JDR MTS

Museum: 129 Jones St., Sandersville 912-552-6965 House: 270 N. Harris St., Sandersville 912-552-6965 (Museum of Washington Co.)

Museum is on the west side of the courthouse square.

Washington County, created in 1784, claims to be the first county named for George Washington. It was located on the stagecoach route between Louisville and Milledgeville before the advent of railroads, and became an important cotton producing county in the 19th century, with a short railroad spur connecting it to the Central Railroad at Tennille. Sandersville suffered when Gen. W.T. Sherman and his entire Left Wing marched into town early in the morning on Nov. 26, 1864, but it almost was worse. His Left Wing had split after Milledgeville, but now it converged on two separate roads just outside of town. The night before, C.S. Gen. Joe Wheeler's cavalry had galloped into town with 13 prisoners, a dozen of which he placed in an improvised barrack in a store and one which was taken to the Methodist parsonage and placed in the care of the Rev. J.D. Anthony. Around midnight, an unknown vigilante mob subdued Wheeler's sentries, seized the prisoners, and took them out to a field, and shot them. Local citizens, fearing Sherman's wrath, quickly buried the bodies before sunrise. The next morning, Wheeler's cavalry briefly skirmished with the Union troops as they approached the town, firing from the court house and other buildings, before saddling up and heading out in the opposite direction.

When Sherman reached town and learned of the skirmish and execution of Federal prisoners, he decided to burn the town of 500 to the ground. The Rev. J.D. Anthony pleaded with the General to spare the town, asserting that Confederate vagabonds killed the prisoners, and Wheeler's men — not the town — fired on Federal troops. The Rev. Anthony informed Sherman that only four men — three old and feeble — were left in town, the rest of the citizens were women and children. (Of Washington County's 1,460 eligible men, 1,502 signed up in 15 different Confederate companies (some signing up twice), perhaps the best record in the Georgia and maybe the South.) Something the Rev. Anthony said must have convinced Sherman, because he only burned the courthouse and downtown district, four cotton warehouses, and destroyed track. Worse, his men looted the county of all available food, creating hardship for the Georgians. But they were spared their homes. On Nov. 27, the Left Wing left town moving toward Louisville, and Sherman switched to the Right Wing in Tennille. Jefferson Davis, in his flight at the end of the War, arrived in Sandersville about noon on May 6, 1865, where the last official business of the Confederate States Treasury was transacted.

Top, Union infantry enter town next to the Masonic building in Sandersville. Middle, Washington County Confederate veterans gather in front of the Masonic building April 26, 1915. Bottom, the Brown House.

Today, you can visit the **county museum**, located in an 1891 sheriff's house and jail, which has on display the couch Sherman slept on the night he stayed in Sandersville; a trunk belonging to William G. Brown (veteran of Gettysburg, The Wilderness, Spotsylvania, Cold Harbor, and many other battles), who owned the house Sherman used as his headquarters in Sandersville; and many other interesting Civil War artifacts. In 1989, the Washington County Historical Society purchased the **Brown House**, circa 1854, and is renovating it now with plans to move the museum into this historic home. A **monument** to Jared Irwin of Washington County, an early governor, is located in front of the current courthouse and reportedly bears scars from the firefight when Sherman came to town. An unmarked, bricked over **tomb** in the old **city cemetery** reportedly contains the remains of the executed Yankee prisoners. Note the old roadbed in the cemetery where the Union marched into town. The Historical Society has a guide to Sandersville with 36 historic sites, and another guide to the homes designed by architect Charles E. Choate.

WAYNESBORO & LOUISVILLE

THE ACTIVITIES IN THIS AREA INvolved the crossing of the Ogeechee River — the last major natural barrier before Savannah — by Sherman's Left Wing on his "March to the Sea," and a series of running cavalry battles between C.S. Gen. Joe Wheeler and U.S. Gen. Judson Kilpatrick, known as the Battle of Waynesboro. Sherman's plan was to feign at Macon with his Right Wing and feign at Augusta with his Left Wing, causing Confederates to organize defenses there, and meanwhile march to Savannah to resupply his 60,000 troops. The first duty of Kilpatrick's cavalry was to protect the Right Wing and convince Confederates they were moving on Macon. In doing this, he encountered Wheeler's cavalry in a series of light skirmishes. When the Right Wing was past Macon and on its way to Savannah,

Kilpatrick was ordered to circuit the Left Wing to the north and ride to Camp Lawton, a huge Confederate prison near Millen, to free the prisoners there, and threaten toward Augusta, creating the illusion that it was the next Federal objective. On his way to Millen, Kilpatrick had been bested in a series of hot cavalry fights with Wheeler in Burke County from Nov. 25-28, 1864, then he retreated to Louisville. When he returned, he brought two brigades of infantry from the Left Wing, and drove Wheeler north out of Waynesboro in battles from Dec. 2-4. Union bummers destroyed the town before Sherman's Left Wing marched through the county. In Augusta, only 25 miles north of Waynesboro, C.S. Gen. Braxton Bragg waited with 10,000 men for Sherman's approach, which never came, as the Left Wing and Kilpatrick turned to their true objective of Savannah. Today, Waynesboro has a **county museum** with Civil War artifacts; a

county **monument** to the Confederates, memorializing the dead in the city cemetery; and a historic **plantation home** which was the site of a cavalry skirmish. The **Burke County Courthouse**, guarded by Civil War cannon, dates to 1857. It was partially destroyed by Kilpatrick's men but repaired. In Louisville stands reportedly Georgia's only remaining **slave market**, built between 1795-98. Known as the Market House, this fascinating, hand-hewn oak structure bore witness to many public economic events, including the sale of cotton, property, and slaves. The bell in the cupola was cast in France in 1772 and bound for a New Orleans Convent, when it was hijacked by pirates and sold in Savannah. The Market House stands in a square that was the hub of transportation routes when the State Capital was located here from 1794 to 1807. Louisville was the home of noted statesman, Sen. Herschel V. Johnson.

Burke County Museum

🏠 🏛 GI MTS

536 Liberty St., Waynesboro 706-554-4889

U.S. 25/GA 121 to Waynesboro turns into Liberty St. Museum is one block south of the courthouse square.

The **county museum** is located in the antebellum home just off the main square. Civil War artifacts include cannonballs, shotguns that Gen. Sherman's men used, and a historic photograph of the first group of men to leave Burke County to fight for the South.

Confederate Memorial Cemetery

HM R.I.P. 🏴 GI MTS

GA 24/Sixth St. and Jones St., Waynesboro

Three blocks west of the courthouse square.

The **cemetery** has the remains of 45 Confederate soldiers who died fighting Sherman's men in Burke County. Twelve are unknown. In the center of the graves is the Burke County **Confederate Monument**, a 15-foot shaft made of granite, dedicated on April 26, 1878, at the cost of $375.

Bellevue Plantation

HM 🏠 ⚔ R.I.P. MTS

Old Buckhead Church Rd., Burke County

Three miles west of U.S. 25 on Old Buckhead Church Rd.

This historic **plantation home**, established from a royal grant from King George III in 1767,

was the scene of a cavalry skirmish Nov. 27-28, 1864, between Wheeler and Kilpatrick's cavalry, as Wheeler pushed the Federals back from Waynesboro. The private residence, believed to be built in the 1760s, has three holes made from minie balls fired during the battle. The soldiers who died here were buried behind the house. The Union dead remain, but the Confederates were reinterred in the **Waynesboro Confederate Memorial Cemetery**.

Confederate Cavalry great Gen. Joseph Wheeler, also known as "Fightin' Joe" and the "War Child."

MILLEN

Camp Lawton/Magnolia Springs State Park

HM 🚂 🏛 GI MTS

U.S. 25, Millen 912-982-1660

Located 5 miles north of Millen on U.S. 25. One hour south of Augusta.

Camp Lawton, a huge prisoner of war camp occupying 40 acres and designed to hold 40,000 men, was built in September, 1864 to relieve congestion at Camp Sumter at Andersonville and to remove the possibility of Gen. W.T. Sherman's army freeing prisoners there. Built by a force of 300 prisoners and 500 slaves, the camp was a log stockade, with guard towers on the walls, and a ditch dug within the walls for a deadline. On high ground surrounding the prison, three earthen forts were excavated and armed with cannon to prevent escape and guard from attacks. One of the reasons the prison was located here was the large, pure spring, which could supply ample water to the prisoners; and the second reason involved the Augusta Railroad, located one mile from the camp. If the camp was threatened, prisoners could be loaded on trains and moved north to Augusta or south to Savannah, and to other points from there.

The first prisoners began arriving in October, 1864. By November, 10,299 were held here.

On Nov. 25, 1864, the camp was abandoned in advance of Sherman's "March to the Sea," and the prisoners were first sent to other camps, including temporary ones in Blackshear and Thomasville, Georgia, then back to Andersonville. The camp was not much better than Andersonville, and more than 700 prisoners died of disease, exposure, and malnutrition in the brief time it was open. When the Left Wing entered the prison, they were enraged at the conditions they found there, including a long, freshly filled pit with a board that read, "650 Buried Here."

The Left Wing burned the stockade. Today, the spring is the site of **Magnolia Springs Park**. The **earthworks** remain and **historical markers** outside and inside the park tell part of the story. The railroad town of Millen had a beautiful depot and hotel which were burned when Sherman's men came through on Dec. 3, 1864. The local Chamber of Commerce, located in the new depot, built in 1915, has a large picture of the prison, various displays, and a historical tour guide to homes in the county.

Buckhead Church

HM 🏠 ✕ MTS

State Route 81, Perkins

Heading south from Waynesboro on U.S. 25, go right at Perkins on S.R. 81 for 4 miles.

Big **Buckhead Church**, named for Buckhead Creek which flows east of the building, was the scene of another one of the Wheeler/Kilpatrick cavalry fights on Nov. 28, 1864 during Sherman's "March to the Sea." This was the site of a Confederate victory. Kilpatrick crossed a nearby bridge, burned it, and defended the other side. Wheeler moved farther up the creek to cross, and pushed the Federals back toward Louisville, where Kilpatrick came under the protection of the Left Wing. The current building is the fourth church built on this site, the first being a log cabin in 1787, and the present one being built in the 1830s.

Above, Magnolia Springs. At left, Buckhead Church.

The Magnolia Midlands witnessed Sherman's March in 1864, when his men came through Screven and Bulloch counties on their way to Savannah; and this region has two of the most unique sites in Georgia: **Jefferson Davis' capture site and Museum** and the "Yank-Reb" town of **Fitzgerald**, founded by Union veterans in the heart of Dixie 30 years after the Civil War. In **Sylvania,** Robbins Mill is located, which still operates every first and third Saturday using only the power provided by a nearby pond. The mill was first built at this location in 1807, was destroyed by Sherman's troops and was eventually rebuilt. The Magnolia Midlands, in southeast central Georgia, is a traditional southern area of rich farmlands, beautiful rivers, and friendly small towns. **Plantation Trace**, in the southwest corner of Georgia, is famous for its beautiful plantations and productive farmlands. This area was the breadbasket of the Confederacy, with its rich, rolling agricultural land helping to feed its armies. There are few major Civil War sites here, but the area witnessed the building of a Confederate battleship at Saffold, Early County, a temporary Confederate **prison camp** and **cemetery** at Thomasville, a **fort, hospitals** and **cemeteries** at Albany, Cuthbert, and Fort Gaines, **cemeteries** at Quitman and Colquitt County (at Greenfield Church), and the **last surviving Confederate flagpole** in Blakely.

One of Fitzgerald's local artists painted this portrait to represent the city's unique history. The painting, which hangs in the Blue and Gray Museum, became the city seal.

Top, a photograph of "Fitzgerald In Shacktown Days" taken in 1895. Middle, a mortar and pestle on display in the Blue and Gray Museum. Bottom, this painting, on display in the Blue and Gray Museum, represents the spirit of unity behind the founding of Fitzgerald.

FITZGERALD

Blue and Gray Museum

HM 🏛 GI

Municipal Building, Fitzgerald 912-423-5375

I-75 to Fitzgerald exit (exit 28), east apx. 30 miles to town. Museum is parallel to railroad tracks in the old depot off West Central Ave.

Nothing happened in **Fitzgerald** during the Civil War because the town didn't exist, but what happened here after the War makes it unusual, and a Civil War site. Fitzgerald has one of the most unique founding stories in the history of the U.S. A **historical marker** titled "Fitzgerald, The Colony City," tells the story well: *Founded at Swan in 1895 by Mr. Philander H. Fitzgerald, lawyer, veteran and publisher of the American Tribune of Indianapolis, as a soldier's colony in the South. Fitzgerald was settled by Union veterans who, tired of Northern winters, flocked from 38 states and two territories to this benign and fertile land which, only 30 years before, had been deep in enemy territory. In the early 90s, devastating droughts had impoverished the farmers of the Mid-West and Georgians had sent trainloads of food to relieve their plight. Impressed, Mr. Fitzgerald conceived his plan and formed the American Tribune Soldiers Colony Company, (non-profit). Despite offers from neighboring states, the Company chose this site, acquired 50,000 acres of land, and laid out a town. By December, 5,000 colonists had*

arrived. The next fall, the schools opened with 501 pupils, the first in Georgia to offer free tuition and texts and a nine-month term. On Dec. 2, 1896, Fitzgerald was incorporated and elected officials took charge. With principal streets named to honor the great leaders of both armies, and with Confederate veterans joining their former enemies in this unique community endeavor, Fitzgerald has symbolized through the years an enduring unity born of that unfailing respect which brave men hold for each other. The town has always been progressive and pro-development, and it quickly grew, building businesses and a 1,200 seat opera house.

The idea of unity was evident among the colonists not only in their street names but in other ways as well. The town was maybe the only one in the U.S. which observed two memorial days, Confederate and Union. When the town built a four-story, 150 room hotel — the largest wooden structure in the state at that time — they named it the Lee-Grant. When Fitzgerald carved out of the frontier a county for itself, it named it Ben Hill for the famous Civil War orator and Confederate.

The aptly named **Blue & Gray Museum** tells the story of Fitzgerald and has an excellent collection of Civil War artifacts, including a Medal of Honor; the Confederate Flag used to drape the coffin of Georgia's last surviving Confederate veteran, a Fitzgerald resident; and a mortar and pestle of Jefferson Davis' doctor, captured with him in nearby **Irwinville**. Be sure to tour the town and see if you can guess which Civil War generals were honored in the Yank-Reb City. At 608 West Suwannee, is **Gen. William J. Bush's home,**

the last survivor of the 125,000 Georgians who fought for the South. He died in 1952 at the age of 107.

IRWINVILLE

Jefferson Davis Memorial Park and Museum

HM 🏛 🐾 GI JDR WR

Jeff Davis Hwy., Irwinville 912-831-2335

I-75 South to Irwinville exit, exit 26. Go east on GA 32 apx. 15 miles to Irwinville. At caution light, turn left and travel apx. 1 mile.

Confederate President Jefferson Davis was captured near Irwinville on the morning of May 10, 1865, the final major event of the Civil War. Had Davis — who discussed fighting on with remnants of the Confederate army in the trans-Mississippi Department — escaped as he had planned, there may have been more history to write. Davis was making his way south across Georgia, pursued by a detachment of Wilson's cavalry which had recently received the surrender of Macon. He reunited with his family in Dublin on May 7 and travelled to Abbeville where he camped on May 8. The next day he travelled to Irwinville, unaware that his pursuers were close behind, and camped there with his staff for the night. A detachment of Wilson's cavalry quietly surrounded him that evening and

Jefferson Davis monument in Irwinville.

waited for dawn. The next morning a separate detachment of cavalry, in a mix-up, rode in to seize Davis, and a skirmish broke out between two sets of Union troops, killing two and wound-

ing four before they realized their mistake.

Davis had heard the firing just before daylight, and snatched up his wife's cloak by mistake as he left the tent and ran to a horse. Just as he reached the reins, a Federal officer yelled, "Halt!" As Davis turned to look at the soldier, his wife Varina ran up to him and threw her arms around him, fearing he would resist and be shot. In all the confusion, not a single Confederate gun was fired. U.S. Lt. Col. B.D. Pritchard rode up and reportedly said, "Well old Jeff, we've got you at last." The Confederacy was dead.

The **Jefferson Davis Museum** has many fine artifacts and displays relating to the capture and Confederacy, including a battle flag and other items. In the **park**, which consists of almost 13 acres, you find various **plaques**, **historical markers**, and picnic tables. But the main feature is a **12-foot high memorial** to the captured president, featuring a bronze bust of Davis on a granite base of Oglesby granite. An engraving on the side of the monument shows the moment of his capture with Davis in a cloak. U.S. Gen. James Wilson, in his report about the capture, wrote that Davis was wearing women's clothing when he tried to escape, a false rumor which delighted the Yankees and embarrassed Jeff Davis. The monument's sculptor was Laurence Tompkins, the great nephew of Robert Toombs, secretary of state in Jefferson Davis' first cabinet.

JESUP

Defense of the Altamaha Bridge

HM ⚔ ◎ MTS

Doctortown Rd., Jesup

Travel north out of Jesup on U.S. 301, and turn right on Doctortown Rd.

On Dec. 1, 1864, the Georgia Militia Fourth Brigade under Brig. Gen. H.K. McKay arrived in Wayne County to prepare a defense of the Savannah and Gulf Railroad bridge over the Altamaha River. The Rebels built earthworks on the north bank of Morgan's Lake, which is bisected by the railroad and located just north of the river. On the southern side of the river, two 32-pound rifled guns were mounted at Doctortown (also spelled Doctor Town), to sweep the bridge if attacked. A light gun mounted on an engine supported two companies of Confederates at Morgan's Lake. On Dec. 16, Gen. W.T. Sherman, stalled outside Savannah, sent Union troops to destroy the railroad from the Ogeechee River all the way to the bridge. A brigade of Gen. Judson Kilpatrick's cavalry under Col. Smith Atkins attacked the bridge and destroyed trestlework past Morgan's Lake, but was unable to capture the bridge or

seize the Confederate battery at Doctortown on Dec. 19. The Yankees withdrew to the Ogeechee River. A **historical marker** (U.S. 301 on the north side of the river) stands near the location of the Confederate victory. Local legend states that the original **railroad bridge** from the battle still stands in Doctortown, but some

experts refute this. After the Civil War, one of the Rebel cannon used in the battle was spiked and loaded with a dangerous charge. It was defused and given to Waycross in 1887. Today, it stands in front of the Ware County **Confederate Monument** in Phoenix Park in Waycross.

The railroad trestle was the site of a Rebel victory during the Civil War. The ironwork at left is an old drawbridge which would raise to allow steamboat paddlewheelers to pass.

THOMASVILLE/FORT GAINES/ ALBANY/CUTHBERT/BLAKELY/ COLQUITT CO./QUITMAN

Thomasville Prison Camp & Cemeteries

 GI

Prison Camp: Wolf St., Thomasville
Old City Cemetery: Madison St. at Webster St., Thomasville
Laurel Hill Cemetery: Hwy. 319 (E. Jackson St.), Thomasville

I-75 South to Hwy. 319 to Thomasville.

Thomasville, founded in the 1820s, was a popular health resort town where wealthy Northerners gathered to avoid the yellow fever and malaria epidemics common to lowland areas. Northerners enjoyed the high elevation, southern climate, and fertile land and bought up huge tracts of land and established fabulous plantations. When the Panama Canal was built and the cause of these diseases discovered, Thomasville lost its appeal as these lessons were applied to lowland areas. The beautiful plantations, farms, and homes remain in Thomasville, many open to tours, including the beautiful 1820 **Pebble Hill Plantation**. A historic walking/driving tour, with 59 sites, is available from the **Visitors Center**.

During the Civil War, Thomasville was the last stop west on the Atlantic and Gulf Railroad line running southwest from Savannah. Fearing a raid on Camp Sumter prison camp at Andersonville, Confederate authorities decided to establish a temporary camp in Thomasville. The **camp** was a 5-acre square bounded by a ditch six to eight feet deep and 10 to 12 feet wide, which was dug by slaves. The second week of December, 1864, as Gen. W.T. Sherman knocked on the gates of Savannah, 5,000 Union prisoners were brought here from Blackshear. When Sherman occupied Savannah on Dec. 20, the camp was evacuated and the prisoners marched north to Albany, entrained, and rode back to Andersonville, where they arrived on Christmas Eve, 1864. A **historical marker** stands near the prison grounds, and **lines of the trench** can be seen. While in Thomasville, several hundred prisoners died of disease, malnutrition, and exposure, and they were buried in a mass grave in the **Old City Cemetery**. Established 1842, this cemetery contains the graves of 38 Confederate soldiers, many unusually adorned with scallop shells pressed into concrete. The first black graduate of West Point and former Thomasville slave, Henry O. Flipper, is interred here. Buried in **Laurel Hill Cemetery** in Thomasville is Confederate General

John C. Vaughn, who commanded C.S. Gen. John Hunt Morgan's forces after their surrender and was Confederate President Jefferson Davis' escort through Georgia until his capture in Irwinville. Also in this cemetery is a statue called **Judgment**, which first had its home in Savannah as part of the Chatham County memorial, but was rejected by art critics and transported to Thomasville.

Fort Gaines was the location of a Confederate fort, hospitals, and cemetery. A lively walking tour of Fort Gaines is available on weekdays at the Clay County Library, 208 S. Hancock St., and daily at the George T. Bagby State Park (GA Hwy. 39). The frontier town and fort were first established and garrisoned on a bluff overlooking the Chattahoochee River in 1814. It was manned twice more, during the Indian Uprising of 1836 and the Civil War in 1863 to protect Columbus from invasion by river. An original **Civil War cannon**, in its original position, marks the site of the Confederate fort on Bluff St. near the river. The **McRae House**, at 103 Jefferson Street, served as barracks for Confederate officers stationed here. The **Brown Cottage**, at 108 Jefferson Street, was the home of James Mason Brown, who left this house to fight for the Confederacy at the age of 14. At the end of the War, Brown rode a train from Virginia to Atlanta, standing up the whole way, then walked 180 miles from Atlanta to Fort Gaines, and fell asleep on the porch, refusing to let his family touch him because he didn't want them exposed to lice and germs. The next day, he burned his clothes, shaved all the hair from his body, and bathed. Then the family had a joyous reunion. The **Wayside Home**, at 106 Commerce Street, was a temporary hospital used after the Battle of Olustee in North Florida. Nine unknown Confederate dead are buried in **New Park Cemetery**.

In **Albany** seven unknown soldiers are buried in Riverside/Oakview Cemetery (200 Cotton Ave.). The graves stand next to the city's Confederate monument. In **Cuthbert's Greenwood Cemetery**, located on Hamilton Ave., an estimated 24 Confederate dead are buried. Most died in local hospitals between 1863 and 1865. On the courthouse lawn in **Blakely** (U.S. 27) stands the **last original Confederate flag staff** still standing in Georgia. It was hauled to Blakely by a yoke of oxen and erected in 1861. There were no battles fought in **Colquitt County** but the **Greenfield Church** was used as a hospital. Today there is an unconfirmed **Confederate cemetery** at Greenfield Church (GA 133 south of Moultrie to the Pavo Rd. to Greenfield Church Rd.). White crosses mark the graves of 75-100 unknown soldiers. The 17 unknown soldiers buried in **Quitman** are a mystery. They are believed to be Confederate soldiers who rode the train as far as Quitman on their way to the Battle of Olustee in Florida. They died mysteriously, probably in a skirmish or as a result of disease, and were buried in the **West End Cemetery** (U.S. 84).

VALDOSTA

Lowndes Co. History Museum

GI

305 W. Central Ave., Valdosta 912-247-4780

Take GA 38/U.S. 84 into Valdosta. Turn left onto Toombs St. and left onto Central Ave.

This **museum** has a section devoted to the county's role in supporting the Confederacy during the Civil War, including uniforms, weapons, and documents. A Civil War memorial is found on the courthouse lawn.

The Lowndes County Confederate Monument and Courthouse in Valdosta.

The Colonial Coast is dominated by the Civil War history found in and around historic and beautiful Savannah. With Richmond, Charleston, Mobile and New Orleans, Savannah was a premier city of the Confederacy, and is a major historic treasure today. Located on a bluff on the Savannah River, the town's fortunes were based on cotton commerce and trade. Early in the War, Georgians seized Federal **Fort Pulaski**, located at the mouth of the river, on Jan. 3, 1861, only to see it fall to big Union guns on Tybee Island on April 11, 1862. Savannah's next big Civil War event was preparing for Gen. W.T. Sherman's armies, which marched across the state from Atlanta to seize the city on Dec. 21, 1864. Darien, located at one of the channels of the Altamaha River, saw some of the first action by black troops stationed on St. Simons Island. Today, the best Civil War sites in the Colonial Coast travel region include **Fort Pulaski National Monument**; the entire historic district of Savannah including the **Green-Meldrim House**; **Fort McAllister State Historic Site**; and **Fort Jackson**. At Midway, a **museum**, **historic church**, and **cemetery** are well worth the trip. A **historical marker** in Blackshear marks the location of a temporary **prison camp**. The Colonial Coast features unforgettable scenery, including hundreds of miles of coastal plain drained by scenic rivers which flow into lush, fertile salt marshes, protected by Georgia's beautiful golden isles.

Top, the Confederate Monument in Savannah's Forsyth Park. Bottom, Fort Jackson.

SAVANNAH IS ONE OF AMERICA'S great cities and is rich with history from the colonial days to the present. During the Civil War, it was one of the most important cities for the Confederacy, and the goal of Gen. W.T. Sherman's army as he marched to the sea to resupply his men in late 1864. Today it boasts more than 1,200 historic structures, 20 beautiful squares, and much, much more. You can begin your tour by going to the **Savannah Visitors Center**. Several days are needed to see all the area has to offer. There are some general Civil War sites not to be missed. **Factors Walk**, located along the river bluff on Bay St., was a 19th century meeting place and center of commerce for cotton merchants. It looks much like it did when Sherman's men occupied the town. The **Andrew Low House**, 329 Abercorn St., was built in 1848 by a wealthy cotton merchant whose son married Juliette Magill Gordon, founder of the Girl Scouts. The home hosted Robert E. Lee, Union generals, and many other famous people. For tour information, call 912-233-6854. The **Juliette Gordon Low birthplace** home, 142 Bull St. is also available to tour. Low, as a young girl, is said to have told U.S. Gen. O.O. Howard, who was missing an arm, "I shouldn't wonder if my papa did it!

He's shot lots of Yankees!" Sherman visited many times. 912-233-4501. The **Olde Pink House**, 23 Abercorn St., 912-232-4286, was built in 1771 and used as a headquarters for Union General York. Today it is a restaurant and tavern. The **Sorrel-Weed House**, 1840, at Harris St. in Madison Square, was the home of G. Moxley Sorrel, who won fame as one of Lee's lieutenants. Sorrel became brigadier general at age 26 and was called the "best staff officer in the Confederate Service." At Bull and Taylor Streets in Monterey Square is the **Comer House**, where Jefferson Davis was a guest in 1886 for the celebration of the cen-

Top, Savannah's riverfront during the Civil War, photographed by George N. Barnard. Bottom, Savannah's riverfront today.

tennial of the Chatham Artillery, during which many parties and celebrations were held. Union Army headquarters for Howard were at Bull St. at Gaston St., named the **Jackson House** for Henry Jackson, a brigadier general for the Confederacy.

After the War, **Gen. Joe Johnston** worked and lived in Savannah at 105 E. Oglethorpe Ave., and was visited by many luminaries of the Civil War, including Robert E. Lee, shortly before Lee's death. A marker on the home commemorates this fact. **Forsyth Park** (Bull St. between Gaston St. and Park Ave.), a 20-acre park laid out in 1851, was a campground for Union soldiers during the occupation of Savannah. A huge **Civil War memorial**, one of the largest in the South and the most expensive in the state, is located in the park, honoring Chatham's war dead. With thousands of citizens present, the monument was unveiled in 1875, with a statue called "Judgment" on the top and a statue called "Silence" in a cupola. The reaction to the memorial was negative, so a philanthropist stepped forward and the memorial was "fixed" and unveiled a second time in 1879, at a total cost of $35,000. A soldier was on top, the cupola was bricked up, "Silence" was sent to Laurel Grove Cemetery in Savannah, and "Judgment" was sent to Thomasville.

Fort Jackson

🏛 ⚔ ⚓ 🚂 🏛 GI MTS

1 Fort Jackson Rd., Savannah 912-232-3945

From Savannah, go east on Bay St. to President St. Ext. towards Tybee Island apx. 2.5 miles from town. Turn left at sign for Fort Jackson.

Fort Jackson, one of the interior brick forts guarding Savannah's river approach during the Civil War, was never taken by naval vessels. Today, the nation's oldest standing brick fort houses a museum featuring the naval history of the area and artifacts from the C.S.S. *Georgia*, scuttled 300 yards away in the Savannah River by evacuating Confederates on Dec. 20, 1864. A red buoy in the river marks the location of Georgia's first ironclad. When Union troops under Sherman first seized Savannah, they occupied Fort Jackson and raised Old Glory over the fort. The iron-ram C.S.S. *Savannah*, displeased with this display, fired on the Federal troops from the river. The fort has 20-foot high walls, a nine-foot deep moat, and it held nine cannon, including a 32-pounder, the largest blackpowder cannon still fired in the U.S. Fort construction began in 1808 under President Thomas Jefferson's administration, and the fort was inspected by Gen. Robert E. Lee and C.S. President Jefferson Davis during the Civil War.

Green-Meldrim House

🏛 🏠 GI MTS

St. John's Church, 14 West Macon St., Savannah 912-233-3845

Downtown Savannah at Madison Square.

This Gothic Revival style **home**, built in 1853 at the princely sum of $93,000, served as the headquarters of Gen. W.T. Sherman from Dec. 22, 1864 to Feb. 1, 1865. Charles Green, an English immigrant and cotton trader who made his fortune with Andrew Low & Company in Savannah, was in Europe in 1861 when the War began. Making his way back to the U.S. through Canada, he was arrested in Detroit, charged with spying, and sent to Fort Warren prison in Boston Harbor for three months. When released, he returned to Savannah.

In December of 1864, when Sherman occupied the town, Green offered his home, considered to be the town's finest, to the General, thinking this would spare it the treatment others had received at the hands of Sherman's army. Sherman accepted, and his men did not disturb Green's possessions. From here, Sherman sent his famous message to President Lincoln, reprinted in many newspapers of the day: "I beg to present to you as a Christmas gift, the City of Savannah with 140 heavy guns and plenty of ammunition and also about 25,000 bales of cotton." While Sherman stayed here, he learned of the death of his son Charles, whom he'd never seen, and planned his march through South Carolina. After the War, Sherman returned to Savannah and stayed again at Green's home. This National Historic Landmark has many fascinating features and is open for tours.

Savannah Visitors Center & History Museum

🏛 🏠 🏛 GI MTS

301 Martin Luther King, Jr. Blvd., Savannah 912-944-0460

I-16 East until it ends in Savannah at Montgomery and Liberty Streets. Turn left onto Liberty St.

This is the place to start your visit to Savannah. The **Visitors Center and Museum** are housed in the former building of the Central of Georgia Railroad Station, Georgia's first railroad and the first chartered railroad in the U.S. It is located on the ground of an important Revolutionary War battle. Inside are trained personnel, tour guides, brochures and other information, along with a local history museum with displays on the Civil War, a film, and a bookstore. Outside are a variety of tour companies, using transportation ranging from horse-drawn carriages to air-conditioned buses.

Top, an aerial view of Fort Jackson. Middle, the Green-Meldrim House, Sherman's Savannah headquarters. Bottom, the Savannah Visitors Center and History Museum's copy of native Georgian and defender of Savannah Gen. William J. Hardee's book, *Rifle and Light Infantry Tactics,* the classic West Point training manual used by both sides during the Civil War.

Fort Pulaski National Monument & Tybee Lighthouse

⌂ ✕ ▦ 🏛 GI

U.S. 80, Savannah 912-786-5787

From Savannah take U.S. 80 east toward Tybee Island for apx. 15 miles to park entrance.

On Jan. 3, 1861 in one of the first military actions of the Civil War, Georgia troops under Alexander Lawton bloodlessly seized **Fort Pulaski** from two Federal caretakers. Fifteen months later, a military lesson would be learned here about rifled cannon and brick forts which would effect the way war was fought for the next century. The fort had been built as a response to lessons learned during the War of 1812, which proved America's ports were easy targets for enemy navies. Savannah's main fort was built on Cockspur Island at the mouth of the Savannah River, 15 miles downstream from Savannah. When construction began in 1829, one of the engineers was 2nd Lt. Robert E. Lee, fresh from graduation at West Point. Eighteen years, 25 million bricks, and a million dollars later, Fort Pulaski was born. With five faces 7 and 1/2 feet thick and 25-feet high, surrounded by a moat 48-feet wide, and armed with 39 guns, it was a formidable sight. Now two months before

Lincoln's inauguration, Georgia was seizing Federal military property. Col. Charles Olmstead, a 25-year-old, was commanding the fort on Oct. 29, 1861 when Robert E. Lee, after inspecting the fort and studying the Tybee shoreline almost a mile away, confidently told him that the fort was secure from cannon fire there. "They will make it pretty hot for you with shells, but they cannot breach your walls at that distance," he said.

On Nov. 24, 1861 having found Tybee evacuated, Federal troops landed and took possession of the island. A Union topographical engineer, Lt. James H. Wilson, who would return to Georgia in 1865 as a general leading 15,000 cavalry, had discovered channels in the marsh where Federals could cut around the fort and place guns upstream, effectively cutting the fort off from its supply base in Savannah. Meanwhile, Maj. Gen. Quincy Gillmore was struggling in the swampy muck of the marsh to secretly build 11 batteries and place 36 guns on Tybee so he could fire on the fort. This required incredible labor and engineering, all at night, with 250 men pulling each mortar weighing 8 and 1/2 tons into place. Part of his arsenal included the new James rifled cannon — two 84-pounders, two 64-pounders, and one 48-pounder. Finally, with the guns aimed on Pulaski, Gilmore asked for Olm-stead's surrender. Olmstead replied, "I am here to defend the fort, not surrender it." Minutes later on April

Top, the northwest wall of Fort Pulaski. Bottom, the Tybee Lighthouse.

10, 1862, Gilmore opened fire. The bombardment lasted 31 hours, hurling 5,275 shots and shells at the fort. The Union's rifled cannon started to break through the walls, threatening the powder magazine. At 2 p.m., April 11, Olmstead raised a white flag and surrendered his garrison of 385 men. After the fort was surrendered, it became a Federal stronghold, preventing Confederate use of Savannah as a seaport.

The destruction of Fort Pulaski marked the end of masonry fortifications, a radical change in the history of warfare. The fort today is a national park and one of the best Civil War sites to tour in the state. Living history events include a **Siege and Reduction Weekend**, sponsored annually on the weekend closest to the battle anniversary (April 10-11). Other living history programs take place on St. Patrick's Day, July 4, Labor Day, Veterans Day and Christmas. Call Fort Pulaski for details. You might want to tour the **Tybee Lighthouse**, located on Tybee Island, built in 1773. Confederates burned the interior wood stairs to prevent approaching Federals from using it, but Union troops rebuilt the stairs and watched the bombardment of Fort Pulaski from the top. **Fort Wimberly**, located at Wormsloe Plantation Historic Site on Skidaway Island, is a series of still visible **breastworks** and a large **earthen battery** used to guard a water approach to Savannah.

Scars left by Union cannon can still be seen on the east wall of Fort Pulaski, a testament to the effectiveness of rifled cannon.

Confederate Cemeteries: Laurel Grove & Bonaventure

Bonaventure: Wheaton St. to Bonaventure Rd., Savannah Laurel Grove: Old Ogeechee Rd., Savannah

Laurel Grove: From the Visitors Center, travel south down W. Broad (MLK Blvd.) and turn right onto Anderson St. Main gates will be straight ahead. Bonaventure: U.S. 80 (Victory Drive) East to Thunderbolt, turn left on Bonaventure Rd., cemetery on your right.

Savannah has more Confederate general graves than any other city in the state, with six at **Bonaventure Cemetery** and eight at **Laurel Grove Cemetery**. Laurel Grove, established in 1852, also has a large Confederate soldiers section with 1,500 soldiers (101 of whom died at Gettysburg), watched over by "Silence," the former Chatham Memorial statue. Laurel Grove was split into North and South sections by Interstate 16, and the Civil War interments are in the North section. Located in this cemetery are generals Francis Bartow, Jeremy F. Gilmer, Paul J. Harrison, Sr., Gilbert M. Sorrel, LaFayette McLaws, Peter McGlashan, Henry C. Wayne, and Edward C. Willis, along with Col. Charles Olmstead, who surrendered Fort Pulaski.

Gilmer was a military engineer who married a sister of C.S. Gen. E.P. Alexander; Harrison, whose son was also a general, fought with the Georgia Militia and was captured; McLaws fought in the Eastern Theater, at Chickamauga, and he commanded the district of Georgia during Sherman's "March to the Sea"; McGlashan

was Scottish and fought in the Eastern Theater and was captured at Sayler's Creek; Sorrel served with Longstreet and became a famous staff officer in the Eastern Theater; Wayne served with the Georgia Militia opposing Sherman; and Willis commanded in the Eastern Theater and was killed at Bethesda Church. Francis Bartow, a Savannah native, had since 1856 been a captain of a volunteer militia unit in Savannah known as the Oglethorpe Light Infantry. When the act authorizing the organization of Confederate troops was passed, he notified his troops and they were the first to sign up for the War. At the Confederate Congress, Bartow was chair-

"Silence" stands in Laurel Grove Cemetery.

man of the Committee of Military Affairs, and he was responsible for the gray color of Confederate uniforms. At the Battle of First Manassas, on July 21, 1861, he was leading his brigade when he was shot from his horse. Col. Lucius J. Gartrell, later to be a general, caught him and held him while he was dying. Bartow uttered his historic last words, "They have killed me, boys, but never give up the fight!" Cass County was renamed Bartow in his honor.

At Bonaventure, what some consider the most beautiful cemetery in the state, are buried Confederate generals Robert J. Anderson, Henry R. Jackson, Alexander R. Lawton, Hugh W. Mercer, Claudius C. Wilson, and Commodore Josiah Tattnall. Anderson commanded cavalry in the Atlanta Campaign under Wheeler; Jackson served in Western Virginia and Georgia; Lawton, president of the Augusta and Savannah Railroad, was educated at West Point and Harvard, and married the sister of Gen. E.P. Alexander. Until he was severely wounded at Sharpsburg, when his brigade lost 565 of 1,150 men, Lawton was the leader of the famous Lawton-Gordon-Evans brigade — one of the hardest fighting in the War — under Stonewall Jackson. When Lawton recovered, he became quartermaster general of the Confederate Army until the end of the War. After the War, he became president of the American Bar Association and was U.S. Minister to Austria. Mercer commanded in the Atlanta Campaign; Wilson commanded at Chickamauga and Chattanooga and died of disease in Ringgold 13 days after Missionary Ridge; Tattnall's naval record includes action in the War of 1812, the burning of the ironclad *Merrimack*, and the naval defense of Savannah.

Above, ancient cypress trees in Ebenezer Creek, the scene of a famous controversy when Union troops during Sherman's March abandoned recently freed slaves to pursing Confederates.

SPRINGFIELD

Ebenezer Creek & Jerusalem Church

🏛 🏠 🏛 GI MTS

GA 275, New Ebenezer

From Springfield go south on GA 21 to GA 275. Turn left and go apx. 5 miles to Jerusalem Church. Farther down GA 275 is a boat landing where Ebenezer Creek meets the Savannah River.

Located here was a town called New Ebenezer, settled by the Salzburgers, a persecuted Protestant sect which fled to Georgia from Austria in 1736. The town had 2,000 citizens when the British captured it in 1779. After the Revolutionary War, the Salzburgers moved away. Their old **church** remains, as does their **cemetery**. A **museum** nearby tells the story of the Salzburgers. During Sherman's "March to the Sea" on Dec. 8, 1864, Federal troops under Union Gen. Jefferson C. Davis filed across **Ebenezer Creek** and destroyed their pontoon bridge behind them, leaving behind over 600 slaves which had been following the army column. With Confederate cavalry under Wheeler approaching, many slaves panicked and drowned as they tried to flee by attempting to cross the creek. The creek today has some of the state's oldest trees, ancient cypress with huge swollen bases. Davis' men marched past the Salzburger Church on their way to Savannah.

King-Tisdell Cottage

🏠 🏛 GI

514 East Huntingdon St., Savannah 912-234-8000 (King-Tisdell Foundation)

In the southern part of the historic district, east of Forsyth Park.

Historic **King-Tisdell Cottage** has museum exhibits which interpret the history of blacks in Savannah and the surrounding islands, including documents which reveal the role blacks played during the Civil War. In Franklin Square next to City Market is the **First African Baptist Church**, 1859, which is reportedly the first brick building built by African Americans for their own use. Church membership was derived from the oldest black congregation in the U.S. (1788) at nearby Brampton Plantation.

RICHMOND HILL

Fort McAllister
State Historic Park

HM ✕ ⚓ 🚂 🏛 GI MTS

3894 Fort McAllister Rd., Richmond Hill 912-727-2339

Exit 15 off I-95, 10 miles east to site.

In sharp contrast to the strategic failure of the brick Fort Pulaski is the success of **Fort McAllister**, a Confederate earthwork fort on the bank of the Ogeechee River, which survived every attack from the sea. Fort McAllister defended the "back door" to Savannah for blockade runners. Built by Capt. John McCrady, the engineer who designed the defenses of Savannah, the fort survived seven attacks by Federal naval vessels, including ironclads, attempting to reduce the fort with the largest shells fired by a naval vessel in the Civil War. On Jan. 27, 1863, the *Montauk*, the second monitor-class ironclad constructed, led a five-ship armada up the Ogeechee to within 1,500 yards of the fort, and opened up its artillery. Captain John Warden, who had captained the original *Monitor* against the C.S.S. *Virginia* (or *Merrimack*) in the classic battle at Hampton Roads, Virginia, hurled 61, 15-inch shells at the fort over five hours. That night, the Confederates snuck out of their bomb proofs and filled the craters in with sand, making the fort as good as new. Frustrated, the Federals returned several other times, only to be disappointed with the results of their bombardment. Fort McAllister was to fall, however, to Gen. W.T. Sherman's men, who stormed the fort from the mainland on Dec. 13, 1864. Sherman, frustrated at the defenses of Savannah, was desperate to open up a supply line from the Ogeechee River for his hungry troops, but Fort McAllister was protecting the entrance to the river. The fort's big guns were trained on the river, and it was garrisoned by little more than 200 men. The Union had approximately 4,000 troops, which simply overran the fort's defenses and fought the Confederates hand-to-hand. "The fort was never surrendered, it was captured by overwhelming numbers," reported C.S. Maj. Georgia W. Anderson, who was in command of the fort. When C.S. Capt. Nicholas Clinch was called on to surrender during the assault, he responded with a blow from his sword, and hand-to-hand combat ensued, with Clinch going down only after three saber, six bayonet, and two gunshot wounds. Capture of this fort sealed the doom of Savannah, which was evacuated Dec. 19-20, 1864. Considered to be the best preserved earthwork fortification of the Confederacy, today the fort is a 1,700-acre **state park** thanks to preservation efforts by automobile industrialist Henry Ford, who had timber interests here and a home in Richmond Hill. A **museum** is located at the site, which has books and a video related to the history of the area. Beside the parking area are large pieces of **machinery** salvaged from the wreck of the *Nashville* (or *Rattlesnake*), a Confederate blockade runner which was sunk by the *Montauk*. A living history event, **The Civil War Soldier**, is held yearly on Labor Day weekend.

Top left, earthen mounds at Fort McAlister. Bottom and at right, heavy guns at Fort McAlister.

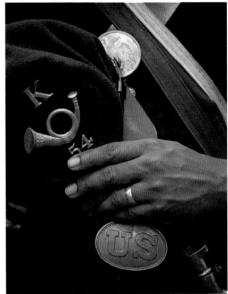

At left, the Altamaha River at sunset. At right, a reenactor from the U.S.C.T. Massachusetts 54th. Below, the Midway Church and cemetery.

DARIEN

The 54th Massachusetts

🏛️ ⊚ GI

Darien

I-95 to exit 10. Darien is south on U.S. 17.

Darien, established on the mighty Altamaha River in 1736 by Scottish Highlanders, saw some of the first action of black troops in the Civil War when Federals looted and burned the town "to the ground" on June 11, 1863. Involved in the action was the 2nd South Carolina and the Massachusetts 54th, the U.S.C.T. regiment commanded by 25-year-old Col. Robert Gould Shaw and made famous in the movie *Glory*. Darien was an important shipping port before the War, exporting cotton grown inland and rafted down the river. During the War, the port was used by blockade runners and consisted of 75 to 100 residences, including three churches, a market house, a courthouse, and an academy.

Shaw's troops, stationed on St. Simons Island June 10-24, 1863, were ordered to Darien by Col. James Montgomery. The next day, the town was looted and burned, with the light from the fires visible from St. Simons Island, 15 miles away. Col. Shaw, the son of a famous Boston abolitionist, did not approve of burning the town and wrote letters to superiors about his feelings on the matter. Twenty-five days after leading troops to Darien, Shaw would be dead and buried in a mass grave with many of his men. He led the Massachusetts 54th on a suicidal assault of Battery Wagner, South Carolina, forever proving the battle courage of black troops in U.S. history.

Darien recovered from the Civil War to become the second largest lumber shipping port on the southern coast from 1870-1910. When timber resources were depleted, Darien became what it is today, a fishing village. Thirty-two historic sites are featured in a driving tour available at the **Welcome Center**. The only remains from the Civil War days are some tabby ruins, constructed from 1815-30, near the river on the west side of the bridge at Broad Street. Darien was the birthplace of John McIntosh Kell, a famed Confederate naval officer, who was executive officer of the *Alabama* throughout its brilliant career, and was present at its sinking at the hands of the *Kearsarge* off Cherbourge, France.

MIDWAY

Midway Church & Museum

🏛️ 🏠 R.I.P. 🏛️ GI MTS

U.S. 17, Midway, 912-884-5837

Take exit 13 on I-95. Go west on U.S. 84 to U.S. 17. Go north four miles to Midway.

Midway Church is an excellent New England-looking structure that was built by Puritans in 1754, burned by the British during the Revolutionary War, and rebuilt in 1792. During Sherman's "March to the Sea," Union cavalry under Gen. Judson Kilpatrick occupied Midway and Sunbury, and Kilpatrick made his headquarters inside the church. His cavalry spent a month in Liberty County, destroying plantations and the railroad. Next to the church is **Midway Museum,** a replica of an 18th-century coastal cottage, which houses exhibits and materials about Midway's history, including exhibits and information on the Civil War period. Many famous figures came from or trace their descendants back to Midway, including Oliver Wendell Holmes, Samuel Morse, Theodore Roosevelt, Jr., and Woodrow Wilson. Across the street is **Midway Cemetery**, which contains the graves of a large number of distinguished persons. A walking tour is available from the museum. **Fort Morris Historic Site**, 912-884-5999, is located seven miles east on GA 38 from exit 13 off I-95. Here is Fort Morris, which saw action in the Revolutionary War and War of 1812. The fort was located near Sunbury, which briefly rivaled Savannah as a seaport, until the British burned the town. Kilpatrick and his cavalry visited the town in 1864, burning a historic church as a signal to Sherman. It is portrayed in a mural in the **Visitors Center.**

LOCATION	NAME	FACTS
Albany	Riverside/Oakview Cemetery	Large Confederate monument and seven unknown soldiers.
Americus	Oak Grove City Cemetery Confederate Section	Graves of 129 Confederate soldiers, 45 of them unknown, who died in local hospitals.
Andersonville	Andersonville National Cemetery	Believed to be 13,699 Union soldiers killed in prisoner of war camps, hospitals, and on battlefields. More than 16,000 total interments, including prisoners of war from all wars.
Athens	Oconee Hill Cemetery	Graves of 12 unknown soldiers. Generals T.R.R. Cobb, Howell Cobb, Martin Smith, and William M. Brown are buried in their family plots.
Atlanta	Oakland Cemetery	Apx. 2,500 Confederate dead and 20 Union dead. Also buried here are John Brown Gordon, Alfred Iverson, Jr., Clement Anselm Evans, Joseph E. Brown.
	Utoy Primitive Baptist Church Cemetery	Buried here are apx. 25 Confederates who died in the Battle of Atlanta and the Battle of Utoy Creek.
	Westview Cemetery	Confederate Memorial and 347 Confederate veterans in the Confederate section.
Augusta	Magnolia Cemetery	More than 300 Confederate soldiers who died in local hospitals. In fortified east wall, patches where cannons were placed still visible.
Barnesville	Greenwood Cemetery	Reported to be 115 Confederate dead, 84 unknown, who died in local hospitals, and two Union soldiers.
Cassville	Confederate Cemetery	Graves of 300 unknown Confederate soldiers. Grave of Gen. William T. Wofford.
Chattanooga, TN	Confederate Cemetery	Tablets feature names of units of Confederate dead. Graves of two Union soldiers.
	Chattanooga National Cemetery	More than 12,000 Union dead, 5,000 unknown, who died at Chickamauga, Chattanooga, and other area battles. Union raiders who stole the General in the "Great Locomotive Chase" are buried here.
Columbus	Linwood Cemetery	More than 200 Confederates lie in the army and navy sections.
Covington	Covington Confederate Cemetery, inside Covington City Cemetery	Buried here are 67 known and eight unknown Confederates.
Cuthbert	Greenwood Cemetery	An estimated 24 Confederate dead buried here.
Dalton	West Hill Cemetery	A total of 421 unknown Confederate, four known Confederate and four unknown Union soldiers.
Forsyth	Forsyth Soldier's Cemetery, inside Forsyth City Cemetery	Graves of 299 unknown Confederate soldiers and one known. Note grave of Honora Sweeney, who died while serving in a Confederate hospital.
Fort Gaines	New Park Cemetery	Graves of nine unknown Confederate soldiers who died in local hospitals.
Fort Valley	Oaklawn Cemetery	Apx. 20 unknown Confederate soldiers who died in a local train wreck and in local hospitals.
Greensboro	Greensboro City Cemetery	A total of 45 Confederate soldiers buried here, most died in local hospitals.
Griffin	Stonewall Cemetery	More than 500 Confederate and one Union soldier buried here.
Jonesboro	Patrick R. Cleburne Memorial Cemetery	An estimated 600-1,000 Confederate soldiers who died in the Battle of Jonesboro and in local hospitals.
Kingston	Confederate Cemetery	Graves of 250 unknown Confederate and two Union soldiers.
LaGrange	Confederate Cemetery	Apx. 300 Confederate soldiers are buried here.
Macon	Rose Hill Cemetery	In Confederate Square lie approximately 600 Confederate and Union soldiers.
Madison	Old City Cemetery	Graves of 51 unknown and one known Confederate soldier and one Negro hospital attendant.
Marietta	Confederate Cemetery	Apx. 3,000 Confederate soldiers, representing every Southern state, buried here.
	Marietta National Cemetery	Graves of more than 10,000 Union soldiers, 3,000 unknown, who died south of Resaca.
Milledgeville	Memory Hill Cemetery	Over 20 unknown Confederate soldiers are buried in one plot. In a separate location are three Union soldiers. General Doles of the Doles-Cook Brigade is buried here.
Milner	Confederate Cemetery	More than 100 unknown soldiers are buried here.
Moultrie	Greenfield Church Cemetery	White wooden crosses mark 75-100 graves. Believed to be unknown Confederate soldiers.
Newnan	Oak Hill Cemetery	Graves of 268 Confederate soldiers, only two unknown.
Oxford	Oxford College Campus Cemetery	Graves of 26 soldiers.
Quitman	West End Cemetery	A total of 17 unknown Confederate dead who mysteriously died on their way to the Battle of Olustee in Florida.
Resaca	Confederate Cemetery	The first Confederate cemetery in Georgia. Graves of soldiers who died in the Battle of Resaca.
Rome	Myrtle Hill Cemetery	In one plot, 377 Confederate and two Union soldiers.
Savannah	Bonaventure Cemetery	Graves of six Confederate generals: Robert J. Anderson, Henry R. Jackson, Alexander R. Lawton, Hugh W. Mercer, Claudius C. Wilson, and Commodore Josiah Tattnall.
	Laurel Grove Cemetery	A total of 1,500 Confederate dead and eight Confederate generals.
Stone Mountain	Stone Mountain Cemetery	Apx. 150 unknown Confederate soldiers who died in Confederate hospitals.
The Rock	Confederate Cemetery	The graves of 12 unknown soldiers who died in the General Hospital.
Thomaston	Glenwood Cemetery	Buried here are 54 Confederate soldiers. The grave of Georgia Dr. Edward A. Flewellen, Medical Director of the Confederate Army of Tennessee, is near the Confederate section.
Thomasville	Laurel Hill Cemetery	Buried here are 13 Confederate soldiers, 12 known and one unknown. General John Crawford Vaughn also buried here.
	The Old City Cemetery	When 5,000 prisoners were brought to a temporary prison camp in Thomasville, several hundred died and 38 are buried here.
Waynesboro	Waynesboro Confederate Memorial Cemetery	An estimated 45 Confederate dead, nine iron crosses mark unknown soldiers.
West Point	Fort Tyler Cemetery	A total of 76 Confederate and Union soldiers who were killed or died of wounds in the siege of Fort Tyler on April 16, 1865. Gen. Tyler is buried here.

APPENDIX - BIBLIOGRAPHY/PRESERVATION ORGANIZATIONS

Left, Kennesaw Mountain today is besieged by urban development; right, the Cassville WPA marker needs preservation help.

The landmark *Civil War Sites Advisory Commission Report on the Nation's Civil War Battlefields* stated in 1993 that "This nation's Civil War heritage is in grave danger. It is disappearing under buildings, parking lots, and highways." The Commission list of recommendations included more government leadership, private sector preservation, and funding to help preserve and protect this valuable and important chapter of America's heritage. The following organizations are devoted to statewide preservation:

Georgia Civil War Commission
Department Of Natural Resources
Historic Preservation Division
500 The Healey Building
57 Forsyth St., N.W.
Atlanta, GA 30303
(404) 656-2840

The Atlanta Preservation Center
156 Seventh St., Suite 3
Atlanta, GA 30308
(404) 876-2041

Georgians For Preservation Action (GaPA)
1516 Peachtree St., NW
Atlanta, GA 30309-2916
(404) 881-9980

Georgia Trust For Historic Preservation
1516 Peachtree St., NW
Atlanta, GA 30309-2916
(404) 881-9980

Selected Bibliography

Atlanta Campaign
Bailey, Ronald H. *Battles For Atlanta: Sherman Moves East.* Alexandria: Time-Life Books, 1989.
Castel, Albert. *Decision In The West: The Atlanta Campaign Of 1864.* Lawrence: University Press of Kansas, 1992.
Scaife, William R. *The Campaign For Atlanta.* Saline: McNaughton & Gunn, Inc., 1993.

Black Troops In Georgia
Emilio, Luis F. *A Brave Black Regiment: History Of The Fifty-Fourth Regiment Of Massachusetts Volunteer Infantry 1863-1865.* Salem: Ayer Company Publishers, Inc., 1990.

Chattanooga
Cozzens, Peter. *The Battles For Chattanooga: The Shipwreck Of Their Hopes.* Urbana: University of Illinois Press, 1994.

Chickamauga
Tucker, Glenn. *Chickamauga: Bloody Battle In The West.* New York: Smithmark Publishers Inc., 1961.

Civil War Magazines
Blue & Gray Magazine. Blue & Gray Enterprises, Inc., 130 Galloway Road, Galloway, Ohio 43119.
Civil War. The Country Publishers, Inc., 133 East Main Street, P.O. Box 798, Berryville, Virginia 22611.
Civil War Times Illustrated. Cowles Magazines, 2245 Kohn Road, P.O. Box 8200, Harrisburg, Pennsylvania 17105-8200.

Famous Georgians In The Civil War
Evans, Clement Anselm. *Intrepid Warrior: Life, Letters, And Diaries Of The War Years.* Edited by Robert Grier Stephens, Jr. Dayton: Morningside House, Inc., 1992.

General Georgia Reference
Arnsdorff, Jimmy E. *Those Gallant Georgians Who Served In The War Between The States.* Greenville: Southern Historical Press, Inc., 1994.
Boyd, Kenneth W. *Georgia Historical Markers — Coastal Counties.* Atlanta: Cherokee Publishing Company, 1991.
Boyd, Kenneth W. *The Historical Markers Of North Georgia.* Atlanta: Cherokee Publishing Company, 1993.
Georgia Civil War Historical Markers. Georgia Department of Natural Resources

State Parks, Recreation, and Historic Sites Division, 1982.
Jones, Charles Edgeworth. *Georgia In The War 1861-1864.* Fayetteville: Americana Historical Books, 1994.
McKenney, Frank M. *The Standing Army: History of Georgia's County Confederate Monuments.* Alpharetta: WH Wolfe Associates, 1993.
Kerlin, Robert H. *Confederate Generals of Georgia and Their Burial Sites.* Fayetteville: Americana Historical Books, 1994.

Georgia Civil War Naval Battles
Turner, Maxine. *Navy Gray: A Story Of The Confederate Navy On The Chattahoochee And Apalachicola Rivers.* Tuscaloosa: The University of Alabama Press, 1988.

Prison Camps in Georgia
Marvel, William. *Andersonville: The Last Depot.* Chapel Hill: The University of North Carolina Press, 1994.

Sherman's March to the Sea
Nevin, David. *Sherman's March: Atlanta To The Sea.* Alexandria: Time-Life Books, 1986.
Scaife, William J. *The March To The Sea.* Saline: McNaughton & Gunn, Inc., 1993.

The Confederate Government
Davis, Burke. *The Long Surrender.* New York: Vintage Books, 1985.

Tour Guides
Kelly, Dennis. *Kennesaw Mountain And The Atlanta Campaign.* Marietta: Kennesaw Mountain Historical Association, Inc., 1945.
Miles, Jim. *Fields of Glory: A History And Tour Guide Of The Atlanta Campaign.* Nashville: Rutledge Hill Press, 1989.
Miles, Jim. *Paths To Victory: A History And Tour Guide Of The Stone's River, Chickamauga, Chattanooga, Knoxville, And Nashville Campaigns.* Nashville: Rutledge Hill Press, 1991.
Miles, Jim. *To The Sea: A History and Tour Guide of Sherman's March.* Nashville: Rutledge Hill Press, 1989.

Wilson's Raid
Jones, James Pickett. *Yankee Blitzkrieg: Wilson's Raid Through Alabama And Georgia.* Athens: The University of Georgia Press, 1976.